MAKING GOOD DECISIONS

FOCUS ON SOCIAL WORK LAW
Series Editor: Alison Brammer

Palgrave Macmillan's Focus on Social Work Law series consists of compact, accessible guides to the principles, structures and processes of particular areas of the law as they apply to social work practice. Designed to develop students' understanding as well as refresh practitioners' knowledge, each book provides focused, digestible and navigable content in an easily portable form.

Available now

Looked After Children, Caroline Ball
Child Protection, Kim Holt
Capacity and Autonomy, Robert Johns
Making Good Decisions, Michael Preston-Shoot

Forthcoming titles

Court and Legal Skills, Penny Cooper
Adoption and Permanency, Philip Musson
Youth Justice, Jo Staines
Children in Need of Support, Joanne Westwood
Safeguarding Adults, Alison Brammer

Author of the bestselling textbook *Social Work Law*, Alison Brammer is a qualified solicitor with specialist experience working in Social Services, including child protection, adoption, mental health and community care. Alison coordinates the MA in Child Care Law and Practice and the MA in Adult Safeguarding at Keele University.

Series Standing Order

ISBN 9781137017833 paperback
(*outside North America only*)

You can receive future titles in this series as they are published by placing a standing order. Please contact your bookseller or, in the case of difficulty, write to us at the address below with your name and address, the title of the series and the ISBN quoted above.

Customer Services Department, Macmillan Distribution Ltd
Houndmills, Basingstoke, Hampshire RG21 6XS, England

MAKING GOOD DECISIONS

LAW FOR SOCIAL WORK PRACTICE

MICHAEL PRESTON-SHOOT

palgrave
macmillan

First published 2014 by
PALGRAVE MACMILLAN

Palgrave Macmillan in the UK is an imprint of Macmillan Publishers Limited, registered in England, company number 785998, of Houndmills, Basingstoke, Hampshire RG21 6XS.

Palgrave Macmillan in the US is a division of St Martin's Press LLC, 175 Fifth Avenue, New York, NY 10010.

Palgrave Macmillan is the global academic imprint of the above companies and has companies and representatives throughout the world.

Palgrave® and Macmillan® are registered trademarks in the United States, the United Kingdom, Europe and other countries

ISBN: 978–1–137–30242–7

This book is printed on paper suitable for recycling and made from fully managed and sustained forest sources. Logging, pulping and manufacturing processes are expected to conform to the environmental regulations of the country of origin.

A catalogue record for this book is available from the British Library.

A catalog record for this book is available from the Library of Congress.

Typeset by Cambrian Typesetters, Camberley, Surrey

Printed and bound in the UK by The Lavenham Press Ltd, Suffolk

CONTENTS

Table of cases	viii
Table of legislation	xvi
Acknowledgments	xix
Abbreviations	xx
Using this book	xxi
Legal skills guide: accessing and understanding the law	xxvii
INTRODUCTION	**1**
Relating law to social work	4
Contexts for decision-making	6
Shifting responsibilities	11
Duty of care	12
The book's scope	13
Chapter outline	15
Further reading	17
1 FIRST PRINCIPLES	**19**
Administrative law	21
Lawful decision-making	22
Further reading	36
2 FOUNDATIONS OF GOOD DECISION-MAKING	**37**
Defining acceptable standards	39
Social work standards of professionalism	41
Accountability	43
Employer accountability	46
Registration and fitness to practise	47
Getting to good	48
Further reading	52

3	**HUMAN RIGHTS AND EQUALITY**	**53**
	Making rights meaningful	54
	Social work and human rights	58
	Equality Act 2010	62
	Social work and equality duties	64
	International conventions	66
	Further reading	68
4	**PARTNERSHIPS WITHIN DECISION-MAKING**	**69**
	Partnership with children	72
	Partnership with parents	74
	Partnership with adults to promote well-being	76
	Partnership with other professionals	79
	Further reading	83
5	**WHO DECIDES?**	**85**
	Principles for assessing capacity	87
	Deprivation of liberty safeguards	93
	Advocacy	95
	Young people's capacity to take decisions	96
	Legal and relationship literacy	98
	Further reading	99
6	**WHAT CAN WE AFFORD?**	**100**
	Local authorities as corporate bodies	103
	Needs versus resources	104
	Organizational resources	110
	Further reading	111
7	**DECIDING TO SHARE INFORMATION**	**112**
	Information-sharing between agencies and professionals	114
	Sharing information with service users and their families	118
	Recording	121
	Accessing personal information	122
	Supporting good information-sharing practice	124
	Further reading	125

**8 LEARNING FROM THE UNCOMFORTABLE AND
    UNTHINKABLE**   **126**
    It couldn't happen here, could it?   127
    Barriers to learning within and across organizations   138
    Looking forward   140
    Further reading   140

9 EMBEDDING AND ENSURING BEST PRACTICE   **142**
    Complaints procedures   144
    Whistleblowing   145
    Reviews   147
    Professional standards   148
    Taking good practice forward   155
    Further reading   156

    Useful websites   157
    Glossary   158
    Bibliography   163
    Subject index   178
    Author index   183

TABLE OF CASES

A v UK [1999] 27 EHRR 611 56

A and Another v Essex County Council [2003] EWCA Civ 1848 34

A and Others v Secretary of State for the Home Department [2004] UKHL 56 56

A and S (Children) v Lancashire County Council [2012] 15 CCLR 471 44, 62, 73, 110, 137

A County Council v SB [2010] EWHC 2528 (Fam) 120

A Local Authority v K (by the Official Solicitor), Mr and Mrs K and an NHS Trust [2013] EWHC 242 (CoP) 89

AH (by his Litigation Friend RH) v (1) Hertfordshire Partnership NHS Foundation Trust and (2) Ealing Primary Care Trust [2011] 14 CCLR 301 86

AR v Homefirst Community Trust [2005] NICA 8 61

Associated Provincial Picture Houses v Wednesbury Corporation [1948] 1 KB 223 26

B v Lewisham London Borough Council [2008] EWHC 738 (Admin) 25

Barrett v Enfield London Borough Council [1999] 3 All ER 193 25, 28, 44, 60

Barrett v Kirklees Metropolitan Borough Council [2010] EWHC 467 (Admin) 35

Bath and North East Somerset v A Mother and Others [2008] EWHC B10 (Fam) 23, 110

Bolam v Friern Hospital Management Committee [1957] 2 All ER 118 39, 111, 148, 149

Bolitho v City and Hackney Health Authority [1997] 4 All ER 771 40, 151

Borley v Care Council for Wales [2010] UKFTT 404 (HESC) 47

C v Flintshire County Council [2001] 2 FLR 33 44

CC v KK and STCC [2012] EWHC 2136 (CoP) 86, 92

Cheshire West and Chester City Council v P [2011] EWCA Civ 1257 95

Cordingley v Care Council for Wales [2009] UKFTT 213 (HESC) 47, 104

Council of Civil Service Unions v Minister of State for the Civil Service [1984] 3 All ER 935 26

D v East Berkshire Community Health NHS Trust and Others [2005] UKHL 23 43

Davis v West Sussex County Council [2012] EWHC 2152 (QB) 27, 33

DL v A Local Authority and Others [2012] 15 CCLR 267 98

DL v South London and Maudsley NHS Foundation Trust and Secretary of State for Justice [2010] UKUT 455 (AAC) 36

DM (A Person under Disability) Acting by his Next Friend, Kathleen McCollum, for Judicial Review [2013] 16 CCLR 39 14, 77

Donoghue v Stevenson [1932] AC 562 12

E and Others v UK [2002] *The Times*, 4 December 60

Edwards and Another v UK [2002] 35 EHRR 19 56

Forbes v General Social Care Council [2008] CST 1267 SW 47, 104

Fraser v Winchester Health Authority [1999] *The Times*, 12 July 150

G v E (by his Litigation Friend, the Official Solicitor), Manchester City Council and S [2010] EWHC 2042 (Fam) 24, 76, 95, 99

Gaskin v UK [1989] 12 EHRR 36 122

Gillick v West Norfolk and Wisbech Area Health Authority [1986] AC 112 96, 123

GJ v The Foundation Trust [2009] EWHC 2972 (Fam) 94

H and L v A City Council and B City Council [2010] EWHC 466 (Admin) 116

HC (A Child) v Secretary of State for the Home Department and Another [2013] EWHC 982 (Admin) 57

Heinisch v Germany [2011] IRLR 922 146

Hillingdon London Borough Council v Neary (by his Litigation Friend, the Official Solicitor) and Mark Neary (Interested Party Equality and Human Rights Commission) [2011] EWHC 1377 (CoP) 24, 30, 32, 35, 59, 95

HL v UK [2004] 40 EHRR 761 59, 93

HN (A Minor) [2010] NIQB 86 23, 107

Hunter v Hanley [1955] 1st Division, Court of Session, Scotland 39

JE v DE and Surrey County Council [2006] EWHC 3459 (Admin) 95

Johnson v UK [1997] ECHR 88 29, 61

K v (1) WSX, (2) L (by his Litigation Friend the Official Solicitor) and (3) M [2012] EWCA Civ 79 89

Keenan v UK [2001] 33 EHRR 913 12

L v UK (Disclosure of Expert Evidence) [2000] 2 FLR 322 116, 120

LA v General Social Care Council [2007] CST 985 SW 47, 104

Lancaster v Birmingham City Council [1999] *The Times*, 6 July 150

Lawrence v Pembrokeshire County Council [2007] EWCA Civ 446 xxviii, 43

M (Minor) v Newham London Borough Council [1994] 4 All ER 602 39

MG v UK [2002] *The Times*, 11 October 122

Mabon v Mabon [2005] 2 FLR 1011 34, 67, 73, 98

Maddock v Devon County Council [2004] EWHC 3494 116

Manchester City Council v T and Another [1993] *Children Act News*, June 1994 117

Merthyr Tydfil County Borough Council v C [2010] EWHC 62 (QB) 45

NXS v Camden London Borough Council [2009] EWHC 1786 (QB) 41, 44

P and Q [2011] EWCA Civ 190 95

P, C and S v UK [2002] *The Times*, 16 August 59, 60

Pierce v Doncaster Metropolitan Borough Council [2008] EWCA Civ 1416 26, 44, 60

R v Avon County Council, ex parte Hazell [1995] *Family Law*, 66 76, 105

R v Birmingham City Council, ex parte Killigrew [2000] 3 CCLR 109 25, 107, 108

R v Brent London Borough Council, ex parte Connery [1990] 2 All ER 353 108

R v Devon County Council, ex parte Baker [1995] 1 All ER 73 33

R v Gloucestershire County Council, ex parte Barry [1997] 2 All ER 1 108, 109

R v Gloucestershire County Council, ex parte RADAR [1996] 4 ALL ER 421 108

R v Haringey London Borough Council, ex parte Norton [1998] 1 CCLR 168 33, 108

R v Islington London Borough Council, ex parte Rixon [1996] *The Times*, 17 April xxv, 24

R v Kensington and Chelsea Royal London Borough Council, ex parte Kujtim [1999] 2 CCLR 340 151

R v Kent County Council, ex parte Marston [1997] Unreported 120

R v Lancashire County Council, ex parte Ingham and Whalley [1995] CO/774/95 107

R v Lancashire County Council, ex parte RADAR and Another [1996] *The Times*, 12 July 76

R v Manchester City Council, ex parte Stennett [2002] UKHL 34 101

R v North Yorkshire County Council, ex parte Hargreaves [1997] 1 CCLR 104 76, 145

R v Sefton MBC, ex parte Help the Aged and Charlotte Blanchard [1997] 1 CCLR 57 25

R v Staffordshire County Council, ex parte Farley [1997] 7 CL 186 26, 107, 108

R v Wigan Metropolitan Borough Council, ex parte Tammadge [1998] 1 CCLR 581 108

R (A) v Lambeth London Borough Council [2010] EWHC 1652 (Admin) 95

R (A and B and X and Y) v East Sussex County Council [2003] 6 CCLR 194 32

R (A, T and S) v Newham London Borough Council [2008] EWHC 2640
    (Admin) 145
R (AB and CD) v Haringey London Borough Council [2013] EWHC 416
    (Admin) 24
R (AB and SB) v Nottingham City Council [2001] 4 CCLR 295 24, 28
R (AH) v Cornwall County Council [2010] EWHC 3192 (Admin) 27
R (Ahmad) v Newham London Borough Council [2009] UKHL 14 5
R (AM) v Birmingham City Council [2009] 12 CCLR 407 64
R (B) v Barnet London Borough Council [2009] EWHC 2842 (Admin) 25,
    29
R (B) v Cornwall County Council [2009] EWHC 491 (Admin) 25, 33
R (B) v Merton London Borough Council [2003] 6 CCLR 457 31, 34
R (B and Others) v Worcestershire County Council [2009] EWHC 2915
    (Admin) 33
R (Behre and Others) v Hillingdon London Borough Council [2003] *The
    Times*, 22 September 24
R (Bernard and Another) v Enfield London Borough Council [2002] 5 CCLR
    577 25, 28, 61
R (Bewry) v Norfolk County Council [2010] EWHC 2545 (Admin) 34
R (Birara) v Hounslow London Borough Council [2010] EWHC 2133
    (Admin) 33
R (Boyejo and Others) v Barnet London Borough Council [2010] 13 CCLR
    72 65
R (Brown) v Secretary of State for Work and Pensions [2008] EWHC 3158
    (Admin) 26, 63
R (C) v Secretary of State for Justice [2008] EWCA Civ 882 63, 67
R (C) v South West Mental Health Review Tribunal [2001] EWCA Civ 1110
    29
R (CD) (A Child by her Litigation Friend VD) v Isle of Anglesey County
    Council [2004] 7 CCLR 589 7, 10, 23, 73
R (Chavda) v Harrow London Borough Council [2008] 11 CCLR 187 65
R (D) v Worcestershire County Council [2013] 16 CCLR 323 77
R (Dudley) v East Sussex County Council [2003] 6 CCLR 18 38
R (EHRC) v Secretary of State for Justice [2010] EWHC 147 (Admin) 63
R (ET, BT and CT) v Islington London Borough Council [2013] EWCA Civ
    323 27
R (FZ) v Croydon London Borough Council [2011] EWCA Civ 59 34
R (G) v Nottingham City Council [2008] 11 CCLR 273 24, 25
R (G) v Southwark London Borough Council [2009] UKHL 26 34, 81
R (G and H) v North Somerset Council [2011] EWHC 2232 (Admin) 109
R (Goldsmith) v Wandsworth London Borough Council [2004] 7 CCLR 472
    107

R (Grogan) v Bexley NHS Care Trust and South East London Strategic
  Health Authority and the Secretary of State for Health [2006] 9 CCLR
  188   81

R (H, Barhanu and B) v Wandsworth London Borough Council, Hackney
  London Borough Council and Islington London Borough Council [2007]
  10 CCLR 439   24

R (J) v Caerphilly County Borough Council [2005] EWHC 586 (Admin)   29

R (JF) v Hackney London Borough Council [2010] EWHC 3130 (Admin)   27,
  29

R (JL) v Islington London Borough Council [2009] EWHC 458 (Admin)   32,
  65

R (JM and NT by their Litigation Friends) v Isle of Wight Council [2012] 15
  CCLR 167   33, 65

R (Kaur and Shah) v Ealing London Borough Council [2008] EWHC 2062
  (Admin)   65

R (KB and Others) v Mental Health Review Tribunal and Another [2002]
  EWHC 639 (Admin)   61

R (KM) (A Child) v Lambeth London Borough Council [2011] EWCA Civ
  1125   34

R (KM by his Mother and Litigation Friend JM) v Cambridgeshire County
  Council [2012] UKSC 23   14, 35, 77, 107

R (L and Others) v Manchester City Council [2002] 1 FLR 43   25, 26, 61

R (LH and MH) v Lambeth London Borough Council [2006] 9 CCLR 622   26

R (Liverpool City Council) v Hillingdon London Borough Council and AK
  [2009] EWCA Civ 43   98

R (M) v Barking and Dagenham London Borough Council and Westminster
  City Council (Interested Party) [2003] 6 CCLR 87   81

R (M) v Birmingham City Council [2009] EWHC 688 (Admin)   65

R (M) v Hammersmith and Fulham London Borough Council [2008] UKHL
  14   73, 107

R (Madden) v Bury Metropolitan Borough Council [2002] 5 CCLR 622   33,
  60

R (McDonald) v Royal Borough of Kensington and Chelsea [2011] UKSC 33
  xxviii, 54, 102, 109

R (Meany and Others) v Harlow District Council [2009] EWHC 559 (Admin)
  65

R (MM) v Lewisham London Borough Council [2009] EWHC 416 (Admin)
  29, 30

R (Munjaz) v Mersey Care NHS Trust [2005] UKHL 58   24

R (NA) v Croydon London Borough Council [2009] EWHC 2357 (Admin)
  10, 31, 34, 73

R (Nassery) v Brent London Borough Council [2010] EWHC 2326 (Admin)   27

R (Phillips) v Walsall Metropolitan Borough Council [2002] 5 CCLR 383 38, 61

R (Rahman) v Birmingham City Council [2011] EWHC 944 (Admin) 29, 33, 65

R (Roose) v Parole Board and Secretary of State for Justice [2010] EWHC 1780 (Admin) 30

R (S) v Croydon London Borough Council [2011] EWHC 2467 (Admin) 109

R (S) v Hampshire County Council [2009] EWHC 2537 (Admin) 33, 145

R (S) v Plymouth City Council [2002] 5 CCLR 251 119

R (S) v Sutton London Borough Council [2007] EWCA Civ 790 24

R (Savva) v Kensington and Chelsea Royal London Borough Council [2010] EWCA Civ 1209 32, 35

R (Selwood) v Durham County Council, Tees, Esk and Wear Valleys NHS Foundation Trust and Northumberland, Tyne and Wear NHS Foundation Trust [2012] EWCA Civ 979 47, 56

R (SSG) v Liverpool City Council and Others [2002] 5 CCLR 639 55

R (Stewart) v Wandsworth London Borough Council, Hammersmith and Fulham London Borough Council and Lambeth London Borough Council [2001] 4 CCLR 466 81

R (TG) v Lambeth London Borough Council [2011] EWCA Civ 526 23

R (V) v South London and Maudsley NHS Trust and Croydon London Borough Council [2010] EWHC 742 (Admin) 29

R (W) v Birmingham City Council [2011] 14 CCLR 516 65

R (Watts) v Wolverhampton City Council [2009] EWCA Civ 1168 33

R (WG) v Local Authority A [2010] EWHC 2608 (Admin) 27, 39, 76

R (Wright and Others) v Secretary of State for Health and Another [2007] 11 CCLR 31 56

Rabone and Rabone v Pennine Care NHS Trust [2012] UKSC 2 56

Re A (Children) [2010] EWCA Civ 344 29, 30, 35, 38

Re B [2007] 1 FLR 482 5

Re B (Children: Patient Confidentiality) [2003] *The Times*, 1 July 116

Re B (Disclosure to Other Parties) [2001] 2 FLR 1017 120

Re C and B (Care Order: Future Harm) [2001] 1 FLR 611 32, 35, 61

Re C (Care Proceedings: Disclosure of Local Authority's Decision-Making Process) [2002] 2 FCR 673 34, 75, 121

Re D [2008] EWHC 1306 (Fam) 5

Re E and Others (Minors) (Care Proceedings: Social Work Practice) [2000] *The Times*, 10 May 75, 121

Re F (A Child) [2008] EWCA Civ 439 5, 9, 38, 121

Re G (Care: Challenge to Local Authority's Decision) [2003] EWHC 551 (Fam) 120

Re M (Care Proceedings: Judicial Review) [2003] 2 FLR 171 61

Re O (A Child) (Supervision Order) [2001] 1 FLR 923 61

Re R (A Minor) (Wardship: Consent to Treatment) [1991] 3 WLR 592 98

Re SA (Vulnerable Adult with Capacity: Marriage) [2005] EWHC 2942 98

Re W (A Minor) (Medical Treatment: Court's Jurisdiction) [1992] 3 WLR 758 98

Re W (An Infant) [1971] AC 682 26

Re W and B (Children: Care Plan) [2002] UKHL 10 61

Re X (Emergency Protection Orders) [2006] 2 FLR 701 5, 38, 75

Re Z (Local Authority: Duty) [2004] EWHC 2817 13

RH v South London and Maudsley NHS Foundation Trust [2010] UKUT 32 (AAC) 36

S and Marper v UK [2008] ECHR 1581 57

S (by the Official Solicitor) v Rochdale Metropolitan Borough Council and Another [2008] EWHC 3283 (Fam) 40

Savage v South Essex Partnership NHS Trust [2008] UKHL 74 56

SC v UK [2004] 40 EHRR 11 56

S, C and D v Secretary of State for the Home Department [2007] EWHC 1654 67

St Helens Metropolitan Borough Council v Manchester Primary Care Trust [2008] EWCA Civ 931 81

Storck v Germany [2005] ECHR 406 93

TF and London Borough of Lewisham [2009] Unreported High Court Case Claim Number 5MY02198 and EWCA Civ 1051 45

Torney v Information Commissioner and the Regional Health and Social Care Board [2013] UKFTT EA/2012/0143 123

TP and KM v UK [2002] 34 EHRR 2 34, 38, 61, 75

TTM (by his Litigation Friend TM) v Hackney London Borough Council and East London NHS Foundation Trust [2011] EWCA Civ 4 41

W v Chief Constable of Northumbria [2009] EWHC 747 (Admin) 116

W v Egdell [1989] 1 All ER 1089 116

W and Others v Essex County Council and Another [2000] 2 All ER 237 34, 44, 61

Walker v Northumberland County Council [1995] IRLR 35 (QBD) 47, 151

Woolgar v Chief Constable of Sussex Police and UK Central Council for Nursing, Midwifery and Health Visiting [2000] 1 WLR 25 116

Worcestershire County Council and Another v HM Coroner for the County of Worcestershire [2013] EWHC 1711 (QB) 117

X Council v B (Emergency Protection Orders) [2004] EWHC 2015 38

YL (by her Litigation Friend the Official Solicitor) v Birmingham City Council [2007] 10 CCLR 505 57

Z v UK [2001] 2 FLR 612 12, 25, 44, 59, 60

ZH v Secretary of State for the Home Department [2011] UKSC 4 67

Ombudsman decisions

Local Government Ombudsman and Bristol City Council (2011)
(09/005/944) 44, 89
Local Government Ombudsman and Bury MBC (2009) (07/C/03887) 28
Local Government Ombudsman and Kent County Council and Dover
District Council (2012) (08/08/2012) 24
Local Government Ombudsman and Liverpool City Council (2010)
(08005858) 38
Local Government Ombudsman and Nottinghamshire County Council
(2002) (01/C/5968) 26
Local Government Ombudsman and Surrey County Council (2008)
(07/A/11108) 28, 30, 39, 107
Local Government Ombudsman and West Lindsey District Council (2009)
(07/C/01269) 28, 107
Local Government Ombudsman and Worcestershire County Council (2011)
(09/013/172) 38, 89
Public Services Ombudsman for Wales v Cardiff City Council (2011)
(200900981) 89
Public Services Ombudsman for Wales v Cardiff Local Health Board (2009)
(200701329) 25, 39, 107, 145
Public Services Ombudsman for Wales v Merthyr Tydfil Council (2010)
(200800881) 25, 38
Welsh Administration Ombudsman v Carmarthenshire County Council
(2009) (1999/200600720) 35

TABLE OF LEGISLATION

Statutes

Adoption and Children Act 2002 9, 40, 62, 64, 72, 95, 174
Adult Support and Protection (Scotland) Act 2007 61, 78, 86, 88, 96, 143, 154, 173
Adults with Incapacity (Scotland) Act 2000 86, 92, 96
Care Standards Act 2000 47
Carers and Direct Payments (Northern Ireland) Act 2002 78
Carers (Equal Opportunities) Act 2004 78
Child Poverty Act 2010 64
Childcare Act 2006 64
Children Act 1989 xxiv, 10, 23, 24, 27, 32, 55, 64, 66, 72, 73, 74, 79, 97, 116, 117, 118, 120, 144
Children Act 2004 58, 80, 117, 175
Children and Young Persons Act 2008 74, 174
Children's Commissioner for Wales Act 2001 58, 67
Children, Schools and Families Act 2010 117
Children (Scotland) Act 1995 64, 72, 74, 96, 118, 144
Chronically Sick and Disabled Persons Act 1970 77
Commissioner for Children and Young People (Scotland) Act 2003 58
Community Care and Health (Scotland) Act 2002 78
Corporate Manslaughter and Corporate Homicide Act 2007 148
Crime and Disorder Act 1998 116
Data Protection Act 1998 16, 112, 114, 115, 116, 117, 118, 120, 122, 124
Enterprise and Regulatory Reform Act 2013 146
Equality Act 2006 174
Equality Act 2010 xxiv, 15, 53, 62, 64, 66
Freedom of Information Act 2000 120, 123
Freedom of Information (Scotland) Act 2002 120, 123
Health Act 1999 154
Health Act 2009 147
Health and Personal Social Services (Northern Ireland) Act 2001 47
Health and Safety Offences Act 2008 149

Health and Social Care Act 2008 57, 173
Health and Social Care Act 2012 47, 78, 154
Health and Social Care (Community Health and Standards) Act 2003 144
Health and Social Care (Reform) Act (Northern Ireland) 2009 144
Human Rights Act 1998 xxi, 15, 43, 53, 54, 55, 56, 59, 60, 63, 66, 102, 104, 115, 176, 177
Local Authority Social Services Act 1970 xxv, 24, 102, 177
Mental Capacity Act 2005 xxv, 15, 55, 59, 66, 86, 89, 90, 91, 93, 96, 97, 117
Mental Health Act 1983 xxv, 64, 86, 90, 93, 94, 106, 174
Mental Health Act 2007 15, 64, 86, 90, 93, 96, 106, 117
Mental Health (Care and Treatment) Scotland Act 2003 86, 90, 96
Mental Health (Scotland) Act 1984 86, 90
National Assistance Act 1948 27
National Health Service Act 2006 154
National Health Service and Community Care Act 1990 66, 77, 79, 144, 174
Protection of Freedoms Act 2012 48
Protection of Vulnerable Groups (Scotland) Act 2007 48
Public Interest Disclosure Act 1998 133, 146
Regulation of Care (Scotland) Act 2001 47
Safeguarding Vulnerable Groups Act 2006 48

Orders, directions and regulations

Children (Northern Ireland) Order 1995 64, 72, 74, 96, 118, 144
Commissioner for Children and Young People (Northern Ireland) Order 2003 58
Community Care Assessment Directions 2004 77
Data Protection (Subject Access Modification) (Social Work) Order 2000 122
Guidance on National Assistance Act 1948 (Choice of Accommodation) Directions 1992 (LAC (2004) 20) 105
Health and Social Care Complaints Procedures Directions (Northern Ireland) 2009 144
Local Authority Social Services (Complaints Procedure) Order 2006 xxv
Local Authority Social Services and NHS Complaints (England) Regulations 2009 144
Management of Health and Safety at Work Regulations 1999 111
Mental Health (Amendment) (Northern Ireland) Order 2004 86
Mental Health (Northern Ireland) Order 1986 86
National Assembly for Wales (Legislative Competence) (Social Welfare and Other Fields) Order 2008 SI 2008/3132 12

National Assistance Act 1948 (Choice of Accommodation) Directions 1992 105
Public Interest Disclosure Act (Northern Ireland) Order 1998 146
Rights of Children and Young Persons (Wales) Measure 2011 66
Safeguarding Vulnerable Groups (Northern Ireland) Order 2007 48

Other

European Convention on Human Rights and Fundamental Freedoms 12, 25, 32, 40, 44, 54, 55, 56, 57, 59, 60, 61, 62, 66, 67, 86, 89, 93, 97, 102, 107, 115, 116, 119, 120, 122, 146
European Social Charter 66, 67, 68, 102
United Nations Convention on the Rights of the Child 58, 66, 67, 72, 98
United Nations Convention on the Rights of Persons with Disabilities 66

ACKNOWLEDGMENTS

This book began life as a joint endeavour with Professor Suzy Braye, University of Sussex. It was her idea for a book on lawful decision-making, drawing on principles of administrative law, and she was very much involved in the initial configuration of the chapters. The writing too was meant to have been a partnership. Unfortunately, however, ill-health prevented her from making a written contribution but her influence is within the pages and I hope that I have done justice to her hopes for the book.

I would like to acknowledge the support of Stuart Vernon, Gwyneth Roberts and Alison Brammer, from whom I have learned much on teaching, researching and writing about the interface between law and social work. I would like to thank all those service users, social work students, practitioners and managers who have engaged with me in learning about and reviewing the impact of law on their lives and work. Their contributions have helped me to refine my analysis of the interface between legal rules and social work's values and professional standards. Finally, I would like to acknowledge Roger Kline for his perspective as a trade union official, passion for the highest standards of service provision, and enthusiastic advocacy for health and social care practitioners.

I dedicate the book to Suzy Braye and also to Hannah, who has joined the ranks of legal practitioners seeking to make a social justice difference, and Sebastian who is also making his contribution to a better world.

Professor Michael Preston-Shoot
August 2013

ABBREVIATIONS

CC	City Council/County Council
CQC	Care Quality Commission
CSCI	Commission for Social Care Inspection
CSSIW	Care and Social Services Inspectorate Wales
DC	District Council
DCA	Department for Constitutional Affairs
DCSF	Department for Children, Schools and Families
DfE	Department for Education
DH	Department of Health
DHSSPS	Department of Health, Social Services and Public Safety
ECHR	European Convention on Human Rights and Fundamental Freedoms
EHRC	Equality and Human Rights Commission
GP	General Practitioner
GSCC	General Social Care Council
HCPC	Health and Care Professions Council
IRO	Independent Reviewing Officer
LBC	London Borough Council
LGO	local government ombudsman
LSAB	Local Safeguarding Adults Board
LSCB	Local Safeguarding Children Board
MoJ	Ministry of Justice
NHS	National Health Service
NISCC	Northern Ireland Social Care Council
OFSTED	Office for Standards in Education, Children's Services and Skills
PHSO	Parliamentary and Health Service Ombudsman
QAA	Quality Assurance Agency
SWIA	Social Work Inspection Agency
SWTF	Social Work Task Force
UNCRC	United Nations Convention on the Rights of the Child
WAG	Welsh Assembly Government

USING THIS BOOK

Aim of the series

Welcome to the Focus on Social Work Law Series.

This introductory section aims to elucidate the aims and philosophy of the series; introduce some key themes that run through the series; outline the key features within each volume; and offer a brief legal skills guide to complement use of the series.

The Social Work Law Focus Series provides a distinct range of specialist resources for students and practitioners. Each volume provides an accessible and practical discussion of the law applicable to a particular area of practice. The length of each volume ensures that whilst portable and focused there is nevertheless a depth of coverage of each topic beyond that typically contained in comprehensive textbooks addressing all aspects of social work law and practice.

Each volume includes the relevant principles, structures and processes of the law (with case law integrated into the text) and highlights clearly the application of the law to practice. A key objective for each text is to identify the policy context of each area of practice and the factors that have shaped the law into its current presentation. As law is constantly developing and evolving, where known, likely future reform of the law is identified. Each book takes a critical approach, noting inconsistencies, omissions and other challenges faced by those charged with its implementation.

The significance of the Human Rights Act 1998 to social work practice is a common theme in each text and implications of the Act for practice in the particular area are identified with inclusion of relevant case law.

The series focuses on the law in England and Wales. Some references may be made to comparable aspects of law in Scotland and Northern Ireland, particularly to highlight differences in approach. With devolution in Scotland and the expanding role of the Welsh Assembly Government it will be important for practitioners in those areas and working at the borders to be familiar with any such differences.

Features

At a glance content lists

Each chapter begins with a bullet point list summarizing the key points within the topic included in that chapter. From this list the reader can see 'at a glance' how the materials are organized and what to expect in that section. The introductory chapter provides an overview of the book, outlining coverage in each chapter that enables the reader to see how the topic develops throughout the text. The boundaries of the discussion are set including, where relevant, explicit recognition of areas that are excluded from the text.

Key case analysis

One of the key aims of the series is to emphasize an integrated understanding of law, comprising legislation and case law and practice. For this reason each chapter includes at least one key case analysis feature focusing on a particularly significant case. The facts of the case are outlined in brief followed by analysis of the implications of the decision for social work practice in a short commentary. Given the significance of the selected cases, readers are encouraged to follow up references and read the case in full together with any published commentaries.

On-the-spot questions

These questions are designed to consolidate learning and prompt reflection on the material considered. These questions may be used as a basis for discussion with colleagues or fellow students and may also prompt consideration or further investigation of how the law is applied within a particular setting or authority, for example, looking at information provided to service users on a council website. Questions may also follow key cases, discussion of research findings or practice scenarios, focusing on the issues raised and application of the relevant law to practice.

Practice focus

Each volume incorporates practice-focused case scenarios to demonstrate how the law is applied to social work practice. The scenarios may be fictional or based on an actual decision.

Further reading

Each chapter closes with suggestions for further reading to develop knowledge and critical understanding. Annotated to explain the reasons for inclusion, the reader may be directed to classic influential pieces, such as enquiry reports, up-to-date research and analysis of issues discussed in the chapter, and relevant policy documents. In addition students may wish to read in full the case law included throughout the text and to follow up references integrated into discussion of each topic.

Websites

As further important sources of information, websites are also included in the text with links from the companion website. Some may be a gateway to access significant documents including government publications, others may provide accessible information for service users or present a particular perspective on an area, such as the voices of experts by experience. Given the rapid development of law and practice across the range of topics covered in the series, reference to relevant websites can be a useful way to keep pace with actual and anticipated changes.

Glossary

Each text includes a subject-specific glossary of key terms for quick reference and clarification. A flashcard version of the glossary is available on the companion website.

Visual aids

As appropriate, visual aids are included where information may be presented accessibly as a table, graph or flow chart. This approach is particularly helpful for the presentation of some complex areas of law and to demonstrate structured decision-making or options available.

Companion site

The series-wide companion site www.palgrave.com/socialworklaw provides additional learning resources, including flashcard glossaries, web links, a legal skills guide, and a blog to communicate important developments and updates. The site will also host a student feedback zone.

Key sources of law

In this section an outline of the key sources of law considered through-out the series is provided. The following 'Legal skills' section includes some guidance on the easiest ways to access and understand these sources.

Legislation

The term legislation is used interchangeably with Acts of Parliament and statutes to refer to primary sources of law.

All primary legislation is produced through the parliamentary process, beginning its passage as a Bill. Bills may have their origins as an expressed policy in a government manifesto, in the work of the Law Commission, or following and responding to a significant event such as a child death or the work of a government department such as the Home Office.

Each Bill is considered by both the House of Lords and House of Commons, debated and scrutinized through various committee stages before becoming an Act on receipt of royal assent.

Legislation has a title and year, for example, the Equality Act 2010. Legislation can vary in length from an Act with just one section to others with over a hundred. Lengthy Acts are usually divided into headed 'Parts' (like chapters) containing sections, subsections and paragraphs. For example, s. 31 of the Children Act 1989 is in Part IV entitled 'Care and Supervision' and outlines the criteria for care order applications. Beyond the main body of the Act the legislation may also include 'Schedules' following the main provisions. Schedules have the same force of law as the rest of the Act but are typically used to cover detail such as a list of legislation which has been amended or revoked by the current Act or detailed matters linked to a specific provision, for instance, Schedule 2 of the Children Act 1989 details specific services (e.g. day centres) which may be provided under the duty to safeguard and promote the welfare of children in need, contained in s. 17.

Remember also that statutes often contain sections dealing with inter-pretation or definitions and, although often situated towards the end of the Act, these can be a useful starting point.

Legislation also includes Statutory Instruments which may be in the form of rules, regulations and orders. The term delegated legislation collectively describes this body of law as it is made under delegated authority of Parliament, usually by a minister or government department. Statutory Instruments tend to provide additional detail to the outline scheme provided by the primary legislation, the Act of Parliament. Statutory Instruments are usually cited by year and a number, for example, Local Authority Social Services (Complaints Procedure) Order SI 2006/1681.

Various documents may be issued to further assist with the implementation of legislation including guidance and codes of practice.

Guidance

Guidance documents may be described as formal or practice guidance. Formal guidance may be identified as such where it is stated to have been issued under s. 7(1) of the Local Authority Social Services Act 1970, which provides that 'local authorities shall act under the general guidance of the Secretary of State'. An example of s. 7 guidance is *Working Together to Safeguard Children* (2013, London: Department of Health). The significance of s. 7 guidance was explained by Sedley J in *R v London Borough of Islington, ex parte Rixon* [1997] ELR 66: 'Parliament in enacting s. 7(1) did not intend local authorities to whom ministerial guidance was given to be free, having considered it, to take it or leave it . . . in my view parliament by s. 7(1) has required local authorities to follow the path charted by the Secretary of State's guidance, with liberty to deviate from it where the local authority judges on admissible grounds that there is good reason to do so, but without freedom to take a substantially different course.' (71)

Practice guidance does not carry s. 7 status but should nevertheless normally be followed as setting examples of what good practice might look like.

Codes of practice

Codes of practice have been issued to support the Mental Health Act 1983 and the Mental Capacity Act 2005. Again, it is a matter of good practice to follow the recommendations of the codes and these lengthy documents include detailed and illustrative scenarios to assist with interpretation and application of the legislation. There may also be a duty on specific people charged with responsibilities under the primary legislation to have regard to the code.

Guidance and codes of practice are available on relevant websites, for example, the Department of Health, as referenced in individual volumes.

Case law

Case law provides a further major source of law. In determining disputes in court the judiciary applies legislation. Where provisions within legislation are unclear or ambiguous the judiciary follows principles of statutory interpretation but at times judges are quite creative.

Some areas of law are exclusively contained in case law and described as common law. Most law of relevance to social work practice is of relatively recent origin and has its primary basis in legislation. Case law remains relevant as it links directly to such legislation and may clarify and explain provisions and terminology within the legislation. The significance of a particular decision will depend on the position of the court in a hierarchy whereby the Supreme Court is most senior and the magistrates' court is junior. Decisions of the higher courts bind the lower courts – they must be followed. This principle is known as the doctrine of precedent. Much legal debate takes place as to the precise element of a ruling which subsequently binds other decisions. This is especially the case where in the Court of Appeal or Supreme Court there are between three and five judges hearing a case, majority judgments are allowed and different judges may arrive at the same conclusion but for different reasons. Where a judge does not agree with the majority, the term dissenting judgment is applied.

It is important to understand how cases reach court. Many cases in social work law are based on challenges to the way a local authority has exercised its powers. This is an aspect of administrative law known as judicial review where the central issue for the court is not the substance of the decision taken by the authority but the way it was taken. Important considerations will be whether the authority has exceeded its powers, failed to follow established procedures or acted irrationally.

Before an individual can challenge an authority in judicial review it will usually be necessary to exhaust other remedies first, including local authority complaints procedures. If unsatisfied with the outcome of a complaint an individual has a further option which is to complain to the local government ombudsman (LGO). The LGO investigates alleged cases of maladministration and may make recommendations to local authorities including the payment of financial compensation. Ombudsman decisions may be accessed on the LGO website and make interesting reading. In cases involving social services, a common concern across children's and adults' services is unreasonable delay in carrying out assessments and providing services. See www.lgo.org.uk.

Classification of law

The above discussion related to the sources and status of laws. It is also important to note that law can serve a variety of functions and may be grouped into recognized classifications. For law relating to social work practice key classifications distinguish between law which is criminal or civil and law which is public or private.

Whilst acknowledging the importance of these classifications, it must also be appreciated that individual concerns and circumstances may not always fall so neatly into the same categories, a given scenario may engage with criminal, civil, public and private law.

- Criminal law relates to alleged behaviour which is defined by statute or common law as an offence prosecuted by the state, carrying a penalty which may include imprisonment. The offence must be proved 'beyond reasonable doubt'.
- Civil law is the term applied to all other areas of law and often focuses on disputes between individuals. A lower standard of proof, 'balance of probabilities', applies in civil cases.
- Public law is that in which society has some interest and involves a public authority, such as care proceedings.
- Private law operates between individuals, such as marriage or contract.

Legal skills guide: accessing and understanding the law

Legislation

Legislation may be accessed as printed copies published by The Stationery Office and is also available online. Some books on a particular area of law will include a copy of the Act (sometimes annotated) and this is a useful way of learning about new laws. As time goes by, however, and amendments are made to legislation it can become increasingly difficult to keep track of the up-to-date version of an Act. Revised and up-to-date versions of legislation (as well as the version originally enacted) are available on the website www. legislation.gov.uk.

Legislation may also be accessed on the Parliament website. Here, it is possible to trace the progress of current and draft Bills and a link to Hansard provides transcripts of debates on Bills as they pass through both Houses of Parliament, www.parliament.uk.

Bills and new legislation are often accompanied by 'Explanatory notes' which can give some background to the development of the new law and offer useful explanations of each provision.

Case law

Important cases are reported in law reports available in traditional bound volumes (according to court, specialist area or general weekly reports) or online. Case referencing is known as citation and follows particular conventions according to whether a hard copy law report or online version is sought.

Citation of cases in law reports begins with the names of the parties, followed by the year and volume number of the law report, followed by an abbreviation of the law report title, then the page number. For example: *Lawrence v Pembrokeshire CC* [2007] 2 FLR 705. The case is reported in volume 2 of the 2007 Family Law Report at page 705.

Online citation, sometimes referred to as neutral citation because it is not linked to a particular law report, also starts with the names of the parties, followed by the year in which the case was decided, followed by an abbreviation of the court in which the case was heard, followed by a number representing the place in the order of cases decided by that court. For example: *R (Macdonald) v Royal Borough of Kensington and Chelsea* [2011] UKSC 33. Neutral citation of this case shows that it was a 2011 decision of the Supreme Court.

University libraries tend to have subscriptions to particular legal databases, such as 'Westlaw', which can be accessed by those enrolled as students, often via direct links from the university library webpage. Westlaw and LexisNexis are especially useful as sources of case law, statutes and other legal materials. Libraries usually have their own guides to these sources, again often published on their websites. For most cases there is a short summary or analysis as well as the full transcript.

As not everyone using the series will be enrolled at a university, the following website can be accessed without any subscription: BAILLI (British and Irish Legal Information Institute) www.bailii.org. This site includes judgments from the full range of UK court services including the Supreme Court, Court of Appeal and High Court but also features a wide range of tribunal decisions. Judgments for Scotland, Northern Ireland and the Republic of Ireland are also available as are judgments of the European Court of Human Rights.

Whether accessed via a law report or online, the presentation of cases follows a template. The report begins with the names of the parties, the court which heard the cases, names(s) of the judges(s) and dates of the hearing. This is followed by a summary of key legal issues involved in the case (often in italics) known as catchwords, then the headnote, which is a paragraph or so stating the key facts of the case and the nature of the claim or dispute or the criminal charge. 'HELD' indicates the ruling of the court. This is followed by a list of cases that were referred to in legal argument during the hearing, a summary of the journey of the case through appeal processes, names of the advocates and then the start of the full judgment(s) given by the judge(s). The judgment usually recounts the circumstances of the case, findings of fact and findings on the law and reasons for the decision.

If stuck on citations the Cardiff Index to Legal Abbreviations is a useful resource at www.legalabbrevs.cardiff.ac.uk.

There are numerous specific guides to legal research providing more detailed examination of legal materials but the best advice on developing legal skills is to start exploring the above and to read some case law – it's surprisingly addictive!

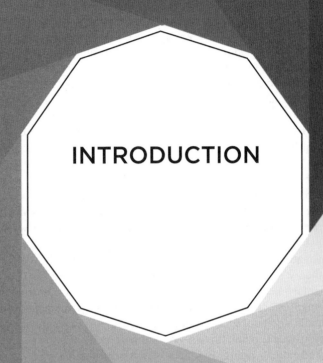

INTRODUCTION

AT A GLANCE THIS CHAPTER COVERS:

- relevance of law to social work decision-making
- research evidence on standards of decision-making
- research evidence on confidence of social workers using legal rules
- territorial scope of the book
- outline of subsequent chapters

Whether working with families where there are children in need or requiring protection, or promoting adults' well-being and safety, law provides one mandate for social work practice through the powers and **duties** given to councils with social services responsibilities. Hence a sound working knowledge of child care, mental health, mental capacity and adult social care law is required. However, that is only half the picture. Social workers also need to understand and apply what the law requires when taking decisions about whether and how to use these powers and duties. That is the purpose of this book. It will set out the key elements of **administrative law**, and of equality and human rights legislation, which must shape how social workers practise and, specifically, how they reach decisions about whether to invoke powers and duties with respect to children and adults. It will link their professionalism and accountability to legal rules and, through use of cases and **case law**, illustrate how social workers can reach decisions lawfully and what may happen when they do not. The book will venture into 'tricky' or 'wicked' issues that routinely confront social workers.

A key feature of the book, therefore, is the link that it makes between law in theory and law in practice, illustrating how knowledge of child care, mental health and adult social care law has to be accompanied by an informed use of legal rules designed to ensure accountable professionalism. In addition, social work's stated goals include empowerment of individuals and communities, and enhancement of equality, social justice and human rights. This book shows how the law can support these goals in everyday practice. The purpose overall is to enable social workers to feel confident to take and to challenge decisions, credible when presenting their assessments and plans, critical when approaching the complexities they face and the information they must consider, and appropriately creative and reflective when working with service users and carers to safeguard and promote their welfare (Preston-Shoot, 2000). In short, the book focuses on using the law as part of making good decisions.

| *On-the-spot questions* | 1 How confident do you feel in your knowledge of legal rules relating to different service user groups? |
| | 2 How confident do you feel in your knowledge relating to taking decisions to implement legal powers or duties? |

PRACTICE FOCUS

Emma, aged three, lives with her mother, stepfather and maternal grandparents in a small rented house in poor condition in a deprived neighbourhood. Emma and her mother are being supported by a local children's centre where staff have become concerned about their welfare. Their attendance has become sporadic. Emma has appeared increasingly wary and withdrawn. Staff have seen bruises on her mother's arms and face but she has avoided answering their questions. They refer Emma to children's services but both mother and stepfather are hesitant about engaging with social workers. Shortly thereafter the police report that they have been called to yet another domestic disturbance at the house, noting in passing that the stepfather is known to them for violent behaviour. The family's General Practitioner (GP) refers Emma's grandmother for adult social care assessment with a diagnosis of dementia.

Some tricky issues arise in social work practice:

- By what standards should professional practice be judged if social workers intervene to assess the needs of Emma and her family (Chapters 1 and 2)?
- Who has what rights in this situation (Chapter 3)?
- How should social workers work in partnership with service users and their carers where statutory powers and duties are being contemplated or used (Chapter 4)?
- How might social workers proceed with the assessment of decision-making capacity where imperatives of autonomy, choice and personalization may appear to clash with a duty of care (Chapter 5)?
- What is the relationship between need and resources (Chapter 6)?
- What information can be shared about Emma, her parents and her grandparents in a multi-layered professional and organizational context (Chapter 7)?
- What might social work practitioners and managers learn from complaints and reviews of cases and serious incidents by courts and inquiries (Chapter 8)?
- How can social work managers ensure management and governance oversight to facilitate safe and effective decision-making when much social work practice takes place away from public view (Chapter 9)?

Relating law to social work

Social work is a profession regulated by law, operating within a framework of legislation and government policy, and with legal and ethical obligations to promote human rights and equality. It involves reaching complex judgments, including decisions about whether to invoke statutory powers (General Social Care Council (GSCC), 2008). Social workers must exercise authority within ethical and legal boundaries, understanding the significance of legislative frameworks, including those relating to standards of service delivery (Quality Assurance Agency (QAA), 2008). The Professional Capabilities Framework for social workers in England (Health and Care Professions Council (HCPC), 2012b; The College of Social Work (TCSW), 2012) includes specific reference to promoting human rights, upholding social justice and respecting diversity.

Even when not explicitly stated, law is implicit or embedded within social work's conceptualization of its roles and tasks. Social workers must respect individual diversity and dignity, and both reach and implement difficult decisions, sometimes involving restriction of liberty. They must manage the complex relationship between justice, care and control, and challenge unacceptable practice responsibly (QAA, 2008). Social workers in England must establish and maintain a safe practice environment, raise and escalate concerns appropriately, maintain confidentiality, provide a rationale for their decisions and review their practice (HCPC, 2012b; TCSW, 2012). Those in Wales, Scotland and Northern Ireland, whose practice must comply with National Occupational Standards, must maintain professional accountability, practise professional social work, assess needs and risks, and promote people's engagement and participation (Care Council for Wales, 2011b; Northern Ireland Social Care Council, 2011; Scottish Social Services Council, 2011).

Service users and carers appreciate social workers who demonstrate an understanding of the law (**Social Work Task Force** (SWTF), 2009). Some researchers have found that legal rules do impact on social workers' decision-making and that law is a constant reference point (Sheppard and Ryan, 2003; Duffy and Collins, 2010). Moreover, in performing their unique role in carrying through key statutory responsibilities to safeguard and promote the welfare of children and adults at risk, and in making and defending complex judgments about when legal powers should be used (HM Government, 2010), social workers have attracted government (Welsh Assembly Government (WAG), 2011a) and judicial recognition for their conscientious approach (*Re F* [2008]), their dedication and commitment (*Re D* [2008]), and their skill and care in meeting people's complex needs (*Re X* (Emergency Protection Orders) [2006]; *Re B* [2007]). Courts recognize that social workers are trained and often experienced and will therefore be slow to intervene in their decisions providing that they act lawfully and rationally (see Chapter 1) (*R (Ahmad) v Newham LBC* [2009]).

The **Office for Standards in Education, Children's Services and Skills** (OFSTED) (2012a) has reported on a range of strategies that effectively support frontline staff and facilitate better child protection outcomes. Management of practice can make a positive difference, facilitating clarity of purpose, identification and management of risk, and confident decision-making. Assessments and child protection plans are improved when informal support and formal supervision are prioritized. The personal qualities of social workers also make a difference, with positive change in families promoted by respectful attitudes and persistent and creative work. Some local authorities demonstrate good or outstanding practice. For example, in one London Borough (OFSTED, 2012b) assessments, case planning and recording were generally comprehensive and good, and multi-agency partnership working was exemplary, leading to positive outcomes for children. Social workers and managers were skilled, highly motivated and knowledgeable about the children with whom they were working. Provision for looked after children was excellent.

However, social work may have taken too little notice of the legal context of practice and been slow to recognize the contribution that techniques of legal reasoning, assessment of evidence and rules of procedural fairness can make to an effective and fairer exercise of social workers' **discretion** (Zifcak, 2009). Keeping abreast of legislative change, especially in child care and youth justice, is challenging. Nor are the legal rules necessarily experienced as easy to understand or to use, especially when legislation concerning adult protection, mental capacity and child care meets requirements relating to human rights and data protection (Dickens, 2007; Perkins et al., 2007; Pinkney et al., 2008).

Levels of legal knowledge and confidence in its skilled use are variable. Laming's assessment (2009) was that too many social workers were not well equipped in law by their training or their employers. The SWTF (2009) concluded that newly qualified social workers lacked some basic legal knowledge to be effective. Researchers have found highly variable use of legislation in decision-making – both amongst newly qualified and more experienced social workers – coupled with gaps in knowledge, inaccurate understanding, a lack of confidence to use the law and to challenge organizational procedures and decisions, and a tendency to conflate rather than recognize the difference between law and agency policy (Drury-Hudson, 1999; McDonald et al., 2008; Braye et al., 2013a). Some social workers, including practice teachers, emphasize agency procedures and appear to experience the law as difficult and hostile; others are both respectful and fearful of the legal rules (Braye et al., 2007); others still will have misgivings about invoking legal proceedings, for example, in child care, because of concern about how social work evidence will be viewed by courts or a preference to work in partnership with parents (Dickens, 2007).

The outcomes of teaching law to social workers

Researchers followed 638 students through their qualifying training across seven universities. Over half of all students on qualifying lacked confidence to challenge their own or other agencies' interpretation of law, even when their legal knowledge was accurate. More than one quarter expressed difficulty with identifying relevant legal rules, applying law to practice, and making lawful decisions.

In core knowledge areas (children in need, child protection, adult safeguarding and mental capacity), under half felt reasonably or fully confident in their knowledge. High levels of anxiety remained about using the law and keeping up to date. Qualifying students had greater confidence in their knowledge than in their skills to apply that understanding.

Qualifying students were more likely to see law as capable of challenging inequality and protecting people at risk but less likely to see the legal rules as agents of social change, protecting socially disadvantaged groups, or meeting people's needs.

Some students had been shocked by the practice they had witnessed on placement, outdated procedures and ignorance of the legal rules, and by the response received when they had raised concerns (Preston-Shoot and McKimm, 2012a; 2012b).

Contexts for decision-making

Social work practice is often effective and unsung. Service users are involved in assessments and decision-making about care plans.

Assessments are timely and needs-led. Care packages restore, maintain and/or enhance an individual's quality of life. Communication with other agencies is effective and managers engage directly with the lived experience of staff at the frontline. However, this is not always the case.

On-the-spot questions

1 What reasons can you think of which might explain poor social work decision-making?
2 When a judge compared a local authority children's services department to a computer system and suggested that its decision-making had become infected by a virus (*R (CD) (A Child by her Litigation Friend VD) v Isle of Anglesey CC* [2004]), to what might the judge have been referring?
3 What viruses do you think affect social work decision-making?

Whilst arguably atypical, one inspection report conveys a blunt assessment of a local authority (OFSTED, 2012c). Finding children's services to be inadequate, despite some examples of timely assessments, effective family work, and good supervision of complex cases, the report recommends immediate action to ensure that children are protected, statutory visits conform to required timescales, assessments are timely and thorough, children are enabled to contribute to assessments and planning, and management oversight of cases is improved. Child protection (OFSTED, 2008; 2009) and adult-safeguarding (Braye et al., 2013b) **serious case reviews** reveal not dissimilar repeating patterns.

Some themes spanning serious case reviews in children's and adults' services

- Lack of compliance with statutory requirements and/or failure to consider options for using legal powers;
- uncertainty about the interface between different legal mandates, for example, children's and adults' social care;
- concerns about the quality of assessments and care plans;
- limited inter-agency cooperation, for example, around information-sharing or acceptance of safeguarding as 'everyone's business';
- unclear roles and overlapping functions;

- lack of management oversight of complex cases;
- ignorance of case chronology and a failure to pool information to achieve a holistic view of a case;
- divergent thresholds, with service users falling through the net;
- poor recording;
- failure to speak to a child or significant others;
- failure to modify assessments and intervention approaches in the light of new information;
- failure to implement agreed action plans and to act in response to increasing levels of concern;
- ineffective case reviews.

Poor decisions can cause harm and have tragic consequences (Duffy and Collins, 2010). However, making good decisions is not straightforward. Social workers may follow a sound decision-making process but fail to secure a beneficial outcome for those with whom they are working. They will routinely face hostility, resistance, distress and scepticism from people whose needs and problems they seek to assess and resolve, thereby complicating the decision-making process. Indeed, the only certainty about social work decision-making is the presence of a greater or lesser amount of uncertainty (Munro, 2012).

Decisions have to be reached in real time; consulting statutes and guidance, and explicitly drawing on research evidence, may have to follow rather than always precede action. The right decision may not be obvious; options may appear so unattractive that practitioners are left searching for the 'least wrong' answer. Decisions may have unintended and unforeseen consequences, especially when working with 'ungovernable actors' (Morrison, 2010). Further complicating the picture are fragmented organizational structures and financial austerity, which social workers may experience as rising thresholds, silo working, escalating workloads, performance management systems that prioritize quantitative over qualitative measurement of practice, and erratic supervision and support (Laming, 2009; SWTF, 2009).

Managers may demand compliance with agency procedures rather than promote collective reflection on the ambiguities and uncertainties that cases present (Morrison, 2010). Organizations may be risk-averse, afraid of possible mistakes and their ramifications, illustrating that the use of legal knowledge is mediated through an organizational context. When social workers become acculturated to an organizational culture that privileges agency procedures and concern with resources above lawful and ethical practice, social work values, empathy with service users and concern for statutory duties, human rights and equality may become casualties (Preston-Shoot, 2010; 2011). The key cases featured in this chapter illustrate what can happen in such organizational cultures and contexts, and lend weight to concerns about agencies failing to meet their statutory duties, for example, in relation to child protection (Department for Children, Schools and Families (DCSF), 2008) and carers (Seddon et al., 2007). They begin also to sketch out not just the need to comply with statutory duties, for example, in child care legislation, but also with principles for decision-making which have been built up through case law.

> **KEY CASE ANALYSIS**

Re F (A Child) [2008]

The Court of Appeal was critical of local authority practice and decision-making in this case where the birth father notified, shortly before his child was placed for adoption, that he intended to seek revocation of the placement order (Adoption and Children Act 2002). The three judges concluded that the father had suffered a manifest injustice and that there had been a travesty of good practice because the local authority had ignored the father's notification and made the placement, which under the construction of the 2002 Act meant that the birth father could not apply for revocation of the placement order. They suspected that the local authority had deliberately set out to prevent the father from being heard by a court and they criticized managers for disgraceful conduct that included a profound and total misunderstanding of their functions under the 2002 Act. The local authority had not been able to produce minutes of meetings to show how the father's late notification was considered and the rationale for the decisions that were reached.

The judges conceded that the local authority may have believed that it was acting in the best interests of the child but reminded social work practitioners and managers that, when dealing with parents, irrespective of how inadequate or abusive they might be, they are dealing with human beings who have feelings and rights. The authority owed a duty to the father and to the prospective adopters. To press ahead without warning the prospective adopters was an abuse of their trust.

> **KEY CASE ANALYSIS**

R (CD) (A Child by her Litigation Friend VD) v Isle of Anglesey CC [2004]

This case revolved around decisions following a review of a respite care package and provides an example of resource-led rather than needs-led decision-making. The judge was critical of the local authority's inflexibility and of a care plan that was contrary to the welfare of the child. The judge concluded that the proposed new arrangements for respite care should be quashed because due consideration had not been given to the child's wishes (s. 20(6) Children Act 1989) and the plan would not meet her needs (s. 23(8)) or minimize the effects of her disability (s. 17(2)). The proposals were also criticized for placing insurmountable responsibilities on the child's mother and for failing to recognize the importance of the child's respite carers in her life.

Indeed, when declaring the care plan for this disabled young person unlawful, the judge compared the local authority to a computer system in which a virus had come to infect decision-making.

> **KEY CASE ANALYSIS**

R (NA) v Croydon LBC [2009]

An age assessment of an asylum seeker was quashed as it was unfairly carried out. The social worker misunderstood the nature of an identity card and failed to analyse whether or not it was genuine.

The social worker's conduct of the interview breached principles set out in case law. The child was not asked if he wanted an independent adult to be present. A solicitor was not informed about the age assessment interview. A second interview was conducted by the same social worker and it was highly doubtful if they could take a fresh decision. There was a two-month gap between the assessment and the recording of it. Supposed inconsistencies in the child's account were not put to him for comment, breaching the rule of procedural fairness. The assessment did not balance for and against factors in order to reach a decision based on the totality of available material.

Shifting responsibilities

Researchers have long critiqued the inadequacy of bureaucratic, managerialistic attempts to secure quality improvements in social work practice, arguing that they undermine performance, transform what should be a professional activity into a technical one, and elevate compliance with procedures over outcomes from effective interactions with individuals and families (Ayre and Preston-Shoot, 2010). Government policy, finally, may now be shifting in a similar direction.

Laming (2009) observed that there had been an over-emphasis on process and targets, jeopardizing reflective social work practice and neglecting the importance of supportive learning environments for the development of professional judgment. Official reviews have recognized that the systems surrounding social workers, including the proliferation of legal rules and **statutory guidance**, may not have helped them to tackle the challenges they encounter (Department for Education (DfE), 2011; Munro, 2012). Stress is now laid on valuing social work expertise, placing greater trust, responsibility and accountability on practitioners whilst supporting their practice and promoting learning. Thus, sustaining quality and safe social services in Wales (WAG, 2011a) requires professionalism, building a workforce that is competent, confident and supported in applying its own judgments, instead of relying on government guidance. Similarly, social work in Scotland is now seen as requiring well-informed decision-making, where social workers use professional judgment and discretion and their creativity is encouraged within a framework of accountability and support, drawing on legislation, social work theory and research evidence (Scottish Government, 2011).

However, in deciding how to exercise professional judgment and discretion, legal rules continue to shape the process by which decisions are reached, the accountabilities owed by the social worker, the framework for what is under consideration and the content of assessment, plans and reviews. Law provides one mandate for intervening in people's lives and a structure or discipline for the professional practice represented by that intervention. It is this structure or discipline that is the focus of this book, rather than the specific mandates to intervene in the lives of children and adults at risk. It is about the 'how' of practice.

Duty of care

Throughout this book reference will be made to a duty of care, such that it is important to give an opening definition here. This will be amplified as the book unfolds, especially in Chapters 1, 2 and 3.

Sometimes experienced as or assumed to conflict with the principle of personal autonomy, expressed through choice and control, is the common law duty of care owed by social workers towards service users (Braye and Brammer, 2012). Established in *Donoghue v Stevenson* [1932], this duty is owed to anyone who may be affected by action taken where injury might be foreseen, and particularly high standards are expected of people with professional expertise. The duty of care encompasses the requirements both to protect from harm (*Z v UK* [2001]; *Keenan v UK* [2001]) and to take positive action to promote rights under the European Convention on Human Rights and Fundamental Freedoms (ECHR) (see Chapter 3). It is a continuing obligation that extends beyond immediate assessment to a requirement for transparent, proportionate monitoring and review of work with service users.

A duty of care is an essential prerequisite in claims of **negligence**, which require the claimant to demonstrate that the duty existed and was breached and that damage ensued. As Chapter 3 explains, and as case law examples throughout the book illustrate, court decisions on whether a duty of care is owed by public authorities to those in whose lives they intervene (or choose not to intervene) have increasingly established that it *is* owed, and have eroded earlier assumed immunity enjoyed by local authorities in the public interest of having freedom to exercise their statutory duties without interference (Preston-Shoot et al., 2001; Braye and Brammer, 2012). Liability in negligence may be more readily established when practice has unreasonably or unlawfully departed from the policy and legislative requirements and social work standards. This underscores the importance of social workers appreciating the legal standards for decision-making, outlined initially in Chapter 1, and social work's own professional standards, discussion of which begins in Chapter 2.

The duty of care exists regardless of whether there is additionally any statutory duty or power to investigate actual or suspected significant harm (Braye and Brammer, 2012). A duty of care may justify information-sharing (see Chapter 7) and intervention, for example, in circumstances where refusal of services by people with capacity is associated with severe and life-threatening self-neglect (Braye et al., 2011). The courts have endorsed the local authority's role in at least investigating the circumstances in which an adult who might be deemed vulnerable appears to be choosing a self-harmful path, whilst stopping short of legitimizing intervention to prevent a mentally competent adult from carrying through such actions (*Re Z (Local Authority: Duty)* [2004]). The court in this case determined that there was no basis in law for preventing a mentally competent person from taking their own life. However, the local authority retained a duty to investigate the position of a vulnerable adult to identify their true intention, to consider whether they were legally competent to make the decision, to consider whether they were subject to any undue influence, and to identify any potential criminal offence (see Chapter 5).

The book's scope

The territorial scope of the book is UK-wide. Specific attention will be drawn where appropriate to the law as it applies distinctively in England, Northern Ireland, Scotland and Wales. Scotland in particular has always had a distinctive legislative system and, arguably, has led developments in the interface between law and social work practice in key fields, such as mental capacity and adult protection. Wales is increasingly diverging from England in the legal rules for social work practice, with its National Assembly now having legislative competence to make measures, which are akin to **primary legislation**, concerning safeguarding and promoting the welfare of children and young people (National Assembly for Wales (Legislative Competence) (Social Welfare and Other Fields) Order 2008 (SI 2008/3132).

The positional scope of the book is that the law is one, but only one, component of sound decision-making. Other skills and knowledge are also necessary to secure good outcomes for children and adults at risk. These include: appraisal and use of research; ethical frameworks; emotional resilience; and communication and relationship skills with service users and other professionals in order to navigate practice dilemmas (see, for example, the forms of literacy discussed in Chapter 2). Here, though, law is foregrounded and other components of decision-making backlit. In particular, considerable use is made of case law and decisions by the **local government ombudsman** (LGO). These cases will often have originated in complaints procedures (see Chapters 8 and 9) and progressed to **judicial review** or the ombudsman when the service user felt dissatisfied with the outcome of their complaint. Social work can learn particular lessons from such cases.

It is important to stress that sometimes local authorities rather than service users succeed at judicial review and emerge positively from ombudsman investigations. Their practice is found to be lawful, rational and reasonable (see Chapter 1). Much good practice goes unnoticed. Inevitably, it is poor practice that reaches the courts and quasi-judicial settings and attracts comment. However dispiriting, such cases can also be instructive, if readers are not diverted by the advantage of hindsight and freedom from budgetary constraint that those who evaluate and judge practice possess.

Care must be taken when thinking of generalizing the implications of ombudsman judgments and case law decisions. They are taken in a particular jurisdiction and the legal rules may be different elsewhere. However, judgments in higher courts, such as the Court of Appeal in England and Wales and the UK Supreme Court, set **precedents**, which may well be referred to in lower courts in other jurisdictions. For example, a court in Northern Ireland (*DM (A Person under Disability) Acting by his Next Friend, Kathleen McCollum, for Judicial Review* [2013]) referred to a Supreme Court decision (*R (KM by his Mother and Litigation Friend JM) v Cambridgeshire CC* [2012]) when deciding that a health and social services trust had erred in law when refusing to make a direct payment by not following the approach that had been approved by the Law Lords. Equally, all judicial and quasi-judicial decisions offer important signposts about quality practice and decision-making.

The book assumes some background knowledge and understanding of core legislative mandates, such as child protection and mental capacity. For this reason, coupled with the book's focus on how well the law is used in practice, the emphasis is placed on case law rather than primary legislation. Equally, a core social work skill is the ability to find, read and understand primary legislation, regulations and statutory guidance. Thus, reference is made where appropriate to such core mandates but extracts are not quoted verbatim. Much is to be gained from reading the source material.

Finally, although the focus is predominantly on local authority social work, it is important to stress the relevance of administrative law to social work and social care provision in the private and voluntary sectors, increasingly important settings for provision across the UK.

Chapter outline

Chapter 1, entitled 'First principles', is an outline of administrative law as the legal framework for accountable professional decision-making. This chapter will set out the principles for decision-making, which are derived from administrative law, and will offer examples to illustrate how these principles should be applied and shape practice. The chapter will focus, for example, on how social work's ethical commitment to partnership working finds expression in administrative law principles and, equally, why it is important to give reasons for decisions.

Chapter 2, 'Foundations of good decision-making', charts the legal underpinnings of accountability and professionalism in social work. This chapter will identify how the legal rules have contributed to the shape of the architecture within which social work is housed, such as professional regulation by the HCPC in England and social care or services councils in Wales, Scotland and Northern Ireland. It will locate how codes of practice and conduct, where applicable, are derived from legal rules and where from the social work profession's own efforts to ensure appropriate practice and decision-making standards. It will similarly trace, for example, the origins of conduct hearings and fitness for practice determinations, offering case illustrations to evaluate the degree to which such mechanisms are capable of ensuring quality outcomes for service users.

Chapter 3, 'Human rights and equality' covers key factors in decision-making. This chapter will focus principally on the Human Rights Act 1998 and the Equality Act 2010, and particularly on such principles and requirements as **proportionality** and impact assessments. Links will be made to primary legislation – such as the Mental Capacity Act 2005 and the Mental Health Act 2007 in England and Wales – and to case law in child care proceedings and setting of eligibility criteria in adult social care, to illustrate the impact that such principles have on decision-making in practice and local policy-setting.

Chapter 4, 'Partnerships within decision-making', deals with partnerships with service users and carers, and with other professionals, as key factors in decision-making. This chapter will connect where administrative law principles link with primary legislation, statutory guidance, practice guidance and case law to embed partnership in practice. Practice application will be illustrated through the use of case examples.

Chapter 5, 'Who decides?', highlights capacity and its role in decision-making, exploring autonomy and best interests in respect of adults and children at risk. The focus here will be particularly on mental capacity legislation and the principles that are meant to safeguard people's decision-making autonomy and to guide practice when people may not have the capacity to make their own decisions. The principles will be illustrated through the use of case illustrations. The chapter will also consider how practitioners and managers should conduct decision-making surrounding deprivation of liberty questions. It will also review how the law views children and young people as decision takers.

Chapter 6, 'What can we afford?', focuses on decision-making about resources and meeting need in a context of financial austerity. Councils with social services responsibilities, when reviewing their eligibility criteria for children's and adults' services, and when making decisions about how to meet people's needs, have sometimes been successfully challenged in judicial review. Through the use of case illustrations, the chapter will outline the principles that elected councillors, practitioners and managers should follow when setting policy and when considering referrals.

Chapter 7, 'Deciding to share information', examines decision-making surrounding sharing information in a multi-layered professional and agency context, including learning lessons from reviews of serious cases. Reviews of the outcomes of professional practice, including of social work, often criticize practitioners for failing to request or to share information, with the result that no one agency has a complete chronology or picture of the circumstances surrounding decision-making. This chapter will consider the Data Protection Act 1998, and subsequent guidance for councils with social services responsibilities, and their statutory partners in child and adult protection, concerning information-sharing and confidentiality. Reference will be made to other pieces of primary legislation and statutory guidance, for example, surrounding child and adult safeguarding – noting in Scotland that it is certainly more usual to refer to adult protection – in order to reinforce the importance of different agencies and professions working closely and cooperatively with social work practitioners and managers. Again, case illustrations will be offered to pinpoint good practice.

Sometimes decisions turn out badly. Chapter 8, 'Learning from the uncomfortable and unthinkable', will explore situations where local authorities have appeared negligent and where complaints procedures and other possible mechanisms for highlighting poor practice have not worked well. This chapter will distinguish between cases where decision-making has been poor and where a framework has been used to reach a good-enough decision but where the outcome has been unexpected. It will identify the standards of organizational behaviour that the law and the social work profession itself expect, and for which managers can be held accountable. Case law will be used to illustrate what courts and **tribunals** have reflected on professional decision-making.

Chapter 9, 'Embedding and ensuring best practice', looks at clinical and organizational governance, exploring the centrality of supervision, safeguarding boards, and overview and scrutiny committees to ensuring accountable, professional and safe decision-making practice. The Social Work Reform Board (2010a), and to a lesser extent parallel processes in other parts of the UK, has reconfigured and codified standards for workloads, supervision, the continuing professional development of the social work workforce, and professional capability. Munro's review of child protection in England (2011) is another example of rethinking and reclaiming social work, to ensure a confident and competent workforce and to promote high practice standards. This chapter will capture the key elements of safe and accountable practice and the management of practice, linking them to legal rules where appropriate. Case examples will be offered to illustrate the importance of oversight of professional practice.

Further reading

Ayre, P and M Preston-Shoot (eds) (2010) *Children's Services at the Crossroads: A Critical Evaluation of Contemporary Policy for Practice.* An edited collection of chapters which critique, in England especially, reforms in children's services, arguing that **managerialism** has diminished social workers' capability to respond effectively to complex challenges.

Braye, S and M Preston-Shoot (2007) *Law and Social Work E-Learning Resources.* A collection of ten reusable learning objects on law and social work, offering diverse opportunities to explore components of the legal rules and to test one's knowledge and understanding. The objects may be found at www.scie.org.uk/publications/elearning.

Guthrie, T (2011) *Social Work Law in Scotland* 3rd edn. This book covers the legal context, accountability and core mandates, including child protection, adults at risk and mental health for social workers in Scotland.

Swain, P and S Rice (eds) (2009) *In the Shadow of the Law: The Legal Context of Social Work Practice.* A perspective from Australia on the relationship between legal rules and social work practice.

Taylor, B (2013) *Professional Decision Making and Risk in Social Work Practice* 2nd edn. A book that explores concepts for and practice of decision-making, wherein law is one component of effective practice.

White, C (2014) *Northern Ireland Social Work Law* 2nd edn. This book covers accountability, the legal system and the core mandates, including equality, youth justice, mental health, community care and child protection for social workers in Northern Ireland.

1
FIRST PRINCIPLES

AT A GLANCE THIS CHAPTER COVERS:

- administrative law as a legal framework for accountable decision-making
- principles for professional decision-making
- case law examples of good and poor decision-making
- congruence of legal principles for decision-making with social work values

All of us have experiences of consulting professionals on whose knowledge, skills and ethics we rely. They possess expertise through training which is beyond our competence and/or have statutory or positional authority on which we depend in order to meet our needs. We will have our own standards or benchmarks by which we differentiate between good and less satisfactory consultations or interactions.

On-the-spot question	What standards or benchmarks for you would comprise a good decision-making consultation with a professional on whose expertise you are relying to meet your needs?

However, what standards does the law require for professional, accountable decision-making? The challenge for social workers is to do the right thing at the right time with the right skills – in effect to get it right every time (HM Government, 2010). Leaving aside, for now, whether such a standard is actually possible for any social welfare or healthcare professional, what would regulatory bodies such as the HCPC in England,

PRACTICE FOCUS

Emma, aged three, lives with her mother, stepfather and maternal grandparents in a small rented house in poor condition in a deprived neighbourhood. Emma and her mother are being supported by a local children's centre where staff have become concerned about their welfare. Their attendance has become sporadic. Emma has appeared increasingly wary and withdrawn. Staff have seen bruises on her mother's arms and face but she has avoided answering their questions. They refer Emma to children's services but both mother and stepfather are hesitant about engaging with social workers. Shortly thereafter, the police report that they have been called to yet another domestic disturbance at the house, noting in passing that the stepfather is known to them for violent behaviour. The family's GP refers Emma's grandmother for adult social care assessment with a diagnosis of dementia.

- By what standards should professional practice be judged as social workers intervene in this case?
- What standards have developed within the legal rules by which to measure good practice?

judges and the Local Commissioner for Administration (ombudsman) consider when subjecting social work decisions to scrutiny?

Administrative law

Social workers, we hope, are familiar with powers and duties for intervening in the lives of children and adults at risk, which are contained in primary legislation and amplified by **secondary legislation** (regulations and directions), statutory guidance and case law. However, whilst these powers and duties outline what may, or in certain circumstances must, be done, decision-making about whether, when and how to use them involves a balancing exercise to reach a reasonable decision based on the merits of the case. Administrative law, dating back at least as far as Magna Carta in 1215, has evolved principles to regulate what, in effect, is the use of discretion, and to mediate between state officials (here social workers) and individual service users, when the former have powers that could impact on people's liberty and other rights. Bingham (2011) captures the point succinctly when noting that public officers must exercise power in good faith, fairly, for the purpose for which powers were conferred, whilst not exceeding the limits of such powers nor acting unreasonably. Similarly, trust between professionals, and between them and service users, is generated by acting with integrity, which includes respect, honesty and fairness, benevolence as in concern for others, humility regarding the limits of one's competence, predictability, and an attitude that is relational and accessible (Hope-Hailey et al., 2012). These principles, as codified by legal rules, correspond closely to social work values (Preston-Shoot et al., 2001).

Law is concerned, therefore, not with whether the right decision is taken. What the correct decision is might not be obvious or it might be contested. Rather, administrative law is concerned that the right decision-making approach was adopted. It is concerned, therefore, with the lawfulness, rationality and fairness of the process. It is concerned with avoiding maladministration, which may result from unreasonable delays, failure to comply with legal requirements, or omitting to investigate an issue and take appropriate action.

> ### ◢ PRACTICE FOCUS
>
> Practice with Emma and her family might be measured against several characteristics of a sound decision-making process:
>
> - openness;
> - fairness;
> - rationality;
> - impartiality;
> - accountability;
> - consistency;
> - participation;
> - efficiency;
> - equity.
>
> As this chapter now explains, the legal rules have codified standards which Emma and her family could expect that those professionals surrounding them should adhere to. Assessments and interventions should comply with statutory duties in primary and secondary legislation, and in statutory guidance. Decisions should be reasonable when considered against professional values and learning from research, serious case reviews, knowledge and practice experience, and should be explained to the family and the professionals who have referred them. Decisions should be timely, including adhering to timeframes where these are specified in law, and all relevant information should be considered from the family and the professionals who know them. Social workers should work with Emma and also involve her parents and grandparents in decisions about her welfare and in discussions about their own needs.

Lawful decision-making

This chapter will consider seven principles – lawfulness, rationality and reasonableness, timeliness, full examination of all relevant factors, not fettering discretion, participation and information-giving, and giving reasons. Each will be illustrated through case law, ombudsman decisions and/or research findings. Other principles, such as meeting acceptable standards of professional competence, the promotion of equality and human rights, and mechanisms to demonstrate accountability or provide for redress, will be explored in subsequent chapters. One case, however, whilst perhaps exceptional, demonstrates a number of these principles in action.

> **KEY CASE ANALYSIS**

Bath and North East Somerset Council v A Mother and Others
[2008]

When reviewing a local authority's handling of a child protection case, the judge found serious failings, amongst which were a social worker who had fabricated evidence and lied under oath (professional competence). The local authority admitted a failure to complete core assessments of the children involved, and family carers were not assessed as foster parents (timeliness, professional competence). The manner in which the children had been removed from home had been emotionally traumatic and extraordinary decisions had been taken about where they would reside (rationality and reasonableness, professional competence, human rights – private and family life). Adults with parental responsibility had not been informed of injuries to the children when being cared for by others, and different parts of the family were kept unaware of what was happening and what the local authority was proposing (lawfulness, participation, human rights – private and family life). The GSCC and the local authority had failed to scrutinize a social worker's criminal record (lawfulness).

Lawfulness

Judicial scrutiny of social work decisions sometimes criticizes *failure to perform a statutory duty*. Supporting homeless teenagers provides one example, where social workers have expected housing departments to provide accommodation rather than recognizing the young person as a child in need, unable to live at home, and therefore using the provisions of s. 20 Children Act 1989 (and equivalent provisions in Scotland and Northern Ireland) (*R (TG) v Lambeth LBC* [2011]). Some care plans, particularly for disabled children, have also been quashed as contrary to the requirements of child care law. For example, one care plan was adjudged unlawful for proposing arrangements contrary to the wishes of the child and parent, and for being unable to demonstrate how social workers would minimize the impact of the young person's disability (*R (CD) (A Child by her Litigation Friend VD) v Isle of Anglesey CC* [2004]).

In Northern Ireland a court has criticized a trust for refusing to assess the needs of carers. Failure to provide services in light of the outcomes of an assessment was also unlawful (*HN (A Minor)* [2010]).

One area where there has been particular judicial scrutiny in England relates to young people, some of whom are unaccompanied asylum seekers. Judges have been particularly critical of local authorities who have sought to sidestep duties to accommodate (s. 20 Children Act 1989), partly to avoid the duties to care leavers that follow, using children-in-need provisions instead (*R (Behre and Others) v Hillingdon LBC* [2003]; *R (H, Barhanu and B) v Wandsworth LBC and Others* [2007];*R (S) v Sutton LBC* [2007]). The ombudsman was severely critical of two authorities for continually failing to assess the housing and support needs of a teenager, who for several months had to live in a tent and experienced physical and mental ill-health as a result (*Local Government Ombudsman and Kent CC and Dover DC* (2012)).

Social workers must not exceed *the limits of their statutory authority.* For example, they must only remove a child with judicial sanction or the active consent of someone with parental responsibility (*R (G) v Nottingham CC* [2008]). Contacting a school and GP without the consent of parents, as a precursor to initiating a child protection investigation, is also unlawful (*R (AB and CD) v Haringey LBC* [2013]). In a case involving deprivation of liberty and best interest assessment of an adult without capacity (*Hillingdon LBC v Neary and Others* [2011]), practitioners and managers were reminded that they must have statutory authority for what they are doing or obtain authority for their proposals from a court. Failure to do so in this case resulted in a breach of the individual's right to liberty. Equally, the complexity of the legal rules surrounding deprivation of liberty is no excuse for ignoring them (*G v E and Others* [2010]). Decisions are also unlawful when they *fail to apply the requirements of secondary legislation (regulations and directions) and statutory (policy) guidance.* In England and Wales, this is guidance issued under s. 7 Local Authority Social Services Act 1970. Indeed, even practice guidance, which is advisory rather than mandatory, such as the Mental Health Act Code of Practice in England and Wales (Department of Health (DH), 2008), should be followed as it outlines standards for good practice (*R v Islington LBC, ex parte Rixon* [1996]; *R (Munjaz) v Mersey Care NHS Trust* [2005]). OFSTED (2009) has noted the importance of social workers following the requirements of legislation, including regulations and statutory guidance, when undertaking assessments and preparing care plans.

Thus, child care assessments must conform to statutory guidance (for England and Wales, HM Government, 2013) (*R (AB and SB) v Nottingham*

CC [2001]). This includes seeing the child, alone when appropriate. A pathway plan for a young mother was quashed as it was not based on a proper assessment, with objectives and plans, as required by regulations for young people leaving care (*R (G) v Nottingham CC* [2008]). Similarly, an assessment of need and a care plan for a disabled child was found to be deficient because it did not comply with statutory guidance. It was descriptive, without a proper assessment of need or detailed plan (*R (B) v Barnet LBC* [2009]).

Local authorities in England and Wales have been criticized for failing to comply with guidance on the rate of financial support given to special guardians (*B v Lewisham LBC* [2008]) and kinship carers (*R (L and Others) v Manchester CC* [2002]; *Public Services Ombudsman for Wales v Merthyr Tydfil Council* (2010)). Redress has also been given where guidance on reviews with looked after children has not been followed, demonstrating carelessness with respect to important decisions in their lives (*Barrett v Enfield LBC* [1999]).

Local authorities in England have been reprimanded for erroneously charging for the first six weeks of re-ablement services, contrary to statutory guidance (DH, 2010), and for ignoring statutory guidance on charges for residential provisions (*R v Sefton MBC, ex parte Help the Aged and Charlotte Blanchard* [1997]). One council (*R (B) v Cornwall CC* [2009]) failed to consider statutory guidance on charging and directions on consultation with service users prior to taking decisions on how needs will be met, when deciding to impose charges for community care provision. Organizations have also been criticized for withdrawing services without reviewing service users' needs, or for failing to provide an adequate analysis of future care proposals when a person's needs have remained unchanged – again contrary to statutory guidance (*R v Birmingham CC, ex parte Killigrew* [2000]; *Public Services Ombudsman for Wales v Cardiff Local Health Board* (2009)).

Social work decisions must also *respect fundamental human rights*. This component of lawful decision-making will be fully explored in Chapter 3. For now, two case illustrations will suffice. A local authority's failure to intervene to protect children from abuse was found to breach their rights to live free of inhuman and degrading treatment (Article 3 ECHR) (*Z v UK* [2001]). A local authority's failure to provide services for disabled parents following a community care assessment was a breach of their Article 8 ECHR right to private and family life (*R (Bernard and Another) v Enfield LBC* [2002]).

Rationality and reasonableness

In law, rationality and reasonableness are defined by their opposites. Thus, irrationality is a decision that is so outrageous in its defiance of logic or accepted standards that no sensible person could have reached it (*Council of Civil Service Unions v Minister of State for the Civil Service* [1984]). Unreasonableness is a decision so extreme that no reasonable authority, in this book's focus a social worker or local authority, could ever have reached it (*Associated Provincial Picture Houses v Wednesbury Corporation* [1948]). Accordingly, two reasonable social workers could reach opposite conclusions on the same set of facts without being regarded as unreasonable (*Re W (An Infant)* [1971]). Put another way, given that exercising discretion is a core feature of social work, practitioners and managers must act in a manner allowable when considering the material available to them before making a decision. The decision must not be plainly wrong but fall within an acceptable and evidenced ambit of disagreement (*R (Brown) v Secretary of State for Work and Pensions* [2008]), or within a range of reasonable decisions open to the decision taker (Bingham, 2011).

Chapter 2 will consider the standards of professionalism that social workers must attain when seeking to justify the reasonableness and rationality of their decisions by reference to research and other sources of knowledge when applied to a particular case. For now, it is important to note that care plans have been quashed when they had no realistic prospect of meeting the needs that assessments and reviews had identified (*R v Staffordshire CC, ex parte Farley* [1997]), or when the assessments themselves were seriously flawed (*R (LH and MH) v Lambeth LBC* [2006]; *Pierce v Doncaster* MBC [2008]). A local authority's decision to approve differential rates of payment to family foster carers, treating them differently from other foster carers, was described as irrational and arbitrary as well as discriminatory and inflexible (*R (L and Others) v Manchester CC* [2002]). Similarly, in a case involving a disabled parent, the ombudsman found that there had been a significant failure to provide the parent and children with proper support and advice, which had resulted in financial hardship, distress and delayed recovery. The local authority agreed to undertake a full needs assessment, prepare an appropriate care plan and ensure service provision (*Local Government Ombudsman and Nottinghamshire CC* (2002)). Decisions must also be reached fairly, and the process leading to them must be fair. If the procedures adopted are judged to be unfair and unjust, for example, exclusion from a case conference considering whether staff members of a residential care home should be referred to regulatory bodies and whether a manager was a fit person to run a home (*Davis v West Sussex CC* [2012]), the resulting decisions will be quashed.

Sometimes, however, local authorities succeed in demonstrating that their decisions are rational. For example, a decision to refuse to accommodate a 17-year-old under s. 20 Children Act 1989 was lawful because there was a rational evidential basis for the conclusions that the social workers had reached (*R (AH) v Cornwall CC* [2010]). A decision not to provide residential accommodation (s. 21 National Assistance Act 1948) to an individual with mental illness was also ruled lawful. The person's mental health needs had been recognized in the assessment, as had been their support network and the help available. There had been a careful consideration of the merits of the case (*R (Nassery) v Brent LBC* [2010]).

A particular feature in adult social care can be difficulties in engaging with service users in order to complete an assessment. Here, local authorities must make reasonable and timely attempts to engage individuals who should not simply be abandoned. In one such case, the council had made sufficient effort, including appointing an advocate for the service user (*R (WG) v Local Authority A* [2010]). Similarly, in child care, lack of cooperation from a parent and/or child is no reason for a local authority not to attempt to carry out its obligations and, if obstructed in so doing, case records should evidence the impact on assessment and case planning, and build in contingency plans to deal with episodes of resistance and absence of cooperation (*R (JF) v Hackney LBC* [2010]).

The acid test, therefore, is the degree to which assessments, care plans and service provision fall within standards accepted by social work and the degree to which decisions have a realistic chance of meeting identified needs. Those driven by resources and financial imperatives alone are likely to be struck down. Equally, to meet the test of reasonableness and rationality, any information on which assessments and decisions regarding intervention rely, especially where risk to children or adults is involved, must be properly and thoroughly analysed (*R (ET, BT and CT) v Islington LBC* [2013]).

Timeliness

The no delay principle is firmly established in child care law across the UK. Not surprisingly, therefore, serious case reviews have been critical of delayed or incomplete assessments (OFSTED, 2009; Tiotto, 2012). One local authority has been strongly reprimanded for delays in assessments and progressing decisions to protect children, with drift in planning and a failure to provide agreed services for some young people. Statutory visits within agreed timescales had not been conducted in some cases, nor had timely action been taken in response to referred child protection concerns (OFSTED, 2012c). Practice guidance, for example, relating to transition planning for young people with complex needs (Commission for Social Care Inspection (CSCI), 2007), also emphasizes the importance of timely intervention, with decisions needing to be agreed early enough in order to avoid last-minute changes.

In one case of serious maladministration, amounting to institutional indifference, a local authority took no effective steps over several years to tackle poor housing for a family with severely disabled children (*Local Government Ombudsman and Bury MBC* (2009)). Judgments against local authorities have also involved unacceptable delays in meeting the assessed needs of disabled parents (*R (Bernard and Another) v Enfield LBC* [2002]) and in assessing or reviewing the needs of children and their families within prescribed timescales (*Barrett v Enfield LBC* [1999]; *R (AB and SB) v Nottingham CC* [2001]). Researchers too have emphasized the importance of timely decision-making. Munro and Ward (2008), for example, found delays in concluding care proceedings, including those involving young babies, and lengthy attempts at rehabilitation, which often led to poor outcome. Reder and Duncan (1999) also found that assessments became protracted because of the fear of making a mistake. Such delays can have a detrimental effect on the child's welfare.

Adult social care and mental health law have also seen challenges regarding delays. One local authority had taken no action for months and given the service user no explanation of the delay, which the principle of transparency would require, regarding adaptations in the home following an assessment for a disabled facilities grant (*Local Government Ombudsman and West Lindsey DC* (2009)). In another case involving adaptations to a family home, a local authority had not completed a community care assessment for over three years because of disagreements with a disabled young woman's mother, thereby preventing the individual's move out of residential care. No contingency planning had been undertaken (*Local Government Ombudsman and Surrey CC* (2008)). Delays have also been criticized in hearing applications against detention under mental health legislation (*R (C) v South West Mental Health Review Tribunal* [2001]) and in delayed discharges from psychiatric care because of inadequate community care provision (*Johnson v UK* [1997]). What is a reasonable delay, for example, when deciding whether in mental health law it is practical to consult a nearest relative, will depend on the circumstances of the case and the decision taken must be capable of explanation (*R (V) v South London and Maudsley NHS Trust and Croydon LBC* [2010]). Serious case reviews in adult safeguarding have also emphasized the importance of timeliness. For example, in one instance (Westminster Safeguarding Adults Board, 2011), clear timescales had not been inserted into agreed action plans with the result that measures designed to protect the service user were allowed to drift.

Social workers and their managers would be well advised, therefore, to familiarize themselves with prescribed timescales, set out normally in secondary legislation or statutory guidance.

Taking account of relevant considerations

This standard requires decision-makers to conduct a full examination of all relevant facts, including those that might support an alternative interpretation or conclusion to the one that is favoured. It requires the decision-maker to avoid bias and personal interest (Bingham, 2011). Several cases will illustrate the approach to be taken here. Firstly, detailed inquiries should be conducted and the issues arising considered (*R (MM) v Lewisham LBC* [2009]). In this instance, such an examination would have revealed that a young person was a child in need, their housing and support needs not being met. Child care planning should give serious consideration to the possibility of reuniting children with one or both parents, taking into account their attitudes and actions since child protection inquiries were begun (*Re A (Children)* [2010]). Care plans should involve a proper needs analysis and result in a realistic and detailed action plan, which includes operational objectives – who will do what, how and when (*R (J) v Caerphilly CBC* [2005]; *R (B) v Barnet LBC* [2009]; *R (JF) v Hackney LBC* [2010]). As will be explored in greater detail in Chapter 3, equality impact assessments should address the real issues presented by a case and take proper account of the impact of withdrawing grants or services on disabled and vulnerable people (*R (Rahman) v Birmingham CC* [2011]).

Research routinely draws attention to examining all relevant facts. In some cases social workers appear too readily to accept reassurances about the safety of children rather than to investigate thoroughly; as a result some children are left unprotected (Stanley et al., 2011; OFSTED, 2012c). Sometimes, social workers focus on the needs of parents to such a degree that the needs of the child are obscured (OFSTED, 2009). As serious case reviews demonstrate, assessment must include an articulated understanding of the child's needs alongside exploration of the attributes of family members and consideration of situational factors such as poverty (Sinclair and Bullock, 2002).

Secondly, cases should be approached with an open mind. Social workers should not look for reasons not to provide services (*Local Government Ombudsman and Surrey CC* (2008); *R (MM) v Lewisham LBC* [2009]). Nor should a local authority adopt a closed mind towards the suitability of parents to care for their children, if necessary with support (*Re A (Children)* [2010]). Equally, social workers must be able to demonstrate, rather than simply assume, that state intervention is better than care provided by a family. An adequate assessment must consider whether an individual, in this instant case an adult without capacity, would be better off living at home (*Hillingdon LBC v Neary and Others* [2011]). The same standard also applies to government ministers and those overseeing parole decisions, for example, where again evidence should be scrutinized thoroughly to ensure that a conclusion is justified; received wisdom in a case should be challenged (*R (Roose) v Parole Board and Secretary of State for Justice* [2010]).

Keeping an open mind emerges as a key social work skill. Munro (2010) refers to the mental maps that social workers use of how to act in situations, and recommends that they should become more aware of their theories-in-use through reflection and supervision. Individual practice orientations are influential (Braye et al., 2013a: see Table 1.1), with some practitioners more inclined to prioritize technical/rational knowledge, others ethical principles or rights, and yet others an agency-driven orientation. Each may make a justifiable contribution to how issues are perceived and practice conducted but social workers must be conscious of knowledge-in-use and attitudes-in-use since what is dominant in understanding a situation inevitably means that there will be factors in a case that quite possibly are given insufficient attention or focus. As Clark (2012) and Sinclair and Bullock (2002) have observed, practitioners and managers will bring particular vantage points or dominant perspectives to what they see; they may be risk-averse or risk-accepting; they must be aware of their own prejudgment or bias.

Rational/technical orientation	Law as a set of rules to be applied Technical legal knowledge privileged Whether situations of need or protection meet legal criteria for intervention Emphasis on legal rules for correct practice – doing things right
Moral/ethical orientation	Law as part of a toolkit where practice is driven by ethical goals Law located within a professional morality Legal rules used to contribute to ethical professional goals Emphasis on negotiating dilemmas – doing right things
Rights/structural orientation	Law as a resource for service users where practice privileges social justice and human rights Practitioners emphasize a critical understanding of law Legal rules used to help confront exclusion, oppression and harm Emphasis on right thinking
Agency orientation	Law conflated or assumed within an agency's bureaucratic imperatives Working within but not necessarily challenging organizational procedures Managers influential in determining the approach to be taken Emphasis on local procedures

Table 1.1: Individual practice orientations

Source: Adapted from Braye et al., 2013a

Gower (2011) has drawn attention to the culture of disbelief that can accompany age assessments of young asylum seekers and, in line with judicial pronouncements (*R (B) v Merton LBC* [2003]), recommends that assessors pay due regard to the bewilderment, tiredness and anxiety that young people may feel, allow for the trauma that they may have experienced, and focus not just on personal appearance but also general background, family circumstances, education, ethnic and cultural information, and history.

Thirdly, assessment should weigh up in the balance all relevant factors, such as when conducting age assessments concerning young unaccompanied asylum seekers, in order to reach decisions based on the totality of material and evidence available (*R (NA) v Croydon LBC* [2009]).

Where risks are involved, a proper assessment is required, which includes how likely are the risks and how serious their possible consequences should they arise (*Hillingdon LBC v Neary and Others* [2011]). In family work, too, risks must be fully appraised, often involving the nature and gravity of significant harm, or its likelihood, and the risks of attempting to reunify the family as against seeking permanent substitute placements. When presenting their plans for children in care proceedings, local authorities must consider and balance all the options before reaching a conclusion and proposal for the court (*Re C and B (Care Order: Future Harm)* [2001]).

One area that highlights the importance and difficulty of balancing different factors or imperatives is adult safeguarding. Independence, choice, autonomy and self-determination are strong themes in adult social care policy. However, unthinking promotion of these practice principles may result in inadequate consideration of safeguarding (Fyson and Kitson, 2010). One serious case review demonstrates this phenomenon well (Buckinghamshire Safeguarding Vulnerable Adults Board, 2011). The review concluded that access to direct payments had been promoted without thorough assessment or professional challenge as to need, appropriateness or outcomes. There had been insufficient monitoring of the father–son relationship, passive and remote social work oversight of the father's needs, and an absence of healthy scepticism.

Fettering discretion

A blanket policy, which does not allow exceptions to be made, will be unlawful unless expressly allowed by law. Thus, the automatic prohibition on manual lifting of disabled people by home care workers was not just a breach of human rights, specifically the Article 8 ECHR right to private and family life, but was also unlawful as an example of fettered discretion (*R (A and B and X and Y) v East Sussex CC* [2003]). Similarly, in community care, resource allocation systems should not be used in a formulaic way but as a starting point for the calculation of an individual budget to meet assessed eligible needs (*R (Savva) v Kensington and Chelsea RBLC* [2010]).

The inflexible application of eligibility criteria by local authorities has also been criticized. In one case, for example, inflexibility had resulted in a disabled child and family being denied an assessment and services, breaching duties in the Children Act 1989 to minimize the effect of disability and to ascertain children's wishes and feelings (*R (JL) v Islington*

LBC [2009]). In another case (*R (Birara) v Hounslow LBC* [2010]), a local authority had paid insufficient regard to whether it should act outside its normal policy and provide support beyond the age of 21 to a young person given the circumstances of the case. In community care, all an applicant's needs must be taken into account when decisions are made about whether to enforce usual eligibility criteria regarding needs assessments (*R v Haringey LBC, ex parte Norton* [1998]). Researchers have also found that decision makers appeared to have an inadequate understanding of guidance surrounding eligibility criteria for community care needs assessments (Newton and Browne, 2008). Sometimes, however, local authority practice is exonerated, as in *R (S) v Hampshire CC* [2009]) where social workers had considered whether the case was exceptional and in reaching a decision had not been irrational and unreasonable, and had not fettered their discretion regarding rules on eligibility.

Consultation, involvement and information-sharing

Meaningful participation in decision-making has several elements. Firstly, except in situations of extreme risk and urgency, *consultation should take place before proposals are firmed up*. Secondly, *sufficient reasons for concern and possible proposals must be given* so that those affected can respond. In line with reasonableness, proposals should be based on evidence and be analysed in detail rather than rely on assumptions. Thirdly, *information* on which the decision taker may subsequently rely *should be shared*. Fourthly, those affected should have *sufficient time in which to respond*. Finally, the decision taker must *take representations into account* and show how this has been done when *giving reasons* for the final outcome. Subsequent implementation of the decision reached must be managed carefully.

This sequence has been outlined in several cases involving proposals to close care homes or day centres (*R v Devon CC, ex parte Baker* [1995]; *R (Madden) v Bury MBC* [2002]; *R (B and Others) v Worcestershire CC* [2009]; *R (Watts) v Wolverhampton CC* [2009]), the setting of local authority budgets and decisions to axe funding or raise eligibility thresholds (*R (Rahman) v Birmingham CC* [2011]; *R (JM and NT) v Isle of Wight Council* [2012]), imposition of charges for community care services (*R (B) v Cornwall CC* [2009]), and opportunities to respond to critical reports (*Davis v West Sussex CC* [2012]).

In care proceedings, the principles to ensure effective participation can be seen in the requirement, except in exceptional circumstances approved by the court, that all parties see the evidence on which others might rely (*R (KM) (A Child) v Lambeth LBC* [2011]). In child protection (*Re C (Care Proceedings)* [2002]; *TP and KM v UK* [2002]) and asylum-seeker age assessments (*R (B) v Merton LBC* [2003]; *R (NA) v Croydon LBC* [2009]; *R (FZ) v Croydon LBC* [2011]), records should be disclosed and allegations, inconsistencies or concerns shared so that young people and parents have an opportunity to respond. Local authorities have also been held accountable for failing to share information on which others may rely when taking decisions, for example, whether to proceed with an adoption application (*A and Another v Essex CC* [2003]), or with fostering a young person (*W and Others v Essex CC* [2000]).

In child care law, there are also obligations to enable children to participate in family proceedings when of sufficient age and understanding (*Mabon v Mabon* [2005]), and to ascertain and take into account their wishes and feelings (*R (G) v Southwark LBC* [2009]; HM Government, 2013). It may be appropriate to ascertain the wishes and feelings of other people who have played a significant and prominent role in a child's life, for example, foster carers (*R (Bewry) v Norfolk CC* [2010]). The research picture here appears mixed. Burke (2010) argues that there have been substantial improvements, with young people increasingly feeling able to influence matters of concern to them, for instance, when parents separate, but notes too that child protection, youth justice and asylum processes remain adult-centred and that younger children and disabled children experience their views as having little impact on decisions. Thomas (2011) found that children's level of participation in planning and reviews was highly variable, appearing dependent on the child's age and adult's attitudes. Some young people felt marginalized, disenchanted and helpless, believing that they were excluded from key decisions, in marked contrast to the directions in regulations in England for care planning, placements and reviews. Partnership working with older people, mental health service users and learning disabled people also appears variable (Sullivan, 2009; Braye and Preston-Shoot, 2010) and is explored in more detail in Chapter 4.

Giving reasons

Reasons should be given for decisions, preferably in writing, and the reasons themselves should be reasonable, using the test outlined earlier in this chapter. This standard aligns closely with effective social work practice. Practitioners should state their position, providing grounds and evidence for it, so that their perspective and the conclusion they have reached is capable of justification by reference to evidence; any counter-evidence should be considered and, where appropriate, a conclusion or recommendation qualified, so that others can assess how much weight there is to support the balance finally struck in a case (Duffy, 2011).

Thus, reasons must not be arbitrary but capable of justification (*Re C and B (Care Order: Future Harm)* [2001]). In child care cases, reasons for decisions should be rooted in the welfare checklist and in the right to private and family life (*Re A (Children)* [2010]). In another case involving the payment of allowances, not only did the local authority pay insufficient attention to statutory guidance but it also failed to justify paying a special guardian at a lower rate than the fostering allowance (*Barrett v Kirklees MBC* [2010]).

Similarly, in adult social care, courts have held that service users should be given an explanation of decisions regarding eligible needs and how the calculation of personal budgets has been determined to address the cost of services (*R (Savva) v Kensington and Chelsea RLBC* [2010]; *R (KM) v Cambridgeshire CC* [2012]). The imperative of transparency requires that decisions should be communicated in full to those affected (*Hillingdon LBC v Neary and Others* [2011]), partly so that service users

> **KEY CASE ANALYSIS**

Welsh Administration Ombudsman v Carmarthenshire County Council (2009)

This case draws out several of the key themes highlighted in this chapter and also introduces others that follow later in this book. The council was found guilty of maladministration due to the inadequate investigation of allegations of abuse by day centre staff (taking account of relevant facts). The investigation took too long (timeliness) and failed to give witnesses the opportunity to reveal wider concerns (consultation and participation). Assessment and conclusions lacked rigour (professional competence). Opinion was recorded as fact and the records kept did not contain notes of meetings or the reasons for decisions (giving reasons; Chapter 8 – recording). Staff did not whistleblow for fear of retribution (Chapters 2, 3 and 9) and the investigation looked for reasons not to suspend or to consider the threat posed by some staff (taking account of relevant facts; Chapters 8 and 9 – governance).

and carers can exercise their right to challenge, complain and seek redress (see Chapter 9).

Tribunals hearing mental health cases must also give adequate explanations and reasons for why patients have (not) succeeded and why expert opinion has been relied upon or set aside (*DL v South London and Maudsley NHS Foundation Trust and Secretary of State for Justice* [2010]; *RH v South London and Maudsley NHS Foundation Trust* [2010]).

On-the-spot questions	1 On the basis of what you have read in this chapter, how might your practice change as a result? 2 What will you take into discussions with your tutors, practice teachers and team colleagues? 3 What practice issues will you raise with your managers?

Further reading

Bingham, T (2011) *The Rule of Law.* A very accessible introductory exploration of the law, including the legal rules relevant to decision-making.

Braye, S and M Preston-Shoot (2010) *Practising Social Work Law* 3rd edn. This book provides further examples of where judicial decisions have criticized local authority and social work practice, and where research findings have similarly expressed concern about the content of and approach taken towards decision-making.

Carson, D and A Bain (2008) *Professional Risk and Working with People: Decision-Making in Health, Social Care and Criminal Justice.* This book includes consideration of standards of professional practice when working with situations involving risk. It explores recklessness and negligence and emphasizes that practice should be consistent with legal and professional standards.

Swain, P (2009) 'Procedural fairness and social work practice' in P Swain and S Rice (eds) *In the Shadow of the Law* 3rd edn. This chapter discusses the principles for appropriate use of power and authority, such as where the mandate for decisions exists and how it should be validly exercised. It emphasizes that decisions should be timely, based on evidence, reached impartially and without bias, using relevant evidence and providing reasons.

2

FOUNDATIONS OF GOOD DECISION-MAKING

AT A GLANCE THIS CHAPTER COVERS:

- legal underpinnings of individual and organizational accountability
- legal underpinnings of social work professionalism
- law and professional regulation of social workers
- codes of conduct and decision-making standards
- fitness for practice

One key principle held over from Chapter 1 holds that decision-making must reflect an acceptable standard of professional competence. Thus, in child care, judges have ruled that abruptly denying a parent help, and without explanation, was very poor social work practice (*Re A (Children* [2010]). Professionals must investigate child protection concerns with proper care, including presenting allegations to parents (*TP and KM v UK* [2002]). Evidence given to a court must be full, detailed, precise and compelling, given by a social worker with detailed knowledge of the case, with minutes of case conferences and other decision-making meetings available (*X Council v B (Emergency Protection Orders)* [2004]; *Re X (Emergency Protection Orders)* [2006]).

It is completely unacceptable to fail to keep records of how a placement was made (*Public Services Ombudsman for Wales v Merthyr Tydfil* (2010)), or decisions taken to progress with an adoption placement despite a birth father's late notification of an intention to seek revocation of a placement order (*Re F* [2008]), or questions asked and answers received in an age assessment interview (*Local Government Ombudsman and Liverpool CC* (2010)). This latter case resonates with principles of transparency, fairness and evaluation of relevant considerations outlined in Chapter 1. The young person's ethnicity, culture and customs were not explored, no consideration was given as to whether a medical examination would facilitate determination of age, no opportunity was given for them to comment on alleged inconsistencies in their account, and no reasons were given for the final decision.

In adult social care, where consultation has been fair and individual risk assessments thorough, where benefits and drawbacks to proposals have been evaluated, and where a proper balance struck between public expenditure constraints and individual rights to private and family life, decisions to close care homes have not been struck down (*R (Phillips) v Walsall MBC* [2002]; *R (Dudley) v East Sussex CC* [2003]). Conversely, failure to assess mental capacity and risk in care planning for an older person who self-neglects, confusion over roles and responsibilities between care managers and home care workers, and absence of reassessment when problems arose represented maladministration (*Local Government Ombudsman and Worcestershire CC* (2011)).

Once again, the absence of records of relevant meetings between agencies and the unilateral decision by one organization to withdraw its contribution to accommodation and care costs for a disabled woman meant that the individual's needs were entirely forgotten (*Public Services*

> **PRACTICE FOCUS**
>
> Emma, aged three, lives with her mother, stepfather and maternal grandparents in a small rented house in poor condition in a deprived neighbourhood. Emma and her mother are being supported by a local children's centre where staff have become concerned about their welfare. Their attendance has become sporadic. Emma has appeared increasingly wary and withdrawn. Staff have seen bruises on her mother's arms and face but she has avoided answering their questions. They refer Emma to children's services but both mother and stepfather are hesitant about engaging with social workers. Shortly thereafter, the police report that they have been called to yet another domestic disturbance at the house, noting in passing that the stepfather is known to them for violent behaviour. The family's GP refers Emma's grandmother for adult social care assessment with a diagnosis of dementia.
>
> • What are the underlying principles used when deciding whether social work practice has attained or missed acceptable standards of professional competence?

Ombudsman for Wales v Cardiff Local Health Board (2009)). Difficult service users should not be abandoned; genuine attempts should be made to complete community care assessments *(R (WG) v Local Authority A* [2010]). Assessments of need must be adequate (*Local Government Ombudsman and Surrey CC* (2008)).

Defining acceptable standards

The test against which to evaluate practice is what a responsible body of fellow professionals would define as competent practice: what someone with the skills and knowledge of a competent member of that profession would be expected to demonstrate (*Bolam v Friern Hospital Management Committee* [1957]). In Scotland the similar test is whether how a member of a profession has acted is such that no other similar person would have done the same if behaving with ordinary care and following normal and usual practice (*Hunter v Hanley* [1955]). For this purpose, social workers, by virtue of their training, knowledge and experience, which ordinary members of the public do not possess and on which they may rely, are members of a profession (*M (Minor) v Newham LBC* [1994]). If challenged, social workers must be able to give a rationale, drawn from theory, research and practice experience, capable of justifying their approach in the circumstances of the case (*Bolitho v City and Hackney Health Authority* [1997]).

Put succinctly (Bingham, 2011), the question is whether the social worker's conduct was such that no sensible social work authority would adopt. Thus, a duty of care is owed to children where the standard is that

> **KEY CASE ANALYSIS**

S (by the Official Solicitor) v Rochdale MBC and Another [2008]

This case concerned the duties owed to looked after children in England by local authorities and **Independent Reviewing Officers** (IROs) (s. 118 Adoption and Children Act 2002). Although settled by a compromise agreement between the parties, the case illustrates the challenges that local authorities may expect. The alleged breaches of positive duties towards S to ensure her safety and her right to private and family life (Article 8 ECHR) included:

- failure to take adequate child protection measures, including assuming parental responsibility and effecting a stable placement;
- not allocating a qualified social worker but a trainee without adequate experience in child protection or knowledgeable of available legal options which would promote S's welfare;
- no adequate records of the work done by the trainee social worker with S and no adequate supervision of practice;
- deficient review documentation and procedures, including failing to ensure that S's views were understood and taken into account and that those responsible for implementing review decisions were fully involved;
- no evidence that S was enabled to contribute to her care plan;
- no evidence of pathway planning ahead of S leaving care;
- no personal education plan even though the local authority acknowledged that one was necessary.

The case illustrates that best practice includes periodically reviewing the suitability of the allocated worker for the case, in order to ensure that they have the necessary knowledge and skills (see Chapter 9). Reviews should identify if the needs of the child have been understood and should consider whether the authority should apply for parental responsibility when parents are playing no effective role in the child's life.

of reasonably competent social work practice judged by the professional standards prevailing at that time *(NXS v Camden LBC* [2009]). Social work practice must not betray careless performance or a lack of reasonable care (*TTM (by his Litigation Friend TM) v Hackney LBC and East London NHS Foundation Trust* [2011]).

Social work standards of professionalism

Excellent, dedicated social work practice occurs daily (SWTF, 2009; WAG, 2011a; Devaney et al., 2013) but by what standards should it be judged? One UK-wide benchmark (QAA, 2008) refers to social workers recognizing individual dignity when taking and implementing difficult decisions and practising in ways that maximize safety and effectiveness in situations of uncertainty and incomplete information. Professional authority must be exercised within ethical and legal boundaries and must appreciate models of assessment and intervention. Social workers must challenge unacceptable practice responsibly, which includes drawing attention to heavy caseloads and unsafe allocation of work.

In England social workers must act in the service user's best interests, uphold high standards of conduct, maintain professional knowledge and skills, act within the limits of their competence, behave honestly and keep accurate records (HCPC, 2012a). Social workers must promote human rights and equality, demonstrate reflection and analytic skills, maintain currency of knowledge about values, ethical standards and legislation, and take responsibility for maintaining quality of practice (HCPC, 2012b). With nuances, these standards are replicated elsewhere in the UK. For example, in Northern Ireland (Northern Ireland Social Care Council (NISCC), 2002) social workers are accountable for the quality of their work, wherein they must promote and protect service users' rights and maintain people's trust and confidence. Social workers in Wales (Care Council for Wales, 2002) must examine their own practice, adhere to relevant standards, maintain people's confidence and trust, and seek assistance if they feel unprepared for allocated tasks. They should use evidence of what works, promoting respect, people's safety and values enshrined in international conventions and domestic legislation (WAG, 2011a). In Scotland (Scottish Executive, 2003; Scottish Social Services Council, 2009; Scottish Government, 2011), social workers must uphold professional values and ethics, be clear about their roles and responsibilities, draw on evidence for assessment and risk management, and use legislation and social work theory. They should use supervision, comply with codes of practice, and develop their knowledge and skills. They should be able to justify their decision-making.

On-the-spot questions	1 What difference have codes of conduct and practice made to your work? 2 Has registration made any difference to your practice?

What emerges strongly from this analysis is the foregrounding of accountability to service users, to law and to social work expertise (values, knowledge and skills). Understanding these codes is essential and upholding them an individual responsibility. It may prove insufficient, if decisions are challenged, to plead having had inadequate resources to work safely or having followed employer instructions (Kline and Preston-Shoot, 2012).

The codes help to capture what a wise social worker (Payne, 2007) embodies in their practice. Social workers should draw on legislation, theory and intervention methods, values and research evidence, together with service-user and carer narratives, and use these skilfully in each specific situation, adapting them to fit the uniqueness of each case (Payne, 2007; Gordon and Cooper, 2010). They should scrutinize the mental maps or orientations that they bring to situations (Braye et al., 2013a), demonstrate awareness of dominant theories-in-use (Munro, 2010) and consider alternative possibilities when faced with uncertainties and dilemmas (Sullivan, 2009). This approach recognizes one's own bias (Clark, 2012) and approaches the standard of impartiality (Bingham, 2011), being open to other perspectives and not being swayed by personal prejudice. Clark (2007) sees decision-making as reaching for a reflective equilibrium, a settled judgment, after having explored all relevant issues. Carson (2012) similarly refers to judgment and balance where knowledge is often incomplete, exploring the possible benefits and drawbacks of potential decisions, in a manner demonstrating fairness and rigour, before reaching a conclusion. It is the process and quality of reaching a decision – the how, when and why – that matters. Sachs (2009) refers to decision-making as a process of discovery, involving finding out (amidst uncertainty), justification (verifying evidence and logical reasoning), persuasion (spelling out in a way that convinces) and preening (refinement and presentation of conclusions).

The codes are intended to assist social workers to apply key values, principles and standards in practice (Clark, 2007). However, their general wording and broad aspirations may make it difficult to prove a breach and risk is located predominantly with the individual social worker (Orme and Rennie, 2006; Clark, 2007; van Heugten, 2011). Equally, social workers may not highlight their importance when discussing their practice (Doel et al., 2010; Braye et al., 2013a). Nonetheless, even if the codes cannot guarantee ethical behaviour, reference to the principles of reasonableness and rationality (see Chapter 1) may help to identify poor practice and misconduct.

Accountability

On-the-spot question   To whom do you believe that you owe accountability and a duty of care?

Other than when acting with designated authority as Approved Mental Health Professionals in England (and their equivalent elsewhere in the UK), social workers hold delegated authority. They must act within the authority delegated to them by local authorities from within their statutory powers and duties, following employer guidance only if it is lawful in terms of the statutory mandate and defensible in terms of standards or benchmarks of good professional practice (Kline and Preston-Shoot, 2012). Thus, as outlined above, accountability is owed to practise within the legal rules and to comply with practice standards as set by regulatory bodies. Accountability is also owed to employers, who are **vicariously liable** for social workers' actions, including decisions not to act, providing what practitioners and managers are asked to do does not contradict codified legal and regulatory standards.

Within this complex accountability mosaic, partly as a result of the Human Rights Act 1998 (see Chapter 3), immunity from scrutiny has been eroded and courts increasingly are holding both local authorities and individual practitioners to account.

In child protection investigations and assessments, a duty of care has been recognized in law to the child at the centre of decision-making but has not been extended to cover parents suspected of causing or likely to cause significant harm (*D v East Berkshire Community Health NHS Trust and Others* [2005]; *Lawrence v Pembrokeshire CC* [2007]). It is arguable

> **KEY CASE ANALYSIS**

Examples where councils with social services responsibilities have failed to exercise a professional standard of care

Z v UK [2001] – neglect and ill-treatment had not been prevented by the state. This breached Article 3 ECHR, the right to live free of inhuman and degrading treatment. State authorities should be held accountable when there was a real and immediate risk of ill-treatment, which was known or which should have been known to the local authority.

Barrett v Enfield LBC [1999] – a local authority would be held accountable for a young person's loss of family life and mental health due to inadequate monitoring of a care order.

W and Others v Essex CC [2000] – a local authority and individual social worker were accountable for failing to inform honestly potential foster carers of an accommodated child's history.

C v Flintshire CC [2001] – damages were awarded for psychological injuries suffered in residential care by a young person.

Pierce v Doncaster MBC [2008] – no reasonable authority in this instance could have reached a decision to permit a young person's return home to their family. Conduct was measured against practice standards pertaining at the time.

NXS v Camden LBC [2009] – a successful claim by a young person for personal injury and damages following negligent failure to properly discharge child protection procedures. The council acted negligently by failing to adequately monitor this case of suspected child abuse.

A and S (Children) v Lancashire CC [2012] – a local authority and an IRO failed to protect the human rights of two children, including the failure to find an adoptive family and to provide a settled and secure home life, to ensure sufficient procedures were in place to implement case review recommendations, and to provide them with access to independent legal advice.

Local Government Ombudsman and Bristol CC (2011) – a local authority should have told family members that a residential home had a zero rating. Councils must have effective systems for monitoring the quality of care in residential establishments and must have a safeguarding response when homes fail. This response must address risks to individual residents as well as systems to improve care. The level of monitoring will depend on the context, with increased monitoring for more serious concerns. Lack of regular monitoring was especially troubling when concerns about the home were known.

whether, as judges appear to fear, an additional duty of care towards parents would undermine effective investigations when the cardinal principle is well known, namely that the paramount duty is to safeguard and promote the child's welfare. However, the immunity from negligence claims brought by parents in connection with child protection investigations only extends to parents suspected of abuse (*Merthyr Tydfil CBC v C* [2010]). In this case, a mother was allowed to bring a claim alleging a negligent child protection response when the repeated abuse was perpetrated by another child. The council admitted mistakes, such as focusing too heavily on the needs of the abusing child rather than the abused child, deficient record-keeping, and allocating the same social worker to both families involved, thereby creating a conflict of interest.

$\rightarrow$ **KEY CASE ANALYSIS** $\leftarrow$

TF and London Borough of Lewisham [2009]

Not all claims of negligence against a local authority and its social workers succeed. In this case a young woman alleged that she had been abused when in the care of her mother and when looked after by foster parents. She alleged that she should have been taken into care sooner than she was and that rehabilitation with her mother should not have been attempted because the local authority knew that it was likely to fail. She further alleged that a proposed adoption had been mishandled and that social workers had given insufficient attention to her case.

The judge found that allegations of sexual abuse had been investigated by the police and social workers appropriately and no evidence found. When considered against the statutory framework at the time and the knowledge then available to social workers in the case, the claim for negligence failed. Social workers have to make difficult decisions about whether or not to remove a child from their family. At appropriate times social workers had considered the mother's ambivalence, the claimant child's wishes at the time, and the uncertain outcomes of court proceedings. No drift was apparent. Reasonable and balanced decisions were taken about placements and attempts at rehabilitation, the risks being recognized and considered. The claimant had not established a causal link between any act or omission by social workers and the alleged psychological damage. Equally, for the claim to have succeeded there had to have been manifest incompetence rather than just difficult decisions which did not have a desired outcome.

Employer accountability

In addition, employers are accountable for the standards of their workforce and for the conditions under which social workers practise. In Northern Ireland, Scotland and Wales these are codified in care council guidance (Care Council for Wales, 2002; NISCC, 2002; Scottish Social Services Council, 2009). The guidance with respect to employers is not binding; it does not have statutory force, which potentially is a weakness when having to negotiate conflicts between professional values and organizational expectations. The standards include effective supervision, making available information relating to legislation, commitment to social work values and knowledge, and not placing social workers at risk of losing their registration and licence to practise. In England, the Social Work Reform Board (2010a; 2010b) has updated expectations of employers. Similarly without statutory force, expectations of a good employer include: workload management systems; supervision, induction and continuing professional development, in order to ensure workforce competence to meet the challenges of practice; and an environment where social workers can maintain their registration and escalate concerns about standards without fear of recrimination. Similar themes have been enunciated in Scotland (Scottish Government, 2011) and Wales (WAG, 2011a), namely having systems for developing and sustaining a competent and confident workforce via supervision, training and career reviews. Thus, good employers maintain effective staff support systems, which include having clearly defined standards and expectations alongside systematic audits and evaluation of the quality of practice (OFSTED, 2012a).

Concerns, however, persist concerning working conditions for social workers. These congregate around the quality and frequency of supervision and management support, working environment cultures, staff vacancy levels, and overwhelming workloads (Laming, 2009; SWTF, 2009; Jack and Donnellan, 2010; OFSTED, 2010; Munro, 2011; Devaney et al., 2013). Some practitioners appear to be allocated work beyond their competence and experience and are placed in vulnerable positions as a result (*Bath and North East Somerset v A Mother and Others* [2008]). Chapters 8 and 9 return to the theme of employer responsibility for the context for practice.

A few social workers have successfully appealed to the Care Standards Tribunal in England and Wales to overturn decisions to bar them from the register. They have successfully used lack of supportive and competent managers, inadequate guidance, poor supervision, unsafe systems regarding case closure and allocation of work to practitioners with sufficient experience and training, and inadequate resources to cope with the job's demands (*LA v General Social Care Council* [2007]; *Forbes v General Social Care Council* [2008]; *Cordingley v Care Council for Wales* [2009]). However, the absence of legal advice, supervision and management guidance will not necessarily prevent a sanction for poor practice, such as inadequate recording and giving untrue evidence in care proceedings (*Borley v Care Council for Wales* [2010]). This case resulted in admonishment for one year as the social worker was new and inexperienced.

Social workers have won damages from a negligent employer who knew or ought to have known of the emotional burdens of the role, with consequent mental and/or physical ill-health, and yet failed to take reasonable steps to provide assistance and adjust workloads (*Walker v Northumberland CC* [1995]). Similarly, employers have been negligent for failing to protect social workers when they knew, or ought to have known, of the risks presented by a service user, reinforcing again a duty of care owed to staff (*R (Selwood) v Durham CC, Tees, Esk and Wear Valleys NHS Foundation Trust, and Northumberland, Tyne and Wear NHS Foundation Trust* [2012]).

Registration and fitness to practise

All four UK jurisdictions have passed legislation that requires registration of social workers and, outside England, some social care workers (Care Standards Act 2000; Health and Personal Social Services (Northern Ireland) Act 2001; Regulation of Care (Scotland) Act 2001; Health and Social Care Act 2012). The legislation enables publication of codes of practice and, through secondary legislation, creates systems for management of the professional registers, including the power to impose penalties of admonishment, suspension or removal. Numbers of registered social workers reported for misconduct have grown – examples include inappropriate relationships with service users, leaving people at risk of abuse and harm, or dishonest behaviour – but remain a small percentage overall (Scottish Social Services Council, 2010; Care Council for Wales, 2011a; GSCC, 2011).

Registration aims to safeguard the public and guarantee standards (Roche and Rankin, 2004; DH, 2011). The system aims to be proportionate to risk, consistent, transparent and targeted (DH, 2011). However, it has drawn criticism for being punitive rather than developmental, long drawn-out, and for sanctions that are disproportionate and limited (Devo, 2009; Heath, 2011).

Suitability of social workers is governed further by legislation that covers criminal offences and unsuitability of people to work with children and/or adults at risk (Safeguarding Vulnerable Groups Act 2006; Protection of Vulnerable Groups (Scotland) Act 2007; Safeguarding Vulnerable Groups (Northern Ireland) Order 2007; Protection of Freedoms Act 2012). Social workers must be vetted prior to commencing employment and may be barred if referred for dismissal for misconduct or for resigning prior to the conclusion of capability proceedings triggered by alleged misbehaviour. However, not all employers may be notifying the regulatory authorities when concerns about an individual's suitability for practice arise (SWTF, 2009; ESTYN and Care and Social Services Inspectorate Wales (CSSIW), 2011). Research has advised employers to keep adequate records of induction, supervision, appraisal and training, and of action taken in respect of staff shortages, working conditions and bullying, in order to defend against pleas of mitigation from staff members based on not being well prepared or working in unsafe environments (Hussein et al., 2009). Concern has been expressed too that focusing on individual staff may overlook systemic weaknesses in organizational cultures (Stevens and Manthorpe, 2007). Arguably, the current mosaic for setting and monitoring standards of conduct is complex, incomplete and imperfect. It may yet be the subject of further reform (Law Commission et al., 2012).

Getting to good

It is against these standards of professionalism and accountability that the findings from serious case reviews, for example, must be judged. Reviews of these reviews concerning children continue to uncover poor assessment processes; variable levels of knowledge about risks of harm, child development and attachment; confusion about thresholds; difficulty challenging hostile or resistant families; and failure to talk with children and to consider their perspectives. They find children left unprotected, delayed planning, insufficient management oversight and challenge, and insufficient staff resources (Sinclair and Bullock, 2002; OFSTED, 2009; 2010; 2012c). Reviews of serious case reviews in adult safeguarding uncover similar themes: insufficient management oversight of cases; confusion about thresholds for intervention; the importance of competence in risk assessment and of understanding the range of legal options available; lack of awareness of procedures; delayed implementation of agreed plans; and the need for an assertive and questioning outreach to service users and their carers, which includes discussion of risk, lifestyle choices and potential implications of their decisions (Manthorpe and Martineau, 2011; Braye et al., 2013b).

So, if excellent social work practice is insufficiently widespread (Munro, 2011) and improvement slow to materialize (OFSTED, 2009), what are the foundations of good professional judgment? One conceptualization (Braye and Preston-Shoot, 2010), which captures the themes introduced in this book thus far, refers to legal, ethical and knowledge literacy – a distillation of understanding of research and theory, skills and values that enables practitioners and managers to connect relevant legal rules on decision-making and law relating to service-user needs with professional priorities and the objectives of ethical practice.

In this formulation, *legal literacy* demonstrates an enhanced visibility of law rather than the limited knowledge sometimes found in practice (Drury-Hudson, 1999; McDonald et al., 2008; Braye et al., 2013a). Social workers question whether what is proposed falls within or transgresses legal rules, and demonstrate confidence in using the full range of legal options available. Practice is compliant with primary and secondary legislation, and with statutory guidance, for example, when completing child care and adult social care assessments of need. Legal literacy is a theme permeating this entire book.

Ethical literacy demonstrates a sound understanding and active use of values, including a reflective and self-critical approach to sense-making, rather than idle acceptance of particular principles, especially where competing ethical positions render safeguarding and promoting a person's welfare complex (Clark, 2007; Banks, 2010). Resultant practice should be consistent with accepted social work aims, with social workers able to give a coherent account of their decisions when balancing competing imperatives, such as personalization and a duty to safeguard. This recalls the point made in Chapter 1, namely that two social workers can disagree reasonably on how to intervene legally and ethically in a case. Ethical literacy is certainly highly pertinent when considering questions of human rights and equality (Chapter 3), partnership working

(Chapter 4), and learning from uncomfortable (Chapter 8) and best practice (Chapter 9).

Relational literacy demonstrates that social workers engage with the biographies and lived experiences of those with whom they are working rather than simply decide on whether or how to intervene according to principles such as autonomy or non-maleficence (Clark, 2012). It involves sharing deliberations, perspectives and concerns. It involves expressing curiosity and challenge, in order to elicit information for assessment and understand its meaning, to address service-user needs and to help resolve problems (Morrison, 2007; Driscoll, 2009; Munro, 2012). It is a dialogic practice, involving exchange and debate (Sachs, 2009). It embodies an investigatory and inquisitive mindset. These themes will be picked up noticeably in subsequent discussions of partnership working, capacity assessments and advocacy.

Organizational literacy demonstrates willingness to draw attention to the legality of agency procedures, the wisdom for quality decision-making of targets for performance and, in line with responsibilities outlined in codes of practice, the impact on practice of staff and resource shortages, workload pressures and organizational cultures (Dickens, 2007; Dwyer, 2009; Horwath, 2011). It recognizes that organizational systems, cultures and expectations can create conditions where error or poor practice are more likely (Munro, 2010; Carson, 2012). For example, team structures and workload demands can limit the time that social workers have to engage with children or adults at risk, failing to recognize that relationships and trust take time to build yet are the foundation on which effective assessment and decision-making depend (Laming, 2009; Stanley et al., 2011; Braye et al., 2013a). It challenges unthinking promotion of such principles as independence and choice where, consequently, inadequate consideration is given to safeguarding (Fyson and Kitson, 2010), and practices around assessment and care planning that are designed more for the organization's than the service user's benefit, often betrayed in the foregrounding of practical and physical as opposed to psychological and social needs (Dwyer, 2009; Sullivan, 2009). The importance of organizational literacy particularly permeates the final two chapters of the book.

Emotional literacy is the social worker's ability to act with integrity, generosity, courage and respect in the face of strong emotions, both their own and other people's. It is the capacity to handle stress, anxiety, fear, uncertainty and blame (Morrison, 2007; Munro, 2012). It is a practice characterized by humanity – grace and compassion alongside formal legal and professional structures (Sachs, 2009). Emotional literacy is a theme that permeates the book but is especially prominent in discussions of human rights, equality, partnership working, capacity assessments and advocacy.

Knowledge literacy is the ability to draw upon and weigh the usefulness of diverse sources of information and evidence. This includes being able to articulate for particular cases the applicability of research, for example, on risk assessment and child development, observation, experience and social work theories and methods. In child care, good practice involves being able to give a full account of a child's needs, the capacity of parents and the impact of wider family and environmental factors, critically reflecting on information from a range of sources, including a thorough history (Munro and Lushey, 2012). Researchers have sometimes found that integration of such knowledge into practice is weak or is discouraged by managers (Drury-Hudson, 1999; McDonald et al., 2008; Sullivan, 2009; Jack and Donnellan, 2010; Rixon and Ward, 2012). Chapter 7 highlights the importance of social workers knowing what information to request and being able to evaluate the significance of what they are told. The final two chapters underscore the centrality to good practice of utilizing the best available evidence.

PRACTICE FOCUS

The literacies outlined above capture what Emma and her family, and those who might scrutinize practice in this case, might be looking for. Social workers will know and apply in this case what sources of knowledge have to offer with respect to children who are withdrawn, women who might be victims of domestic violence and older adults experiencing dementia. These sources of knowledge will be tested out for their applicability in this case, with social workers drawing on their relationship and questioning skills, and demonstrating the values codified in codes of conduct. Their employing authority will be providing an organizational context that enables social workers to ask difficult and challenging questions, to keep Emma at the centre of decision-making, and to show resilience and persistence if faced with denial and a refusal to engage.

<table>
<tr><td rowspan="3">On-the-spot
questions</td><td>1 On the basis of what you have read in this chapter, how might your practice change as a result?</td></tr>
<tr><td>2 What will you take into discussions with your tutors, practice teachers and team colleagues?</td></tr>
<tr><td>3 What practice issues will you raise with your managers?</td></tr>
</table>

Further reading

Fairgrieve, D and S Green (eds) (2004) *Child Abuse Tort Claims against Public Bodies: A Comparative Law View*. An interesting comparison of how different jurisdictions have approached the question of legal redress for actions and omissions by state agencies.

Kennedy, R with J Richards (2007) *Integrating Human Service Law and Practice* 2nd edn. This book contains chapters on law, ethics and decision-making and focuses on the relationship between law and practice in human services, including social work. It covers the obligations, rights and regulation of social workers.

Kline, R and M Preston-Shoot (2012) *Professional Accountability in Social Care and Health: Challenging Unacceptable Practice and its Management*. A theoretical and practical review of accountability and professionalism for social workers and health care staff, including obligations relating to a duty of care, whistleblowing, health and safety, and workloads.

3

HUMAN RIGHTS AND EQUALITY

AT A GLANCE THIS CHAPTER COVERS:

- Human Rights Act 1998
- the principle of proportionality
- Equality Act 2010
- the requirement to conduct impact assessments
- the impact on social work practice in mental health, mental capacity and child care
- relevance of international conventions

One principle of lawful decision-making held over from Chapter 1 concerns respect for human rights and equality. Bingham (2011) argues strongly that the law must protect fundamental rights but indicates that there are gaps in the protection it affords in the UK. Nonetheless, human rights law acts as a check, not always welcomed, on arbitrary government, particularly on questions relating to liberty and fair trials. Similarly, Sachs (2009) stresses the importance of commitment to a society founded on human rights. In everything that the state does, recognition should be given to the values of a right to life and dignity. He argues that human rights should be extended beyond civil and political to socio-economic concerns in order to guarantee people the minimum decencies of life. He cautions that people should be sceptical of the law's pretensions but never cynical of its possibilities. The same may equally be said of social work and its espoused commitment to human rights, equality and social justice.

McDonald (2007) argues that the Human Rights Act 1998 sets down the minimum standard of legally acceptable behaviour by the state and suggests that there have been mixed outcomes. She contrasts some positive developments with respect to the right to liberty with some disappointing outcomes with respect to requests for resources to advance the right to private and family life. The case of *R (McDonald) v Royal Borough of Kensington and Chelsea* [2011] provides a good illustration of how resource arguments can be seen to defeat claims of dignity and human rights (Carr, 2012). This raises the question of just how fair and rights-conscious the UK is.

Making rights meaningful

The Human Rights Act 1998 applies to all four UK jurisdictions and incorporates into UK law rights contained within the ECHR. Key ECHR Articles, for the purposes of this book, are the right to life (Article 2), the right to live free of inhuman and degrading treatment (Article 3), the right to liberty (Article 5), the right to a fair trial (Article 6), the right to private and family life (Article 8) and the right to live free of discrimination (Article 14). Article 3 is an absolute right but the others may be limited or qualified by the state as long as this is for a lawful and recognized purpose, such as the prevention of crime and the protection of children or adults at risk. The Human Rights Act 1998 does not permit public officials to override the duties contained in primary legislation. If they follow

> **PRACTICE FOCUS**
>
> Emma, aged three, lives with her mother, stepfather and maternal grandparents in a small rented house in poor condition in a deprived neighbourhood. Emma and her mother are being supported by a local children's centre where staff have become concerned about their welfare. Their attendance has become sporadic. Emma has appeared increasingly wary and withdrawn. Staff have seen bruises on her mother's arms and face but she has avoided answering their questions. They refer Emma to children's services but both mother and stepfather are hesitant about engaging with social workers. Shortly there-after, the police report that they have been called to yet another domestic disturbance at the house, noting in passing that the step-father is known to them for violent behaviour. The family's GP refers Emma's grandmother for adult social care assessment with a diagno-sis of dementia.
>
> - Who has what rights in this situation?
> - How should social workers strike the balance when considering Emma's rights alongside those of her mother and stepfather, or when considering Emma's grandparents' rights, individually and collectively in this family?
> - How does the Human Rights Act 1998 affect the powers and duties that social workers have in other primary legislation, such as the Mental Capacity Act 2005 or the Children Act 1989?
> - Who might be protected in this situation by equality legislation?

such duties and accordingly appear to violate the Articles contained in the 1998 Act, a court may declare the relevant duties in primary legisla-tion to be incompatible with the ECHR and this may prompt amendment to the legal rules, as in the case of the duty to consult with nearest rela-tives in mental health legislation (*R (SSG) v Liverpool CC and Others* [2002]). However, public officials may disapply secondary legislation and statutory guidance where they believe this to breach the requirements of the ECHR.

The Act applies to all public authorities, including councils with social services responsibilities and central government departments, and to any person or organization whose functions are of a public nature, such as private hospitals detaining an individual under mental health legislation or an independent care home commissioned by a local authority to look

> **KEY CASE ANALYSIS**

Holding the state accountable: some outcomes of ECHR and Human Rights Act 1998 principles

- *The state should promote the right to life (Article 2).* Shortcomings in protective mechanisms for prisoners, including poor record-keeping, inadequate communication of information and weak risk assessments breach this Article (*Edwards and Another v UK* [2002]). Mindful of the principle of accountability (Chapter 2), risks were known or should have been known such that there was a reasonable expectation that the public authority would have taken steps to avoid that risk but the individual's medical history had not been disseminated. Thus, the state and its officers have a duty to take steps to protect life where they know, or should know, of a real and immediate risk, for example, of suicide by detained or informal mental health patients, and must do what a competent professional, trained to a high standard, can be reasonably expected to do (see Chapter 2) (*Savage v South Essex Partnership NHS Trust* [2008]; *Rabone and Rabone v Pennine Care NHS Trust* [2012]). Social workers who undertake difficult and dangerous work should be protected as far as practicable (*R (Selwood) v Durham CC, Tees, Esk and Wear Valleys NHS Foundation Trust and Northumberland, Tyne and Wear NHS Foundation Trust* [2012]).
- *The state should protect people from inhuman and degrading treatment (Article 3).* The use of corporal punishment by a parent violates Article 3 as the defence of reasonable chastisement does not provide adequate child protection (*A v UK* [1999]). There is concern that subsequent reform of the legal rules relating to smacking children in each of the UK's four nations may not have gone far enough to implement the judgment of the European Court of Human Rights (Hamilton, 2007).
- *People should not be detained without good reason (Article 5).* Indefinite detention without trial is incompatible with the right to liberty (*A and Others v Secretary of State for the Home Department* [2004]).
- *People should have the right to a fair trial (Article 6).* Thus, individuals should have the right to make representations before a decision is made to bar them from working with vulnerable adults (*R (Wright and Others) v Secretary of State for Health and Another* [2007]), which is now provided for in legislation regulating fitness for practice (see Chapter 2). Children should not be tried in adult courts and must be able to participate effectively in a trial, with proper allowance made for any disabilities (*SC v UK* [2004]).

- *Public authorities must take proactive steps to ensure respect for private and family life (Article 8).* Retaining fingerprints and DNA when suspects have been acquitted violates this Article (*S and Marper v UK* [2008]). The failure to provide an appropriate adult for 17-year-old young people detained in police custody is also incompatible with Article 8 (*HC (A Child) v Secretary of State for the Home Department and Another* [2013]).

after an older person. One criticism of the Act is that its scope is limited to civil and political rights, although some lawyers have argued that it is possible to protect socio-economic rights, even in an age of financial austerity and limited resources (Sachs, 2009). Another criticism is that it has strengthened procedural rights in respect of the use of power and authority by public organizations but done little to break down gate-keeping to services (Braye and Preston-Shoot, 2010). A third is that the coverage of the rights it protects is limited, with, for example, people who receive social care from private and voluntary sector providers excluded (*YL v Birmingham CC* [2007]; s. 145 Health and Social Care Act 2008).

The Forum for a New World Governance (2011) offers one assessment of how individual nation states perform on five domains, namely: peace and security (including the approach towards refugees, asylum seekers and violent crime); rule of law (including independence and effectiveness of the judiciary); human rights and participation (covering respect for civil rights and promotion of equality); sustainable development (embracing employment protection); and human development (including quality of life and promotion of well-being). On overall rankings the UK is placed 18th, behind Scandinavian countries which occupy the first five places, New Zealand, Australia, Canada and France, but ahead of the USA, Israel and South Africa.

This governance index provides one context for reports from social work and legal practitioners of abuses of power. These include the abrogation of civil liberties and human rights in the UK (Bingham, 2011). In the UK, whilst there is a positive picture of public authorities and legal systems using human rights to protect individuals and communities, nonetheless human rights could be protected more fully (**Equality and Human Rights Commission** (EHRC), 2012). The EHRC points to a reluctance to use the language of human rights, a lack of understanding, and fear about the implications of the legislation. It reports failures to protect the rights of children and disabled people, abuse of vulnerable people in institutional care, and degrading treatment towards victims of human-trafficking and unaccompanied asylum-seeking minors.

Perhaps more positively, Northern Ireland and Wales have both appointed Commissioners for Older People. Their role is to encourage best practice that is rooted in awareness of older people's rights and interests. Mindful of equality legislation, they also have a role in challenging discrimination. Their advocacy, promotional, educational and general investigatory roles find parallels in the roles of Commissioner for Children and Young People in Northern Ireland and Scotland, and Children's Commissioners for Wales and for England. How the roles are specifically configured in each jurisdiction depends on the powers and duties contained in primary legislation (Children's Commissioner for Wales Act 2001; Commissioner for Children and Young People (Northern Ireland) Order 2003; Commissioner for Children and Young People (Scotland) Act 2003; Children Act 2004). For example, the Northern Ireland, Welsh and Scottish commissioners can investigate individual cases, are responsible for protecting children's rights and should be influenced by the UNCRC when determining the interests of young people. However, the Children Act 2004 did not give these powers to the Children's Commissioner for England. All the commissioners may promote awareness of children's views and needs. The Children and Families Bill, if passed by the Westminster Parliament, will give the Children's Commissioner in England the mandate to protect and promote children's rights but may not remove all the constraints on holding central and local government accountable for how policy and practice promote good outcomes for young people.

Social work and human rights

On-the-spot questions	1 To what degree do you believe that social work is effective in promoting and safeguarding people's human rights? 2 What reasons do you give for your answer?

Social work is committed to advancing human rights and to dignity and to respect for private and family life (GSCC, 2008; QAA, 2008; HCPC, 2012a). A duty of care includes the promotion of human rights (Kline

> **KEY CASE ANALYSIS** ←

Hillingdon LBC v Neary (by his Litigation Friend, the Official Solicitor) and Mark Neary (Interested Party EHRC) [2011])

A learning disabled young man was deprived unlawfully of his liberty. Individuals should not be detained without lawful authority (Article 5) and assessments must be balanced and give due regard to the views expressed by service users and family carers (see also *HL v UK* [2004]). The local authority's assessment was flawed because an independent mental capacity advocate was not appointed soon enough, as required by the Mental Capacity Act 2005. A best interest assessment was not balanced (see Chapter 1). The disadvantages for the young man living away from home and the significance of the father–son relationship were not acknowledged. Additionally, the local authority tried to prevent proper scrutiny of its intervention and attempted to divert the young man's father from challenging its approach.

and Preston-Shoot, 2012), with the 1998 Act providing a source of authority aligned with social work values (Preston-Shoot et al., 2001; Duffy, 2011).

Views vary on the impact of the Human Rights Act 1998 on social work practice. Some suggest that the Act has been influential in how social workers prepare care plans, involve parents and children in assessments to meet the requirements of Articles 6 and 8, and present evidence in court to overcome the no order principle and to meet the demands of demonstrating proportionality when intervening in private family life (Duffy et al., 2006; Dickens, 2007; Munro and Ward, 2008). Others, whilst emphasizing that the ECHR should be an influential element of social work practice, suggest that social workers are fearful of the Act's implications should their practice be scrutinized, not least because of criticism both for non-intervention (*Z v UK* [2001]) and disproportionate intervention (*P, C and S v UK* [2002]) (Munro and Ward, 2008). Social workers have appeared uncertain how to respond when human rights principles appear to compete against welfare powers and duties in child care/protection and adult services/protection law, or indeed when one ECHR Article, such as the right to private and family life, may clash with another, such as the right to live free of degrading treatment (Duffy et al., 2006; Perkins et al., 2007; Duffy, 2011; Braye et al., 2013a). Some social workers have appeared equivocal when confronted with the prospect of having to challenge organization proce-dures and practices that limit a rights-based approach to assessment and service delivery (McDonald, 2007; Preston-Shoot, 2010; 2011).

McDonald (2007) concedes that the proportionality principle places a heavy burden on the integrity of decision-making when arbitrating between the rights of different individuals. Proportionality requires that, where permitted by law, a state's intervention should be the least restric-tive alternative and just sufficient to address the needs and/or risks that have been identified. It requires social workers, therefore, to have a clear rationale for what action should be taken and why a particular level of intervention is required in a particular case. McDonald argues too that managerialism, the routinization of decision-making, has had a negative impact on the realization of service users' human rights. Social work practice has not necessarily met standards of dignity, fairness and respect (CSCI, 2007; LGO, 2008; LGO and Parliamentary and Health Service Ombudsman (PHSO), 2009) and there have been human rights viola-tions where learning disabled adults have not been safeguarded (Fyson and Kitson, 2010). Some social workers do not mention human rights when giving accounts of their practice (Doel et al., 2010; Braye et al., 2013a) and may harbour variable awareness and attitudes towards human rights (Ellis, 2004). So, what guidance do court judgments give about human rights complaint decision-making and how do these outcomes, which draw on human rights principles, align with the princi-ples for lawful and accountable professionalism outlined in Chapters 1 and 2?

>**KEY CASE ANALYSIS**

Principles in the Human Rights Act 1998 for social work decision-making

- *Positive duty to promote Convention rights*: this includes protection of young people from abuse (Article 3) (*Z v UK* [2001]; *E and Others v UK* [2002]), and adequate monitoring and review of decisions concerning looked after children (Articles 6 and 8) (*Barrett v Enfield LBC* [1999]; *Pierce v Doncaster MBC* [2008]). Individual needs must be considered (Article 8) when proposals are made to close residen-tial care homes (*R (Madden) v Bury MBC* [2002]).
- *Duty to act proportionately when qualifying human rights*: emergency protection orders must be supported by relevant and sufficient reasons, proportionate to the level of risk (*P, C and S v UK* [2002]).

Care plans in care proceedings should consider the appropriate level of intervention necessary to safeguard and promote the welfare of the child (*Re O (A Child) (Supervision Order)* [2001]). Proposals to close residential care homes must be proportionate and beneficial to the individuals who are affected (*R (Phillips) v Walsall MBC* [2002]). Adult protection orders in Scotland must be a proportionate response, capable of providing a benefit to the individual which would not be available otherwise and where, in the circumstances of the case, the order represents the least restrictive alternative available (Adult Support and Protection (Scotland) Act 2007).

- *Practitioners should take timely decisions* (see Chapter 1) (*R (Bernard and Another) v Enfield LBC* [2002]). In keeping with promotion of Article 5, mental health patients should not be detained longer than necessary (*Johnson v UK* [1997]; *R (KB and Others) v MHRT and Another* [2002]).
- *Practitioners should take into account all relevant considerations* (see Chapter 1). All options should be considered rather than only care by the state and a fair balance arrived at (*Re C and B (Care Order: Future Harm)* [2001]). Article 8 rights must be acknowledged and understood, with the option of family reunification considered alongside alternative forms of care (*AR v Homefirst Community Trust* [2005]).
- *People should ordinarily be involved in decisions that affect them and should have relevant information on which they may rely* (*W and Others v Essex CC and Another* [2000]). Thus, removal of a child without the parents having the opportunity to answer allegations, other than in situations of extreme risk, would breach Articles 6 and 8 (*TP and KM v UK* [2001]).
- *Decisions should be reasonable and rational*. Thus, opinion must be supported by evidence and detailed reasoning; evidence for proposals when intervening in family life (Article 8) should be full, precise, detailed and compelling (*Re M (Care Proceedings: Judicial Review* [2003]). Evidence should be carefully weighed, with a determination capable of justification of how to balance Article 8 rights with the welfare principle (*Re C and B (Care Order: Future Harm)* [2001]). Payments should be equitable to kinship carers as well as other foster parents in order to promote family life and avoid discrimination (Articles 8 and 14) (*R (L and Others) v Manchester CC* [2002]).
- *People should have the right to a fair hearing* (Article 6) *and to an effective remedy* (Article 13). Thus, reviews of looked after children must identify when local authorities are failing to implement agreed care plans (*Re W and B (Children: Care Plan)* [2002]).

Thus, as described in Chapters 1 and 2, rights-thinking needs to accompany a technical and ethical approach to using legal rules (Braye and Preston-Shoot, 2010), and practitioners need to integrate the principles of lawful decision-making outlined in Chapter 1 with the principles of proportionality and promotion of ECHR rights outlined above. Only then will values rooted in human rights be underpinned by an analytical framework for decision-making that identifies the complex issues to be managed, evaluates what action may be justified, and engages with service users and their carers in reaching lawful and ethical outcomes (Duffy et al., 2006; McDonald, 2007).

> **KEY CASE ANALYSIS**

A and S (Children) v Lancashire CC [2012]

Failures by the local authority and IRO in this case were found to have breached Articles 3, 6 and 8 ECHR. The IRO was held responsible for delays in advancing the care plan for the two children although it was noted that he had limited access to independent legal advice, had received inadequate supervision and training, and had an unreasonable workload (see Chapters 2 and 9 on employer accountability). The local authority had failed to find an adoptive home for the children and, as an alternative, had not considered revocation of the freeing order and promotion of renewed family contact. The children had been abused in foster care and had not had a settled family life. Neither the local authority nor the IRO appeared to have recognized that the children's human rights were being infringed.

The case lends weight to the argument that safeguards (Adoption and Children Act 2002) to ensure that local authorities in England and Wales are held to account for the implementation of care plans for looked after children are little used and perhaps insufficiently robust, and that the independence of IROs from local authorities should be further reviewed and strengthened (Timms and Thoburn, 2006).

Equality Act 2010

The Equality Act 2010 applies in England, Scotland and Wales. Northern Ireland continues to have separate legal frameworks for race, gender, disability and sexuality in relation to employment and the provision of goods and services. This is extended to age, gender reassignment and religion in relation to employment. Public bodies, as defined by the Human Rights Act 1998, must promote equality by means of policy impact assessments, equality objectives and annual monitoring of the workforce. They must have due regard to the need to eliminate discrimination, harassment and victimization as prohibited by the legislation, advance equality of opportunity, and foster good relations. Advancing equality of opportunity requires taking steps to minimize or remove disadvantages associated with characteristics protected by the legislation (namely age, disability, gender reassignment, marriage and civil partnership, pregnancy and maternity, race, religion and belief, sex and sexual orientation), taking steps to meet people's particular needs, and encouraging people who share protected characteristics to engage in activities where they are under-represented. Fostering good relations means tackling prejudice and promoting understanding of the needs of particular communities. Scotland (EHRC Scotland, 2011) and Wales (WAG, 2011b) have produced specific provisions for how these obligations are to be met.

The phrase 'due regard' means that public bodies must consider how to advance equality rather than just how to avoid discrimination, and any likely impact on equality before decisions are taken on policy implementation or review. Drawing on the principles outlined in Chapter 1, they must ensure that those making a decision take a fully informed view of the likely impact on equality, exercising rigour and an open mind, either through an equality impact assessment or some other means so that sufficient information is available to assess the equality impact on those affected. Adequate records must be kept to show how equality impact was considered and how the duties were complied with (*R (Brown) v Secretary of State for Work and Pensions* [2008]; *R (C) v Secretary of State for Justice* [2008]; *R (EHRC) v Secretary of State for Justice* [2010]; Kline and Preston-Shoot, 2012).

On-the-spot questions	1 How fair do you believe the UK to be? 2 How effective is social work in promoting equality and counteracting discrimination? 3 What reasons do you give for your answer?

Social work and equality duties

On-the-spot question

Think about particular social work roles, such as completing carers' assessments or compiling child protection plans. What relevance to these roles does promoting equality have?

Social work's duty of care also includes promoting equality and counteracting discrimination (QAA, 2008; HCPC, 2012a; Kline and Preston-Shoot, 2012). However, in terms of promoting equality, inspections of local authorities have found leadership and staff training to be variable (CSCI, 2008a; 2008b; 2009). The EHRC (2011) has warned that many commissioning and service provision decisions appear to be based on narrow perceptions of age and disability, with block contracts militating against more personalized or diverse provision. It found that not all groups were able to access support of their choice to enhance their quality of life and cautioned that reductions in public expenditure would make equality of opportunity more difficult to achieve. It concluded that current practice in equality impact assessments was not working effectively.

Certainly, judicial review evidence would, on balance, appear to support this analysis. However, it should be stressed that not all claims for judicial review relating to Equality Act 2010 duties succeed against local authorities. For example, in one case the court decided that social workers had paid proper regard to disability and the need to intervene to protect and promote the service user's interests (*R (AM) v Birmingham CC* [2009]).

Anti-discriminatory practice is good practice. Increasingly, welfare law is expressing principles and duties relating to equality. In England and Wales the Mental Health Act 2007, amending the Mental Health Act 1983, requires that services respect diversity and avoid unlawful discrimination. All four UK nations require those responsible for the welfare of children to ensure that race, culture, religion and language are considered (Children Act 1989; Children (Northern Ireland) Order 1995; Children (Scotland) Act 1995; Adoption and Children Act 2002). The Child Poverty Act 2010 enables the setting of targets to reduce the numbers of children living in poverty, whilst the Childcare Act 2006 requires local authorities in England to reduce inequalities between

→ **KEY CASE ANALYSIS** ←

Equality duties

R (Chavda) v Harrow LBC [2008] – a successful challenge by service users to an amendment to a local authority's adult social care eligibility criteria. The local authority had not considered the impact on disabled people of a proposed policy change.

R (Kaur and Shah) v Ealing LBC [2008] – the local authority must perform a race equality impact assessment before changing funding criteria for voluntary organizations. It must keep transparent records to demonstrate that a proper assessment has been completed.

R (JL) v Islington LBC [2009] – local authority acted unlawfully when using eligibility criteria to deny a disabled child and family a core assessment. It failed to consider equality duties towards disabled people when creating, implementing or amending policies.

R (Boyejo and Others) v Barnet LBC [2010] – an unlawful decision to withdraw resident warden services as the local authority had failed to complete a rational equality impact assessment, to consult adequately, and to inform decision makers of the content of equality duties.

R (Meany and Others) v Harlow DC [2009] – cuts to rights advice funding were ruled unlawful as the council had not paid due regard to equality duties and the impact of the proposed change.

R (JM and NT) v Isle of Wight Council [2012] – a successful challenge to unlawful restriction of eligibility criteria as the council had not complied with guidance and consultation did not give people sufficient information in order to consider and respond to proposals.

R (M) v Birmingham CC [2009] – an unsuccessful challenge by an individual disabled person who had applied for community care assistance as the council had complied with general equality duties and had made service provision decisions based on an assessment of need.

R (W) v Birmingham CC [2011] – when proposing to raise eligibility levels for community care from substantial and critical needs to critical only, as a result of budget restrictions, there had been a lack of clarity in the consultation material and insufficient regard had been paid to the likely impact on disabled people.

R (Rahman) v Birmingham CC [2011] – an unlawful decision to axe funding for voluntary groups as the local authority failed to take proper account of the impact on disabled and vulnerable people.

> ### PRACTICE FOCUS
>
> Each individual family enjoys identical rights from the ECHR. However, the right to private and family life may be qualified according to law. Social workers may therefore intervene, using their powers in the Children Act 1989, the National Health Service (NHS) and Community Care Act 1990 and the Mental Capacity Act 2005, in order to complete assessments and, where appropriate, determine care packages and protection plans. Their involvement should be proportionate to the risks identified and the outcomes desired, particularly those of safeguarding and promoting Emma's welfare, and of enabling her grandmother to exercise choice and receive personalized care. Emma's grandmother is a disabled person and therefore belongs to a group protected by equality legislation. Other family members may come within the ambit of this legislation by association with her.

children in their area, including socio-economic disadvantages. In that context, it is interesting to note that provisions in s. 1 Equality Act 2010, relating to counteracting socio-economic inequality, have not been implemented. Moreover, some groups remain disproportionately represented in the numbers of looked after children and adults compulsorily detained in psychiatric institutions and prisons (Braye and Preston-Shoot, 2010). Questions remain, therefore, whether equality legislation has really transformed individual attitudes and organizational practices.

International conventions

The UK is a signatory to a number of international conventions, for example, the UNCRC, the United Nations Convention on the Rights of Persons with Disabilities and the European Social Charter. However, in contradistinction to the Human Rights Act 1998, these have not been incorporated into UK law, despite pressure from some Members of Parliament. However, in Wales, the Rights of Children and Young Persons (Wales) Measure 2011 requires Welsh ministers to have due regard to the UNCRC when exercising their functions. A similar proposal has been tabled in the Scottish Parliament (Children and Young Persons (Scotland) Bill 2013). Moreover, Scottish policy for child care services (*Getting it Right for Every Child*, Aldgate, 2013) builds on the principles of the UNCRC. Social workers must seek out and consider the voice of the child, plan and review provision in order to improve children's well-being and outcomes, engage actively with young people and consider each child's needs, risks and rights. In Wales, the Children's Commissioner must have specific regard to the UNCRC when safeguarding and promoting the rights and welfare of children (Children's Commissioner for Wales Act 2001). In England, directors of children's services must have regard to the UNCRC and ensure that young people are involved in service development (DfE, 2013).

The UNCRC contains Articles that focus on children's survival, development, protection and participation. Whilst not yet incorporated into domestic law in any of the UK nations, it has been quoted and relied upon in court judgments. Its emphasis on humanity, respect for dignity, involvement of young people in decisions that affect them, and taking into account children's needs, has been referred to in judgments relating to staff behaviour and use of restraint in secure institutions for young people (*R (C) v Secretary of State for Justice* [2008]), children's involvement in court proceedings (*Mabon v Mabon* [2005]), removal of a child's mother from the UK (ruled as a breach of Article 8 ECHR with reference to the UNCRC) (*ZH v Secretary of State for the Home Department* [2011]), and detention of parents and children in immigration removal centres where Article 5 ECHR was to be read in light of the UNCRC (*S, C and D v Secretary of State for the Home Department* [2007]).

As a signatory to the UNCRC, the UK must report periodically to the UN Committee on the Rights of the Child on progress towards full implementation. The committee has been routinely critical of the UK's record, not least around the low age of criminal responsibility, discrimination against disabled children and policy relating to asylum seekers. Arguments for incorporation include that it would ensure systematic consideration of children's rights in all policy and legislative developments, assist with the consistency and accountability of decision-making and give greater force to children's rights (Rights of the Child UK, no date). Meanwhile, social workers should be cognizant of the UNCRC and use the Articles to underpin their practice.

The European Social Charter builds on the argument (Sachs, 2009) that there can be no human rights without social rights. It addresses rights relating to housing, health, education, employment and social protection. It is not possible for individuals to lodge petitions to a court or tribunal but states can allow complaints to be made to a committee by non-governmental organizations and from trade unions. Once again, social workers should be mindful of the provisions of the European Social Charter, especially to challenge decisions taken by central government and local authorities when economic constraint appears to reduce the protection available of social rights, such as social security, legal aid and welfare provision.

On-the-spot questions	1 On the basis of what you have read in this chapter, how might your practice change as a result?
	2 What will you take into discussions with your tutors, practice teachers and team colleagues?
	3 What practice issues will you raise with your managers?

Further reading

Dickens, J (2012) *Social Work, Law and Ethics*. This book explores the relationship and tensions between law and ethics and their contributions to the moral dilemmas that social workers encounter when working with children and adults.

Ellis, K (2004) 'Promoting human rights or avoiding litigation? The introduction of the Human Rights Act 1998 into adult social care in England' 7(3) *European Journal of Social Work* 321–40. An early evaluation of the impact of human rights legislation on social work practice.

Hale, B (2009) 'Dignity' 31(2) *Journal of Social Welfare and Family Law* 101–08. An important essay on how legal rules can uphold people's dignity but also how dignity is itself a complex concept and one which brings local and central government into the realms of social and political responsibility.

Sachs, A (2009) *The Strange Alchemy of Life and Law*. A reflective articulation of how one judge reaches decisions about human rights in practice and views the enforceability of social rights in law.

4

PARTNERSHIPS WITHIN DECISION-MAKING

AT A GLANCE THIS CHAPTER COVERS:

+ partnership with service users and carers
+ partnership with other professionals
+ connecting administrative law principles with primary legislation and guidance on involvement in social work processes

By now it should be clear that service-user involvement is axiomatic to lawful decision-making both in individual cases and when planning service provision. Equally clearly, what will have emerged from the reported case law decisions and ombudsman investigations are occasions where respect for people has broken down. Partnership working with children and adults in need or at risk, with individuals and their communities, is one way of making their humanity visible (Bilson, 2007). Partnership working turns knowledge of need and risk into acknowledgment. It is when the personal dimension of a child's or carer's experiences is recognized through dialogue, and when the formal structures of law and social work processes are infused with empathy and compassion (Sachs, 2009). It is when their perspectives and their horizons, essentially their individuality, become known, their lived experience and biography and its influence on the encounter in the here-and-now (Clark, 2012). Put another way, the act of listening, giving voice to, and exploring options with service users engenders substance into the principle of empowerment.

Relationships, then, are at the heart of practice with children and with adults. Needs are addressed through relationships (Morrison, 2007; Braye et al., 2011). Time is required to build trusting relationships that form the foundation of making sense of people's lives (Laming, 2009). Honesty, respect and working *with* family members count. However, accounts from service users and carers themselves (for example, Flynn, 2004; Goldsmith, 2005; Braye and Preston-Shoot, 2006) tell a different story of at least some encounters. Here are descriptions of social workers prejudging situations, refusing to assess or listen, appearing to lack compassion and to be preoccupied with targets, dissembling about legal powers and duties and ignoring people's wishes and feelings. In these encounters people's humanity has become obscured (Bilson, 2007), in the process of which resources, managerialism, performance targets and even practitioners' own attitudes towards individual help-seeking may all be implicated (Morrison, 2007; Ayre and Preston-Shoot, 2010; Preston-Shoot, 2011).

On-the-spot questions	1 Think of the last time you worked with a child, parent or an adult at risk. If you put yourself in their shoes, anticipating your first visit, what do you think they were feeling, anticipating, hoping for, and anxious about? 2 What do you think were their expectations about your knowledge of law?

On-the-spot questions

3 Now think of that first encounter. To what degree did you leave with an appreciation of the individual's feelings, hopes, fears and expectations?
4 What helped and what got in the way of building a relationship that enabled the individual to talk about and you to appreciate their starting position?
5 To what degree do you think those with whom you were working felt recognized, acknowledged and heard?

The question then becomes to what degree the legal rules can support partnership working and enable social workers to ensure that people achieve and maintain independence, feel respected and included, fulfil their potential, take control, stay safe, make choices and realize their rights (HCPC, 2012a; Aldgate, 2013). In effect, it is about how to put children and their families, and adults in need of services and their carers, (back) at the heart of decision-making.

◤ **PRACTICE FOCUS**

Emma, aged three, lives with her mother, stepfather and maternal grandparents in a small rented house in poor condition in a deprived neighbourhood. Emma and her mother are being supported by a local children's centre where staff have become concerned about their welfare. Their attendance has become sporadic. Emma has appeared increasingly wary and withdrawn. Staff have seen bruises on her mother's arms and face but she has avoided answering their questions. They refer Emma to children's services but both mother and stepfather are hesitant about engaging with social workers. Shortly thereafter, the police report that they have been called to yet another domestic disturbance at the house, noting in passing that the stepfather is known to them for violent behaviour. The family's GP refers Emma's grandmother for adult social care assessment with a diagnosis of dementia.

- How might social workers put Emma at the heart of decision-making?
- How might adult social care staff put Emma's grandmother at the heart of their decision-making?
- What are the core elements of working in partnership?
- How does the use of statutory powers impact on the principle of working in partnership?

Partnership with children

Article 12 of the UNCRC promotes children's participation in proceedings that affect them. Across the UK primary legislation emphasizes the importance of ascertaining and paying due regard to the child's wishes and feelings (Children Act 1989; Children (Northern Ireland) Order 1995; Children (Scotland) Act 1995; Adoption and Children Act 2002). Guidance (for example, Aldgate, 2013; HM Government, 2013) provides additional reinforcement for a child-centred approach – children should be at the heart of decision-making and they should be informed about concerns, heard, respected, involved in discussions, offered advocates where appropriate, and enjoy stable relationships with professionals. Secondary legislation and statutory guidance for IROs in England and Wales (Department for Children, Schools and Families (DCSF), 2010) stresses their role in consulting with children about their care plans at reviews and when significant changes occur at other times. IROs should begin from the child's perspective, listen to their views, involve them fully in the review process and consult with them before every review. An IRO might invite a young person to chair their own review when that would help to increase their ownership of the discussion and its outcomes. They must inform the child of their right to apply with leave for a s. 8 order (Children Act 1989) or for discharge of the care order. Being consulted and seeing the impact on decisions of their expressed views promotes their self-esteem (Thomas, 2011).

However, social work's track record is variable. Children want to be treated with fairness and respect but they do not always feel consulted or heard, for example, when deciding the content of care plans, preparing for or determining the recommendations from reviews, or arranging placements (Timms and Thoburn, 2006; Thomas, 2011). Younger children, disabled children, and those involved in child protection, asylum and youth justice proceedings are less likely to be involved in decision-making (Burke, 2010; Horwath, 2011). Overviews of serious case reviews also routinely report that practitioners have lost sight of the child, have failed to consult and listen, and have not considered the child's perspective (Sinclair and Bullock, 2002; OFSTED, 2008; Devaney et al., 2013). As a result they may doubt their ability to influence decisions and may feel hopeless, helpless, lost and excluded as a result (Timms and Thoburn, 2006).

Losing focus on the child has been attributed to an overemphasis on procedures, compliance with assessment timescales, formulaic completion of assessment schedules, managerialist organizational cultures, and difficulties in establishing meaningful relationships with families (Ayre and Preston-Shoot, 2010; Horwath, 2011). Certainly, the evidence from trials of more flexible timescales for assessments in England (Munro and Lushey, 2012) suggests that reduced prescription allows time to engage with children and explore their wishes and feelings, and increases the scope for additional visits to explain what is happening, build rapport and collect and clarify information. However, social workers may lack effective strategies to engage young people and ensure that their voices

> **KEY CASE ANALYSIS** <

Court and ombudsman judgments concerning children's involvement

A young person's wishes must be ascertained before accommodation (s. 20 Children Act 1989) is provided and the onus should not be on the child to identify and request the services they require (*R (M) v Hammersmith and Fulham LBC* [2008]). Due consideration should be given to the views of disabled children when deciding or reviewing care packages (*R (CD) (A Child by her Litigation Friend VD) v Isle of Anglesey CC* [2004]).

If children have sufficient age and understanding, they should be able to participate in court proceedings. Emotional harm may result if they are denied information or participation (*Mabon v Mabon* [2005]).

Children should be asked if they want an independent adult present at age assessment interviews. Inconsistencies in their account should be explored with them (*R (NA) v Croydon LBC* [2009]).

Local authorities and IROs must not allow cases of looked after children to drift. Due regard must be paid to their human rights and they should be fully involved in decisions about their future, particularly at reviews (*A & S (Children) v Lancashire CC* [2012]).

Social workers have sometimes failed to pay sufficient regard to young people's views about their placements. Children have not always been told of a placement until the decision has been taken, nor have they routinely been given an opportunity to put their views to review meetings. Young people should be offered an advocate and file recording should clearly outline what information has been given to children about possible placements (LGO, 2009).

are central to assessments. *Getting it Right for Every Child* in Scotland (Aldgate, 2013) demands that children feel confident about the help that they and their family is receiving. This requires that social workers listen to their accounts of family life as part of ultimately reaching that finely balanced judgment of the child's right to be safe and the parents' right to bring up their child (Devaney et al., 2013).

On-the-spot question	How can social workers demonstrate that they have seen and spoken to a child, enabled them to contribute effectively to assessment and care planning, and paid due regard to their wishes and feelings?

Partnership with parents

Getting it right for every child also means supporting families, taking early action when this would help to prevent escalation of difficulties, staying involved longer when this would help to consolidate improvements, and involving parents in understanding what is happening and why (Duffy, 2011; Munro, 2011; OFSTED, 2012c; Aldgate, 2013; Devaney et al., 2013). Good outcomes for children follow when parents are effectively included in planning and decision-making, and when trust is built through committed and honest relationship-building (OFSTED, 2012a). Communication, therefore, between social workers and families is at the heart of work with children in need and child protection, helping parents to discuss their difficulties, identify their fears and anxieties and to build on their strengths (Horwath, 2011; Devaney et al., 2013). This may be challenging and complex. It may be difficult to distinguish those who are understandably anxious, fearful and ambivalent from those who are evasive and deceitful (OFSTED, 2008; 2010; Horwath, 2011). Social workers may encounter resistance and hostility, or find it complicated to obtain a clear picture when people are living chaotic lives, especially when mental ill-health, drugs and alcohol, and domestic violence feature strongly (Sinclair and Bullock, 2002; OFSTED, 2008; Harwin and Madge, 2010).

Across the UK, primary legislation emphasizes the importance of ascertaining and paying due regard to parents' wishes and feelings (Children Act 1989; Children (Northern Ireland) Order 1995; Children (Scotland) Act 1995). The Children and Young Persons Act 2008 requires social workers in England and Wales to consider family first when looking for a placement for a child. Regulations govern parental involvement in agreements surrounding placements for their children. Case law too, as earlier chapters have identified, has emphasized the importance of participation.

> **KEY CASE ANALYSIS**

Selected case law on involving parents in child care proceedings

Parents must be involved in decision-making and enabled to answer allegations and criticisms of their parenting and behaviour (*TP and KM v UK* [2002]; *Re C (Care Proceedings: Disclosure of Local Authority's Decision-Making Process)* [2002]).

Parents should be given minutes of case conferences (*Re X (Emergency Protection Orders)* [2006]).

Lack of parental cooperation is never a reason to close a case or step down from concerns about child protection, and family work should take place with clarity about timescales and the changes required (*Re E and Others (Minors) (Care Proceedings: Social Work Practice)* [2000]).

Taking full account of parents' views, sifting and evaluating evidence, and considering contextual factors such as parental capacity and poverty (Harwin and Madge, 2010) are not helped when encounters are prescriptive rather than interpersonal, service-oriented rather than therapeutic (McDonald et al., 2008). Trials of more flexible assessment practices in England (Munro and Lushey, 2012) have shown that reduced prescription concerning timescales has enabled social workers to time visits when convenient for families, and increased the scope for building trust, clarifying information and assessing parental engagement.

Intervention will need to be authoritative, which means having an investigatory mindset and low threshold of concern, being curious and thorough, focusing on the child and having high expectations that parents will do the same, and being challenging in a care-full way. This approach to professionalism, involving challenge and the exercise of authority but also care and concern, requires skill, experience, courage and resilience, hence the importance given in Chapter 9 to supervision and continuing professional development. In a clear reference back to the standards identified in Chapters 1 and 2, good quality assessments will be child-centred, will contain relevant and accurate information, evaluate information from a range of sources and include an analysis between what is known and the recommended plans for the child and family (Munro and Lushey, 2012). Research has shown that social workers, and other professionals, have not always identified patterns that should trigger alarm, have misunderstood thresholds, especially around neglect, or have relied too much on parents to monitor their own behaviour (Dickens, 2007; OFSTED, 2008; 2010; 2012c). Sometimes they have not given reports to family members to enable them to consider the content and to make effective contributions to meetings (OFSTED, 2012c). Sometimes assessments have proved descriptive rather than evaluative, with missing information and little indication of how people's views have been taken into account (Munro and Lushey, 2012).

Partnership with adults to promote well-being

Chapter 3 identified several cases where local authority decisions about eligibility criteria and funding for service provision had been ruled unlawful because service users had not been appropriately involved in consultations. Sometimes local authorities succeed in defending judicial review

$\rightarrow$ **KEY CASE ANALYSIS** $\leftarrow$

Selected case law on involving adult service users and/or their carers in decisions

Difficult service users must not be abandoned but a genuine attempt made to engage them (*R (WG) v Local Authority A* [2010]).

Carers should be involved in decisions when removing someone from their care and when transferring them subsequently between care homes (*G v E (by his Litigation Friend, the Official Solicitor, Manchester CC and S* [2010]).

In line with statutory guidance, local authorities must consult learning disabled people about their needs when conducting assessments and reviews (*R v North Yorkshire CC, ex parte Hargreaves* [1997]).

Statutory guidance on choice of accommodation must be followed (*R v Avon CC, ex parte Hazell* [1995]) and a service user's choices and preferences must be taken into account when the local authority is deciding the content of a care package (*R v Lancashire CC, ex parte RADAR and Another* [1996]).

> **KEY CASE ANALYSIS**

DM (A Person under Disability) Acting by his Next Friend,
Kathleen McCollum, for Judicial Review **[2013])**

This Northern Ireland case found that a health and social services
trust, when implementing s. 2 Chronically Sick and Disabled Persons
Act 1970, had erred in law when refusing to make direct payments.
This was because it had not followed the Supreme Court decision in
R (KM) v Cambridgeshire CC [2012]). This requires that a local authority asks the service user about their needs, considers then whether it
is necessary to make arrangements to meet these needs, then decides
the nature and extent of services to be provided, and finally deter-
mines the reasonable cost of securing necessary provision. In this case
there had not been a detailed assessment of needs or costs, and the
trust had taken resources into account when deciding whether it was
necessary to make arrangements for meeting the service user's needs,
suggestive of a resource-driven decision (see Chapter 6).

claims regarding consultation. In one example (*R (D) v Worcestershire CC*
[2013]) the local authority's approach to consultation concerning the cost
of non-residential care packages was ruled lawful because adequate and
clear information had been given about the proposals, equality duties had
been implemented appropriately and potential consequences had been
mitigated. Nonetheless, case law has sometimes held that service users
and carers have been unlawfully excluded from decision-making.

Primary and secondary legislation, and associated statutory guidance
and practice codes, demonstrate equivocal attitudes towards partnership, with the spectre of resources (see Chapter 6) never far away. In
England and Wales, for example, adult social care service users should be
active partners in their assessments, a written statement of the outcome
of the consultation should be provided if this results in a continuing service, and points of difference should be noted (NHS and Community Care
Act 1990; *Community Care Assessment Directions*, DH, 2004). Increasingly
the role of the local authority is configured as the promotion of people's
well-being, where well-being is defined as the outcomes that individuals
are seeking for themselves. However, assessment is not user-led, despite
social policy emphasizing personalization, and the spectre of resources is
ever present (see Chapter 6). Ultimate responsibility for defining need
still rests with the assessing professional.

Adult protection legislation in Scotland (Adult Support and Protection (Scotland) Act 2007) embeds participation in its provisions. The right of access to an individual at risk of harm is tempered by their right to refuse to participate in assessment or medical examination. Assessment and removal orders do not contain a right to detain the individual, who must be advised that they do not have to cooperate. Protection orders require the individual's consent, unless they are acting under undue influence, and professionals must have regard to their ascertainable wishes and feelings, and to the views of relevant others. Independent advocacy and information provision may be used to promote participation (Patrick and Smith, 2009).

Mental health legislation and associated practice codes (for example, DH, 2008) promote patient involvement as far as possible in the formulation and delivery of care and treatment, taking into account also the views of relatives and friends. Patients must be given information about their rights and their treatment. Mental capacity legislation follows a similar trajectory. Finally, in England, the Health and Social Care Act 2012 requires the involvement of service users in providing advice on the development and review of provision across health and social care.

Once again, researchers uncover a variable picture of partnership working. For instance, older people sometimes experience limited involvement in assessment and care planning (Dwyer, 2009; Sullivan, 2009). Residents in care homes are not routinely supported in making decisions, and examples have been found of poor care planning and reviews (**Care Quality Commission** (CQC), 2011). This against a backdrop of renewed emphasis on dignity where assessment and reviews should be regular and record how service users' preferences have been understood and how they have been involved as active participants in their care (Commission on Dignity in Care for Older People, 2012). Carers are not always routinely engaged as partners and not all assessments take account of the complexity and diversity contained within the caring role, or capture the impact on carers' lives (Seddon et al., 2007). Whilst carers have a right to information about assessment (Carers and Direct Payments (Northern Ireland) Act 2002; Community Care and Health (Scotland) Act 2002; Carers (Equal Opportunities) Act 2004), assessments often have a practical rather than more holistic focus, with delays and inadequate explanations often characteristic (Seddon et al., 2007).

Serious case reviews in adult safeguarding also highlight the importance of communication, partnership working and relationships. Key themes include the absence of healthy scepticism, lack of scrutiny of the service user–carer relationship, and little person-to-person contact with social workers (Buckinghamshire Safeguarding Vulnerable Adults Board, 2011). Staying in contact and building trusting and respectful relationships can prove challenging, both because of care management structures and due to the persistence with which some service users and their carers refuse support. The strength of opposition from carers can sometimes deflect attention away from an adult at risk and/or paralyse action. As in child care, sometimes courageous challenge will be necessary, using skills of assertive and questioning outreach, for example, in order to explore what may lie behind service refusal, discuss risk and consider the implications of their apparent lifestyle choices, which again demands resilience and experience from social workers (Westminster Safeguarding Adults Board, 2011; Braye et al., 2013b). Promoting service user and carer involvement with safeguarding adults boards (England and Wales) and **Adult Protection Committees** (Scotland) has also proved challenging, with some positive and proactive work contrasting with uncertainty about whether and how to involve them in the work of these multi-agency forums (Braye et al., 2012; Cornish and Preston-Shoot, 2013).

On-the-spot questions

1 What guidance does your employer provide on the involvement of service users and carers in adult social care assessments, care plans and reviews?
2 To what degree does the guidance accurately reflect the requirements of the legal rules?

Partnership with other professionals

The core legal mandates available to social workers in the UK, when working with children and their families, and with adults needing services or protection, contain powers and duties with respect to multi-agency working. Invariably these are characterized by social workers having the power to request information and seek assistance from professional colleagues in education, housing and health care, and staff in those organizations being under a duty to comply if what is requested is consistent with their roles and functions (see, for instance, ss 27 and 47 Children Act 1989 and the NHS and Community Care Act 1990). These powers and duties are amplified in nation-specific guidance relating to working together to safeguard children (for example, HM Government, 2013, for England and Wales) and multidisciplinary practice in mental health (for example, again for England and Wales, DH, 2008). Throughout, such guidance emphasizes the need for good working relationships, which comprise understanding of each other's roles and responsibilities, and acting in collaboration. Unsurprisingly, therefore, social workers are expected to be competent in working with other professionals (Care Council for Wales, 2002; NISCC, 2002; Scottish Social Services Council, 2009; HCPC, 2012a). Inter-agency collaboration is a core component of their role (GSCC, 2008) and a key element of getting it right for every child (Aldgate, 2013). However, there is some evidence that suggests that social workers, even when they have an accurate understanding of the legal rules, lack confidence in multi-agency exchanges and in challenging the approach of other agencies (Driscoll, 2009; Preston-Shoot and McKimm, 2012b; Braye et al., 2013a).

Additionally, there are requirements placed on local authorities, health care organizations and the police at a strategic level to work together, for example, through the operation of **Local Safeguarding Children Boards** (LSCBs) and **Local Safeguarding Adults Boards** (LSABs) in England and Wales, and Child Protection Committees and Adult Protection Committees in Scotland. For example, directors of children's services in England must ensure the adequacy and effectiveness of partnership arrangements underpinning child protection systems (Department for Education (DfE), 2013). Such developments often appear as a response to the deaths of children, for example, the duty to work collaboratively and effectively which applies in England and Wales from the Children Act 2004.

Case law and inquiries sometimes reveal obstacles in relation to multi-agency working, at both strategic and operational levels, especially the interface between adult social care and health, and between housing and children's services. Local authorities can also become embroiled in disputes between themselves, especially around ordinary residence and which council should assume responsibility for a person in need.

Rarely do single agencies have a complete picture or understanding of the needs of children or adults at risk. However, serious case reviews, and evaluations of them, in children's services (Sinclair and Bullock, 2002; OFSTED, 2008; 2009; 2010; Devaney et al., 2013), mental health (Stanley and Manthorpe, 2004) and adult services (Buckinghamshire

→ **KEY CASE ANALYSIS** ←

Selected case law and inquiries on multi-agency working

Disagreements have been noted in England between NHS trusts and local authorities as to whether an individual has health care or social care needs, and whether assessments by one organization or professional should be accepted by other parties (*R (Grogan) v Bexley NHS Care Trust and South East London Strategic Health Authority and the Secretary of State for Health* [2006]; *St Helens MBC v Manchester PCT* [2008]).

Detailed guidance has been necessary on how housing departments and children's social care should work together to meet the needs of homeless young people (*R (G) v Southwark LBC* [2009]).

Local authorities can become locked in disputes about who is responsible for service provision when individuals and families move (*R (Stewart) v Wandsworth LBC, Hammersmith and Fulham LBC and Lambeth LBC* [2001]; *R (M) v Barking and Dagenham LBC and Westminster CC (Interested Party)* [2003]).

Poor communication can disrupt the transfer of services between NHS trusts and local authorities and undermine quality of care for individual service users (LGO, 2008).

Strategy meetings must have a multi-agency focus if children are to be safeguarded, enabling all relevant information to be considered when planning action to protect young people. All agencies must engage in providing a fully integrated early support service for children and families. Participation of agencies in case conferences and strategy meetings was variable, weakening their overall effectiveness (OFSTED, 2012c).

Greater familiarity is required across agencies regarding legislation for practice in adult safeguarding (Westminster Safeguarding Adults Board, 2011).

Safeguarding Vulnerable Adults Board, 2011; Westminster Safeguarding Adults Board, 2011; Braye et al., 2013b) have uncovered examples of limited inter-agency cooperation in assessments, discharge planning and reviews; silo working; variable definitions and thresholds of need; unclear roles and fragmented assessments of need and risk; absence of protocols to resolve disagreements; poor sharing of information and case chronologies, and poor communication. They emphasize the importance of an effective interface between social workers practising with children and with adults; of health care professionals alerting local authorities when people at risk fail to keep appointments, and engaging fully in multi-agency working to engage adults at risk; of a coordinated response to people's needs and shared risk assessments and decision-making through case conferences, network meetings and reviews. They note that collaborative working can improve referral practice and coordinate follow-through on service delivery.

Research into the governance of adult safeguarding in England (Pinkney et al., 2008; Braye et al., 2012) and adult protection in Scotland (Cornish and Preston-Shoot, 2013) has found evidence of strong multi-agency engagement but also challenges with respect to the engagement of some professionals, especially in the NHS, and strongly endorses the practice of shared decision-making and shared responsibility for good service-user outcomes. Inspections and research into outcomes of safeguarding children similarly comment on the lack of priority given by some health care organizations and adult services to child protection (HM Government, 2008a; Munro and Ward, 2008) but also suggest that greater flexibility in the timescales for assessments might help social workers to obtain input from other agencies (Munro and Lushey, 2012).

Explanations for poor partnership working include: limited knowledge by other professionals of the powers and duties held by local authorities for children and adults; lack of corporate ownership of safeguarding children and adults; and mistrust of each other's expertise. Additionally, researchers have focused on divergent interpretations of key values, such as confidentiality, different professionals advocating for different family members, perceptions of status, resource constraint and boundary disputes (Johnson et al., 2003; Stanley et al., 2003; Seddon et al., 2007; Sullivan, 2009). Collaboration requires professionals to believe that their combined efforts are not only necessary in legal and professional terms to obtain a desired goal but also that each individual professional is capable and willing to undertake their share of the work and believes that their organizational culture offers them the flexibility and support to participate in decision-making (Johnson et al., 2003). Considerable faith is invested in multi-professional training to break down professional stereotypes, learn about each other's roles and expertise, and develop shared practice. However, rigorous evaluations of training are lacking (Charles and Horwath, 2009; Campbell and Chamberlin, 2012). What evidence exists is tentative about the practice improvements that might follow (Richardson et al., 2002; Carpenter et al., 2010; Pike et al., 2011).

Whilst the law endorses and indeed requires multi-professional working, it is practitioners on the ground who must ultimately realize the ambitions contained in the legal rules. This requires considerable investment of time in relationship-building, both around specific cases and more generally as part of building a community of practice and learning for improvement of the environment (see Chapter 9).

PRACTICE FOCUS

Social workers must talk with Emma and engage in an age-appropriate way. They must place her at the centre of their assessment, planning and decisions, keeping her in focus throughout. They may need to be creative in helping her to contribute her views about her own safety and well-being. They will have to consider how to explain that Emma's views are important but that what she says may not ultimately be what you, as the social worker, decide to follow.

Work with the family should be investigative and where necessary challenging, but Emma's mother, stepfather, grandparents and relevant others, including possibly Emma's birth father, should be involved in decision-making. Social workers may have to draw on their relationship and communication skills and to be resilient and persistent in the face of resistance to engage.

Social workers working with Emma's grandmother should not assume automatically that she lacks decision-making capacity (see Chapter 5) and should involve her in assessment and care planning to ensure a personalized response. Emma's mother and grandfather may be entitled to a carer's assessment.

Social workers for Emma and for her grandmother should ensure that they work closely together. All professionals in this case may have vital information, such as the GP and the health visitor. All those involved should attend strategy meetings to ensure that intervention is coordinated and based on all available and relevant information.

Further reading

General Teaching Council, GSCC and Nursing and Midwifery Council (2007) *Values for Integrated Working with Children and Young People.* A statement of how the values of teachers, social workers and health care practitioners align in order to safeguard and promote the welfare of children.

Social Work Inspection Agency (SWIA) (2005) *An Inspection into the Care and Protection of Children in Eilean Siar.* A forensic account of the challenges of partnership working.

Taylor, B (2013) *Professional Decision Making and Risk in Social Work Practice* 2nd edn. This book contains material on engaging with service users and their families in decision-making.

5

WHO DECIDES?

AT A GLANCE THIS CHAPTER COVERS:

- mental capacity and its place in decision-making
- autonomy, best interests and adults at risk
- mental capacity legislation and principles to safeguard adult self-determination
- decision-making on deprivation of liberty
- children and young people as decision takers
- the role of advocacy

One consistent theme in this book has been that practitioners and managers must have a comprehensive knowledge of the legal rules of the jurisdiction in which they are employed when working with children and adults in need or at risk. This chapter focuses on questions of capacity to take decisions, the relevant legal rules for which vary across the UK. Thus, practitioners and managers in Scotland must have a sound understanding of the Mental Health (Scotland) Act 1984, the Adults with Incapacity (Scotland) Act 2000, the Mental Health (Care and Treatment) Scotland Act 2003 and the Adult Support and Protection (Scotland) Act 2007. Those in England and Wales must have the same understanding of the Mental Health Act 1983 (as amended by the Mental Health Act 2007) and the Mental Capacity Act 2005. Social workers in Northern Ireland operate under the Mental Health (Northern Ireland) Order 1986 and the Mental Health (Amendment) (Northern Ireland) Order 2004. New legislation on mental health and mental capacity in Northern Ireland is anticipated.

Assessing mental capacity emerges through research as a significant challenge for many social workers. They appear to make limited use of government guidance, to be uncertain how to evaluate people's decision-making competence and capacity, and to have limited knowledge of advocacy (Manthorpe et al., 2009; Braye et al., 2013a).

A second consistent theme, to which the book has given specific and detailed consideration because of its focus on the legal rules for good decision-making, has been the principles for the use of statutory authority that have been developed within the law. In this chapter these legal rules are particularly salient because the principles of adult autonomy and self-determination, and the right to private and family life (Article 8 ECHR) and the right to liberty (Article 5), rub up against the principle of protection, the right to live free of degrading and inhumane treatment (Article 3), and the duty of care. Human dignity is especially at stake here (Munby, 2010).

Thus, social work intervention must be lawful, which includes having regard to statutory and non-statutory guidance, and decisions must follow consideration of all relevant information. Balanced judgment is necessary – practitioners should not assume incapacity, and they should guard against the protection imperative (*CC v KK and STCC* [2012]), yet they should not follow policies of personalization and choice when these are unrealistic and would in the circumstances of a case cause significant harm (*AH (by his Litigation Friend RH) v (1) Hertfordshire Partnership NHS*

Foundation Trust, (2) Ealing Primary Care Trust [2011]) (see Chapter 1 on blanket policies). Intervention must be proportionate to a legitimate aim, often the protection and promotion of someone's welfare and interests (Chapter 3), and participatory, where working together means not the imposition of professional control but is characterized by meaningful engagement (Chapter 4) (Munby, 2010). Relationships are once again central to social work practice. At the centre of decisions about who decides is a unique individual who requires understanding, empathy and compassion (Munby, 2010; Westminster Safeguarding Adults Board, 2011). These are core components of professional accountability (Chapter 2).

On-the-spot question	How confident do you feel in your knowledge of the legal rules surrounding assessment of an individual's decision-making capacity in the jurisdiction in which you are working?

Principles for assessing capacity

PRACTICE FOCUS

Emma, aged three, lives with her mother, stepfather and maternal grandparents in a small rented house in poor condition in a deprived neighbourhood. Emma and her mother are being supported by a local children's centre where staff have become concerned about their welfare. Their attendance has become sporadic. Emma has appeared increasingly wary and withdrawn. Staff have seen bruises on her mother's arms and face but she has avoided answering their questions. They refer Emma to children's services but both mother and stepfather are hesitant about engaging with social workers. Shortly thereafter, the police report that they have been called to yet another domestic disturbance at the house, noting in passing that the stepfather is known to them for violent behaviour. The family's GP refers Emma's grandmother for adult social care assessment with a diagnosis of dementia.

- What should social workers consider when assessing Emma's grandmother's capacity?
- How might social workers balance her autonomy with their duty of care?

Social workers have a strong professional commitment to autonomy, which creates a dilemma when this appears to conflict with a perceived duty of care, as in adult safeguarding. In England and Wales particularly, personalization – choice and autonomy – and adult safeguarding have followed parallel tracks (Fyson and Kitson, 2007). In Scotland, by contrast, the Adult Support and Protection (Scotland) Act 2007 has connected the two policy imperatives in order to address situations of harm and abuse (Preston-Shoot and Cornish, 2014). Here protection orders for assessment, and for removal and banning perpetrators from a location, are held in tension with values of self-determination and participation. The tension is resolved by reference to proportionality (see Chapter 3) and involvement (see Chapter 4). The individual must derive a benefit from use of the orders which would not otherwise be available. They must give consent unless there is evidence that satisfies a court of them acting under duress or undue influence. Social workers must pay regard to the ascertainable wishes and feelings of the individual and relevant others, with independent advocacy available (Patrick and Smith, 2009). Proposals for England and Wales to reform adult social care legislation appear to be rejecting this balanced approach towards the use of statutory powers.

Clark (1998) has noted that protective intervention may be justified in value-based terms in the name of beneficence, especially in cases where risks of significant harm are high. McDermott (2011) has observed that autonomy may be interpreted in different ways, both narrowly to protect specific rights or broadly to promote well-being, with active involvement to prevent harm and to promote self-determination. Perhaps then it is unsurprising that inquiries, research and judicial pronouncements have been critical of social work's approach to capacity assessment and to local authority decision-making where risk features prominently in a case. What features prominently are the key principles that should guide use of statutory authority (Chapter 1) and drive professional accountability (Chapter 2), enriched by reference to human rights (Chapter 3) and involvement (Chapter 4).

One overview of serious case reviews involving adults who self-neglect in England (Braye et al., 2013b) found evidence that capacity judgments were being made without formal assessment and that practitioners were confused about the interface between choice and risk. Work appeared to be reactive as a result, rather than characterized by a questioning outreach towards service users, which would include discussion

> **KEY CASE ANALYSIS**

Some critical analytical outcomes of capacity assessments by social workers

Social workers and home care workers did not recognize that the individual lacked capacity to make certain decisions. They appeared to misunderstand the principles of the Mental Capacity Act 2005 (s. 5), namely that caring acts may be performed where the service user lacks capacity to consent, if the carer has taken reasonable steps to ascertain if the person has capacity and acts in their best interests. There was no strategy to address the risks posed by the individual's lack of capacity (*LGO and Worcestershire CC* (2011)).

If the local authority believes that a service user lacks capacity, it must ensure that a formal capacity assessment is completed (*LGO and Bristol CC* (2011)).

The way in which the council decided that an individual did not have capacity was ad hoc. There was a blinkered approach to the case, a lack of urgency and concern, and poor communication between professionals (*Public Services Ombudsman for Wales v Cardiff CC* (2011)).

Decisions should be the least restrictive of a person's rights and freedom of action. Risk management is generally to be preferred to invasive interventions, and a correct balance has to be achieved between protection and empowerment (*A Local Authority v K (by the Official Solicitor), Mr and Mrs K and an NHS Trust* [2013]).

In deciding the best interests of a mentally incapacitated adult, regard must be paid to the right to private and family life (Article 8 ECHR) but there is no starting point that family care is better. All relevant circumstances must be considered (*K v (1) WSX, (2) L (by his Litigation Friend the Official Solicitor) and (3) M* [2012]).

of risks, apparent lifestyle choices and the implications of their decisions (see Chapter 4). There was a lack of awareness of the law, especially the Mental Capacity Act 2005, and of adult safeguarding procedures.

A review of practice with people who self-neglect (Braye et al., 2011) found that practitioners and managers may wrongly understand that the capacity to make simple decisions does not necessarily translate into capacity to implement more complex decisions. Equally, they may not recognize executive dysfunction, the inability to perform activities of daily living even if the person understands the need for them.

Muddled views about whether a learning disabled young man had capacity emerge from another serious case review (Flynn, 2011), which concluded that it was highly questionable whether the assumption that the individual had capacity was reasonable (see Chapter 1). Indeed, it appears that his capacity to take decisions was never assessed despite the evidence available to practitioners and managers that he was taking unwise decisions that placed him manifestly at risk of harm. The review reminds social workers that the presumption of capacity contained within the Mental Capacity Act 2005 does not exempt authorities from undertaking robust assessments where apparent decisions are contrary to a person's well-being. An individual lacks capacity if they are unable to understand information relevant to a decision, including reasonably foreseeable consequences of making a particular decision or not.

The evidence from these serious case reviews highlights the pertinent conclusion that the powerful ethical force of the statutory presumption of capacity, associated with individual autonomy, may render professionals reluctant to question capacity, even when there are clearly problematic elements to a person's decision-making (Keywood, 2010). If a person's decision-making process is not subject to scrutiny, then the statutory presumption may safeguard their liberty but not necessarily their autonomy (Keywood, 2010). Thus, all components of decision-making should be examined, which includes the ability to implement and manage the consequences of particular decisions.

What key principles, then, should be followed for lawful decision-making in this complex field of practice? In England and Wales the Mental Capacity Act 2005 requires a presumption of capacity and endorses the right of individuals to make their own decisions, with support when necessary. It asserts people's rights to make unwise or eccentric decisions and, where capacity is lacking in respect of a particular decision, requires the least restrictive intervention to preserve a person's basic rights and freedoms, based on an understanding of that person's best interests. Similarly, the Mental Health Act 2007 (amending the Mental Health Act 1983), the Mental Health (Scotland) Act 1984 and the Mental Health (Care and Treatment) Scotland Act 2003 require respect for diversity and for people's past and present feelings and wishes. People should be involved in the planning and delivery of their care and treatment, and carers' views should be sought. Intervention again must be proportionate, with the minimum restrictions necessary imposed on liberty.

> **KEY CASE ANALYSIS** ←

Westminster Safeguarding Adults Board (2011)

This case involved an older couple who were well known to adult social care, mental health providers and other health care personnel. The husband had a diagnosis of serious mental illness and subsequently of dementia. He did not always comply with treatment plans. Agencies were concerned that his care and health needs were being neglected. They perceived that his wife's actions hampered their efforts to provide health and social care support, which was often neglected.

The tension between safety and choice was at the heart of difficulties faced by those involved and led to paralysis rather than to a resolve that, to find the right balance, high-quality interventions were required, including tenacity and persistence. The serious case review report is critical of the lack of exploration with the couple of their reasons for declining services, including an absence of appropriate challenge (see Chapter 4). Those involved also appeared to find it difficult to create opportunities to discuss with each of them individually how they saw their needs and those of their partner.

The review is critical of the absence of a collaborative inter-agency approach to risk assessment. Risks did not appear to have been discussed with either the husband or the wife, representing a breakdown in partnership working (Chapter 4). Plans were not updated as risks grew.

In this case there was no formal documented mental capacity assessment and no Mental Capacity Act 2005 compliant best interests assessment. A presumption of capacity was followed without question. Decisions that left the individual vulnerable should have triggered assessment of his mental capacity. The review concludes that practitioners and managers must appreciate and be familiar with the law that underpins practice.

Capacity requires understanding of the need for a decision to be made and why; of the likely consequences of making or not making a decision; the ability to understand, retain, use and weigh up relevant information as part of the decision-making process; and the ability to communicate a decision (DCA, 2007). The ability to use and weigh up information can be read to include executive capacity, namely the ability to implement a decision and to adapt a plan in the light of its consequences (Braye et al.,

2011). It is the salient factors of a decision that is the focus of whether an individual has capacity, not their ability to grasp every nuance and detail; assessors must recognize that different individuals will give different weight to their physical, emotional and other needs; and people must have all relevant information before making a decision, including what a local authority may provide in support, for example, of a return home (*CC v KK and STCC* [2012]). If an individual does not have capacity to take a particular decision, what principles should then guide assessment of best interests?

The Adults with Incapacity (Scotland) Act 2000 contains principles relevant to this question, namely that any intervention must be proportionate to the needs of the individual and capable of providing a benefit that would not otherwise be available. In deciding whether and how to intervene, the individual's present and past wishes and feelings must be ascertained, along with the views of relevant others. In England and Wales similarly (DCA, 2007), practitioners must take account of the individual's past and present wishes and feelings, including beliefs and values, and those of family carers. The individual's participation should be encouraged, and all relevant circumstances should be taken into account. Assumptions should not be made, derived from stereotyping, about the individual's age, appearance or behaviour, and whether the person has capacity to take a particular decision should be kept under regular review. Any intervention should be proportionate and provide the best balance of advantages over disadvantages, and be in line with what a responsible body of professional opinion would consider to be in the person's best interests. The resonance here with principles that have been outlined throughout this book thus far is obvious.

Thus, as Munby (2010) has observed, those exercising authority must guard against stereotyping and must engage meaningfully with individuals and their families. The person's wishes and feelings remain significant at all times, the weight attached to them being case and fact-specific. All relevant circumstances include: the degree of incapacity, with the closer to the borderline the more weight to be attached in principle to the person's wishes and feelings; the strength and consistency of expressed views; the possible impact on the individual of their wishes and feelings being set aside; the degree to which these wishes and feelings can be accommodated within an assessment of best interests; and the extent to which they are capable of sensible and responsible implementation.

Deprivation of liberty safeguards

> → **KEY CASE ANALYSIS** ←
>
> *HL v UK* [2004]
>
> This could also have been a key case in Chapter 3, given its relevance to human rights. This young learning disabled man was taken to a hospital from a day centre where he attended without the knowledge and consent of his carers. The European Court of Human Rights ultimately ruled that he had been deprived of his liberty contrary to Article 5 ECHR. This requires that a procedure recognized by law is followed. In this case the formal safeguards of detention under the Mental Health Act 1983 had not been applied, as he had not been held under s. 2 and s. 3 and the court noted the absence of procedural safeguards to scrutinize detention in hospital under common law in the best interests of a person who did not have the capacity to consent.
>
> As a consequence the Mental Health Act 2007 inserted into the Mental Capacity Act 2005 the Deprivation of Liberty Safeguards. These apply where it is proposed to detain an adult who lacks capacity in hospital or a care home for the purpose of giving treatment or care in circumstances that amount to a deprivation of liberty, where it is necessary to protect them from harm and in their best interests.

Lawful authority is required in order to deprive an adult without capacity of their liberty and there must be a procedure to review such detentions (Article 5(1) ECHR; *HL v UK* [2004]). Deprivation of liberty is distinguished from restriction of liberty by complete and effective control over a person's residence, assessment, contacts and treatment, by a decision not to release the individual into the care of others if so requested, and the possible use of restraint to prevent discharge (*HL v UK* [2004]; *Storck v Germany* [2005]). In England and Wales, the safeguards have been written into the Mental Capacity Act 2005 by the Mental Health Act 2007. Procedures are under discussion in Scotland and Northern Ireland in order to protect people without capacity there from arbitrary detention.

Significantly for this book, with its emphasis on lawful use of authority, the Department of Health, Social Services and Public Safety (DHSSPS) in Northern Ireland (2010) has issued interim guidance on good practice. It advises that:

1 decisions should be taken in a structured way, with a proper assessment of whether the person lacks capacity to decide on the care proposed;
2 care planning should be effectively documented in record-keeping and demonstrate appropriate family involvement;
3 alternatives should be considered and restrictions should be the minimum necessary;
4 individuals and their families should be given appropriate information, especially regarding the purpose and reasons for care and treatment proposals, arrangements to review care plans, the outcomes of such reviews and the availability of complaints procedures through which to challenge decisions;
5 decisions must be formally reviewed.

The Code of Practice for England and Wales similarly refers to decisions being taken in a structured way, evidenced through proper assessment, individual and family involvement, good care-planning and transparent recording. Where appropriate, advocates should be involved and decisions must be proportionate to the needs identified and reviewed routinely (Ministry of Justice (MoJ), 2008). Once again there is a clear resonance with the principles for professional accountability and lawful decision-making processes outlined earlier in this book.

Authorization to deprive someone without capacity of their liberty, in order to prevent harm, does not give authority to treat. That must be established through the wider provisions of mental capacity and, where appropriate, mental health legislation. Assessment involves two key people, whose roles are distinct, namely a best interests assessor and a mental health assessor. There are six requirements to be met, namely that the person is over 18, has a mental disorder, lacks capacity to determine whether they should be accommodated in the proposed location and given care, and has not made an advance declaration refusing some or all of the care and treatment envisaged. The proposed deprivation of liberty must be in their best interests, necessary to prevent harm and proportionate to the risks identified. They must not be already detained under the Mental Health Act 1983 and authorization should not conflict with an obligation under that Act (Braye and Preston-Shoot, 2010). The procedures under the Deprivation of Liberty Safeguards are not to be used as an alternative means of containment for people who ought to be subject to the powers contained in mental health legislation (*GJ v The Foundation Trust* [2009]).

This area of law is complex and subject to ongoing review by the courts. Particularly complex appears to be the definition of what amounts to a deprivation of liberty, especially in relation to objection and lack of objection, and the availability of possible alternative places of residence (*Cheshire West and Chester Council v P* [2011]; *P and Q* [2011]). More clear-cut are cases where there has been a misuse or misrepresentation of authority and an apparent determination to act contrary, and without giving due consideration, to the views expressed by the person themselves and/or family carers (*JE v DE and Surrey CC* [2006]; *Hillingdon LBC v Neary and Others* [2011]). In *G v E and Others* [2010] a family carer had not been adequately involved in decisions relating to the removal of the person from them, or subsequently when transferred between placements. Balanced consideration had to be given to the advantages and disadvantages of where a person might live, including at home with a carer with local authority service support. The council had failed to ensure that staff were conversant with the Deprivation of Liberty Safeguard procedures, with responsibility for poor practice in this case attributed to higher-level management in the local authority rather than to individual social workers.

Advocacy

Advocacy is one crucial element of challenging the balance of power between service users and those with statutory powers. In England and Wales, the Adoption and Children Act 2002 made advocates available to looked after children and to young people leaving care, in order to ensure that their voices are heard in important decisions affecting them and to enable them to make complaints and representations. There is some concern that advocacy provision here may be too standardized and proceduralized to be useful (Boylan and Braye, 2006) and that social workers are reluctant to refer young people to, and to engage with, advocates (Pithouse and Crowley, 2007). In one court judgment relating to young people leaving care, a distinction was made between the role of the social worker, which is to prepare a pathway plan, and the role of a personal adviser, which is to enable the young person to participate in a plan's preparation and to act as their representative or advocate when appropriate (*R (A) v Lambeth LBC* [2010]). IROs in England and Wales must discuss advocacy as an option with young people as part of the process of preparation for statutory reviews (DCSF, 2010). The use of advocates to enable young people to communicate their wishes and feelings emerges too in the Children (Scotland) Act 1995 and the Children (Northern Ireland) Order 1995.

Mental health and mental capacity legislation (Adults with Incapacity (Scotland) Act 2000; Mental Health (Care and Treatment) (Scotland) Act 2003; Mental Capacity Act 2005; Mental Health Act 2007), and in Scotland also adult safeguarding legislation (Adult Support and Protection (Scotland) Act 2007), make provision for the appointment and use of advocates. Familiarity with the legal rules relating to when advocates must or may be appointed is a crucial social work task. The availability of advocates is designed to enable individuals to make representations about their wishes and feelings, to provide information and support in order to promote and protect their rights, and to facilitate understanding of proposed care or treatment. Indeed, advocacy provision should be a stronger part of good governance and oversight of care provision, as the events surrounding Winterbourne View (see Chapter 8) have shown (DH, 2012). Evidence suggests that advocates can help to improve decision-making on issues relating to accommodation, care reviews, adult protection and medical treatment but that referrals in some areas are still low, availability and accessibility remains patchy for some marginalized groups, and staff awareness of when they may or must refer cases to an advocate remains variable (DH, 2009; Manthorpe et al., 2009; Corkhill and Walker, 2010; EHRC, 2011; DH, 2013; Preston-Shoot and Cornish, 2014).

Young people's capacity to take decisions

One further complexity surrounding the question of 'who decides' is the decision-making capacity of children and young people. Chapter 4 discussed the involvement of young people in decision-making and the duties of social workers to ascertain and pay due regard to their wishes and feelings. However, the question remains as to when a young person's views may be determinative of a matter in question.

The key case is *Gillick v West Norfolk and Wisbech Area Health Authority* [1986] which stated that parental responsibility yields to the child's right to make their own decisions when the child reaches sufficient understanding and intelligence to be capable of making up their own mind on a specific decision. Thus, as with mental capacity questions relating to adults, at a particular point in time, a young person may have capacity to take one particular decision but not another. The exercise of parental responsibility is therefore a question of judgment in determining when its exercise is necessary to enable the parent to perform their duties towards a child.

Child care legislation, for example, the Children Act 1989, also captures this approach by allowing a child of sufficient age and understanding to refuse assessment, examinations and medical treatment and, with the court's permission, to seek an order about their future and to instruct directly a solicitor to represent them. As highlighted in Chapter 3, children's participatory rights have also been given significant recognition,

---

PRACTICE FOCUS

For social workers in England and Wales, the Mental Capacity Act 2005 and the code of practice (DCA, 2007) are key here. Social workers will need to draw on their relationship-building and communication skills to enable Emma's grandmother to express clear preferences and to maximize the choices available to her. They should get to know her in order to avoid social stereotypes and to appreciate what she values, enjoys and wants. This will be important if she is judged to lack capacity for a particular decision, with others therefore having to decide how to act in her best interests. It will also be important if there is a clear difference of opinion between the social worker's emerging assessment of her best interests and the views of family members.

Capacity assessments should be approached formally and be carefully documented. Risks should be minimized in the least restrictive manner possible, protecting her right to private and family life (Article 8) and to liberty (Article 5 ECHR), and based where possible on a clear understanding of what she would wish. In order to act in her best interests in respect of a decision for which she lacks capacity, social workers should encourage her participation, appreciate her beliefs and values, and defer any non-urgent intervention if she might regain capacity. The views of her carers will be important. Social workers and others involved should discuss and seek to resolve any tension between being risk-averse and risk-supportive. Emma's grandmother has a family network to support her. If this network did not exist an advocate would be appointed and, if the family is unable to agree on how to act in her best interests, good practice would consider the involvement of an advocate.

especially in Wales and Scotland, with the increasing reference to the UNCRC in how social workers should engage with young people (Boylan and Braye, 2006). Some judgments have acknowledged the importance of the autonomy of young people and their right to freedom of expression and participation (*Mabon v Mabon* [2005]).

However, the welfare imperative remains strong, not least in legal rulings (*Re R* [1991]; *Re W* [1992]) that have overruled a young person's refusal of treatment. The law therefore distinguishes between a *Gillick* principle, which involves consenting to something, and cases involving the right of someone with parental responsibility or a court to disregard a young person's competently reached refusal. Moreover, in welfare decisions, social workers must complete an assessment rather than simply seek to implement the child's wishes and feelings (*R (Liverpool CC) v Hillingdon LBC and AK* [2009]). Thus, whilst children and young people may bring considerable expertise to decision-making, and whilst independent advocates may assist them to participate meaningfully, the law has yet to recognize them fully as social and legal actors, and the challenge for social workers is to ascertain their capacity to understand particular questions that affect them and to maximize the space in which their views are heard and considered (Sawyer, 2006; Boylan and Dalrymple, 2011).

Legal and relationship literacy

Service users have generally welcomed the principles contained within mental capacity legislation but, in line with the principle of consultation that has been emphasized throughout this book, they need to receive clear information and advice, and be given time to absorb and respond to what has been shared (Manthorpe et al., 2009). Even then, however, tensions will continue to exist between autonomy and protection. Local authorities may turn to the courts even in respect of capacitated adults for a safety net to enhance or liberate their autonomy where it is being jeopardized or infringed by the undue influence or coercion of others (*Re SA (Vulnerable Adult with Capacity: Marriage* [2005]; *DL v A Local Authority and Others* [2012]).

What this chapter underscores, and what earlier chapters have similarly emphasized, is the importance of developing trusting relationships, which feature attentive practice and clear scrutiny of possible choices. The involvement of significant others, family and friendship networks, is crucial also, both when deciding to support someone at risk at home and when vulnerable individuals are removed from their family home and carer (*G v E and Others* [2010]).

Further reading

Jones, R (2012) *Mental Capacity Act Manual* 5th edn. An authoritative review of this key but complex piece of legislation for England and Wales.

6

WHAT CAN WE AFFORD?

AT A GLANCE THIS CHAPTER COVERS:

- decision-making about resources and meeting need in the context of financial austerity
- principles to follow when setting social work procedures that involve financial commitment
- principles to follow when determining the relevance of resources when considering people's needs and provision of services
- when resources can and cannot be taken into account by social workers

What topic could be more pertinent for social workers to consider in a context of financial austerity? In fact, however, the tension between needs and resources has been a long-running feature of social work practice, perhaps just brought into starker relief by substantial fiscal retrenchment across the public sector. Indeed, the pressure of meeting financial targets, leading to compromises in levels of medical and nursing care and shortcomings in the standards of care provided to patients, was one significant component in a major recent scandal within the NHS (Francis, 2010; 2013).

Service users have expressed concerns that the pursuit of financial and performance targets, and managing services within constrained resources, have been elevated above their needs in importance (Braye and Preston-Shoot, 2006; Preston-Shoot, 2010). Researchers have also found that one area where the prioritization of agency procedures above strict interpretation of the legal rules becomes especially problematic is when resources are taken into account when deciding how to meet people's needs (Braye et al., 2007; Braye et al., 2013a). Meeting needs inevitably sits adjacent to managing within available resources, which creates tensions within decision-making, the resolution of which managers and practitioners ultimately have to defend. Consequently, reference to the principles being outlined in this book makes practice sense. This chapter will apply those principles to how social workers and their employing organizations should navigate the interface between needs and resources.

The challenge of this interface originates with the realization that social work service users do not have a right to assessment and provision. Rather, social workers operate within a system of absolute duties, discretionary duties, and powers. There are few absolute duties, such as after-care provisions in mental health legislation, perhaps precisely because of their resource implications. Indeed, local authorities cannot impose financial charges for mental health after-care services, which must be provided for as long as the mental health needs endure (*R v Manchester CC, ex parte Stennett* [2002]). Discretionary duties are where social workers must do something once they have decided that a service user's circumstances justify the exercise of that statutory authority. Powers are where social workers may lawfully do something if they decide the circumstances justify it. The principles outlined in the first five chapters are essential ingredients in the mix of deciding when and how to exercise discretion and implement a discretionary duty or exercise a statutory power. The legal rules surrounding the use of resources add to this partic-ular mix, understanding of which is one further way in which social work-ers can assure the quality of practice and maintain public trust (HCPC, 2012a).

However, this system of duties and powers raises a further question. Chapter 3 focused on human rights and equality, noting that the rights guaranteed in the ECHR and Human Rights Act 1998 are civil and polit-ical as opposed to socio-economic. Reference was made to the European Social Charter, which embraces housing, health, education, employ-ment and social protection, but individuals cannot petition a court or tribunal in an attempt to give personal legitimate effect to these rights. So, one question is whether effective human rights are possible without realizable socio-economic rights. A second question is how social work-ers, and indeed legal systems where socio-economic rights are guaran-teed in law (Sachs, 2009), can balance competing interests in a principled and compassionate way, in order to promote dignity, when resources are limited. As this chapter will uncover, these are not simply academic questions.

Evidence suggests that the LGO and the PHSO, together with the EHRC and its predecessor commissions, have been successful through pursuing individual cases and conducting wide-reaching investigations in using equality law and political action to highlight the importance of social rights, notably social inclusion and better health and social care for disabled people (O'Brien, 2012). Evidence also suggests, however, that social work has not enabled some people to secure the minimum decencies of life, their needs having been defined away rather than acknowledged (Sachs, 2009; for an example, see Carr's discussion (2012) of *R (McDonald) v Royal Borough of Kensington and Chelsea* [2011]). Since UK legislation does not, currently, embrace social rights in the manner of the Human Rights Act 1998 for civil and political rights, the struggle for realizable social rights will depend on use of equality legislation and the activation of civil society (O'Brien, 2012). Social work organizations belong to the range of institutions that support civil society. A key challenge then for social workers is how, in adult social care, for example, they use the room for manoeuvre provided in guidance on assessing needs, and the legal rules on resources outlined in this chapter, to push for the protection and promotion of people's social rights.

On-the-spot questions

1 To what degree do you believe that social workers should be and can be human rights workers?
2 How in your practice can you advance people's socio-economic rights alongside their civil and political rights?

Local authorities as corporate bodies

Unless ring-fenced for specific purposes, the annual financial allocation to each local authority does not specify how available resources are to be partitioned. Such decisions are political and taken locally. However, the local authority remains responsible corporately for meeting its statutory duties and, therefore, the decisions taken locally concerning the division of resources into sums for children's services, adult services and other provision for which a council is accountable are indicative only. Social workers are often told that lack of funds in particular budgets means that their recommendations cannot be actioned. However, local authority managers can only plead lack of resources for fulfilment of statutory duties once all budgets, across all council departments, have been spent.

Local authorities must have sufficient staff to perform their statutory social services functions. In England and Wales this duty resides in s. 6 Local Authority Social Services Act 1970. The duty has been amplified by statutory guidance directed at directors of children's services (DfE, 2013) and of adult services (DH, 2006a) who must ensure that there are sufficient resources to maintain standards and discharge statutory functions, and that staff are supported to maintain their codes of practice. What qualifies as sufficient is left to local discretion. However, its exercise must be reasonable and ombudsman judgments have referred to this duty in cases involving substantial delays in assessments and service provision (LGO, 2002; 2007). OFSTED (2012c) has also intervened here, with, for example, a recommendation to one local authority that it must ensure the availability of sufficient social workers and managers to undertake the volume of child protection work, with staff also having the necessary skills and experience to identify and manage risk, and to undertake child protection inquiries to an appropriate standard.

Tribunal decisions concerning the registration of social workers have used the impact of lack of resources on a practitioner's or manager's ability to cope with the volume of demands as a mitigating factor when considering allegations of poor practice (*LA v GSCC* [2007]; *Forbes v GSCC* [2008]; *Cordingley v Care Council for Wales* [2009]). OFSTED (2009), in reviewing learning from serious case reviews, has noted the impact of lack of staff with appropriate expertise on service provision. Laming (2009) also noted the impact of high workloads on effective practice. With the Human Rights Act 1998 having diminished the immunity that local authorities previously enjoyed from claims of negligence (see Chapter 3), it is possible that future claims relating to the quality of provision of child protection and leaving-care services might focus on whether sufficient resources were made available to meet the needs presented.

Needs versus resources

> ◤ **PRACTICE FOCUS**
>
> Emma, aged three, lives with her mother, stepfather and maternal grandparents in a small rented house in poor condition in a deprived neighbourhood. Emma and her mother are being supported by a local children's centre where staff have become concerned about their welfare. Their attendance has become sporadic. Emma has appeared increasingly wary and withdrawn. Staff have seen bruises on her mother's arms and face but she has avoided answering their questions. They refer Emma to children's services but both mother and stepfather are hesitant about engaging with social workers. Shortly thereafter, the police report that they have been called to yet another domestic disturbance at the house, noting in passing that the stepfather is known to them for violent behaviour. The family's GP refers Emma's grandmother for adult social care assessment with a diagnosis of dementia.
>
> - To what degree are resources relevant in law when considering Emma's needs and those of her grandmother?
> - What should be covered in any assessment of Emma's needs and her grandmother's needs?
> - What should be covered when Emma's grandfather is considered as a carer?

This is a key battleground for social workers. Research evidence suggests that social workers often adopt a restrictive rather than broad interpretation of need, influenced strongly by the procedures adopted by their employing authority in response to resource pressures. Some express disquiet, however, about their inability to meet the needs that are presented to them and about the inexorable pressure to adjust services to inadequate levels of funding. They may feel uncertain about the lawful position and even less confident about their ability to challenge the policies that their employing authorities adopt (Braye et al., 2013a).

> **KEY CASE ANALYSIS**

R v Avon CC, ex parte Hazell [1995]

Mark Hazell was a young man with Downs syndrome. The disputed decision in this case concerned to what residential placement he should be transferred as part of a longer-term plan with the goal of independent living. Two placements were available, one locally and one further afield. The local authority chose the cheaper local option.

Mark Hazell successfully challenged the lawfulness of that decision. The case established that for some disabled people assessment should cover psychological as well as social and physical needs. Assessment should follow guidance on the scope of needs assessments. The local authority was also criticized for failing without good reason to follow the outcomes and recommendations of its own internal complaints procedure, which Mark Hazell and his family had used. Finally, the local authority's decision in this case was quashed because it had failed to follow statutory guidance on choice (Guidance on National Assistance Act 1948 (Choice of Accommodation) Directions 1992 (LAC (2004) 20)). This states that a service user succeeds with their choice of accommodation providing that there is a vacancy, that the placement will meet the person's needs, and that the home will not cost the local authority more than it would ordinarily expect to pay. There was a vacancy in the more expensive home which Mark Hazell had chosen. The care manager advised that the placement would meet his needs. Crucially, the local authority had also used the placement for other service users so the third component of the statutory guidance on choice was met. This appeared to have been a resource-driven decision taken contrary to statutory guidance and was quashed.

Across child care, mental health and adult social care, the impact of resource constraint is meaning that people's situations are deteriorating until their needs become critical (Braye and Preston-Shoot, 2010). Researchers in Scotland (Daniel and Baldwin, 2010) and England (Morris, 2010) have argued that children in need are not getting the early intervention and help needed because stretched resources are focused on acute cases. The focus on risk assessment and child protection dominates child care social work, with support services for families uneven and insecurely resourced, despite the policy emphasis on early help. Resource concerns also dominate social work practice with older people (Tanner, 2003) and with carers (LGO, 2002; 2007; Seddon et al., 2007), affecting people's experiences of assessment, help offered and reviews.

Evidence from service users includes managers providing misleading advice and direction about how agencies can balance resource considerations against need (Braye and Preston-Shoot, 2006). Evidence from social workers includes having to hold onto professional judgment about people's needs in the face of managers under pressure regarding resource allocation (Preston-Shoot, 2010; Gower, 2011; Preston-Shoot, 2011). Indeed, in order to secure provision for service users, there is some evidence that social workers inflate levels of need, for example, when working with young people (Daniel and Baldwin, 2010), people with mental distress (Cestari et al., 2006) and with older people (Charles and Manthorpe, 2007).

When may demand be controlled and effectively rationed? There is, of course, an answer in the legal rules but this is also a moral question, which involves people's human rights. Hence, once again, a technical interpretation of the legal rules should be placed alongside both a rights orientation and an ethical orientation, as described in Chapter 2.

These illustrative cases on resources underscore the principles of lawful decision-making (Chapter 1), namely that assessments must be timely, conducted within the legal rules and fairly, and concluded reasonably and rationally, on the basis of analysis of all relevant considerations. So, what are the legal rules on the relationship between needs and resources? Some legislation, for example, the Mental Health Act 2007 in amending the Mental Health Act 1983, sets out principles for its implementation, which include the efficient use of resources alongside other priorities, such as respect for diversity and ascertaining the wishes and feelings of service users and their carers.

Most of the statutory duties delegated to social workers are discretionary and, in considering what is appropriate and reasonable by way of response to presented needs, social workers may be guided by eligibility

> **KEY CASE ANALYSIS**

Illustrative cases on resources

A local authority acted unlawfully by choosing the cheaper option and failing to consider the older person's Article 8 ECHR rights and an assessment that indicated that a move from residential care to nursing care was unnecessary (*R (Goldsmith) v Wandsworth LBC* [2004]).

There was no evidence of commitment from the local authority to ensure that the needs of a young person leaving care were properly identified and the most appropriate services made available (*R (M) v Hammersmith and Fulham LBC* [2008]).

Services provided must have a reasonable chance of meeting the needs identified during assessment and/or review. Care plans must not be resource-led such that there is no reasonable prospect of the identified need being met (*R v Staffordshire CC, ex parte Farley* [1997]; *R v Birmingham CC, ex parte Killigrew* [2000]). Assessment must be focused on need and not on what can be funded (*LGO and Surrey CC* (2008).

Local authorities are entitled to consider the cost of alternative forms of provision to meet assessed need (*R v Lancashire CC, ex parte Ingham and Whalley* [1995]).

The amount of a care package must relate to the assessed cost of meeting assessed eligible needs and involve a detailed presentation of the identified eligible needs and the costs of the necessary required services (*R (KM) v Cambridgeshire CC* [2012]).

Limited resources do not justify a failure to perform a statutory duty, such as a carer's assessment (*HN (A Minor)* [2010], or an assessment or review of needs (*Public Services Ombudsman for Wales v Cardiff Local Health Board* (2009)). Delays are unacceptable when a council has failed to allocate sufficient funds to meet its statutory duties (*LGO and West Lindsey DC* (2009)).

criteria. Thus, one answer to the question posed above – when is a need not a need? – is when a need is presented but is not considered eligible. Put another way, some needs will be determined as falling below a threshold of risk at which the local authority has determined services, beginning with assessment, will be provided. This will mean that addressing need is vulnerable to resource constraints which is why social workers must challenge individual decisions on cases that are wholly irrational and unreasonable (see Chapter 1). In determining whether an approach to a particular case falls within the boundaries of reasonableness, social workers should refer to guidance on what should be considered when assessing children in need and the needs of adults for social care services (for example, in England and Wales, DH, 1991; 2004; HM Government 2013). In setting and reviewing eligibility criteria, essentially what it proposes to do within its statutory duties and powers, a local authority may have regard to its resource position (*R v Gloucestershire CC, ex parte Barry* [1997]). However, it must undertake a lawful process of consultation, namely one that is fair, reasonable and non-discriminatory, as outlined in Chapter 3. The criteria when set must not be operated as a blanket policy (see Chapter 1). Rather, in each referred case social workers must exercise discretion, and that process must be conducted reasonably and rationally, in order to decide whether the eligibility criteria should be applied or set aside (Kline and Preston-Shoot, 2012).

> → **KEY CASE ANALYSIS** ←

Legal rules governing the relationship between needs and resources

Local authorities must allocate sufficient funds to meet their statutory duties and to minimize delay (LGO, 2002; 2007).

A local authority's response to absolute duties, where no discretion is involved, cannot be fettered by resource considerations (DH, 1990; *R v Brent LBC, ex parte Connery* [1990]).

A local authority cannot use its resource position to justify a failure to follow statutory guidance, for example, on reassessment and reviews of an individual's need for community care provision (*R v Gloucestershire CC, ex parte RADAR* [1996]).

Lack of resources cannot prevent service provision once a service has been deemed necessary (*R v Wigan MBC, ex parte Tammadge* [1998]). However, resources may be considered when deciding *how* to meet assessed needs (*R v Gloucestershire CC, ex parte Barry* [1997]) but only if all issues relevant to a case are considered (*R v Lancashire CC, ex parte RADAR and Another* [1996]; *R v Haringey LBC, ex parte Norton* [1998]), including human rights, and if the final care plan for meeting these needs is not so resource-driven that there is no reasonable prospect of the needs being met (DH, 2002; *R v Staffordshire CC, ex parte Farley* [1997]).

Care planning and reviews must follow statutory guidance and contain an adequate analysis, for example, of whether needs have changed and why care packages are being altered or reduced (*R v Birmingham CC, ex parte Killigrew* [2000]).

Courts will not substitute their own judgment for priorities set and assessments undertaken by skilled professionals unless the allocation of resources and the conduct of an assessment or review are entirely unreasonable. They are highly unlikely to direct a council in terms of precisely how a need, for example, of accommodation for a young person, should be met (*R (S) v Croydon LBC* [2011]). Even a decision by a council not to consult with people may in the circumstances of a case be judged reasonable where it involves the protection of public funds, for example, the proper use of direct payments, and where the service user's needs continue to be met (*R (G and H) v North Somerset Council* [2011]).

Nonetheless, the gymnastics and contortions that sometimes result are well illustrated by the majority and minority Supreme Court judgments in *R (McDonald) v Royal Borough of Kensington and Chelsea* [2012]. Here the question turned on what need the service user actually had – either for night-time assistance in using a commode or a night-time toileting need. If the former, then a waking night-sitter would meet this assessed need but incontinence pads would not; if the latter, then incontinence pads would have a reasonable chance of meeting the identified need. The majority decision of the court reaffirmed the principle established by *Barry* [1997], namely that a local authority is entitled to take resources into account when determining how to meet an assessed need. However, the case illustrates the complexity that social workers face when completing written assessments of need in terms of how a person's wishes and needs are actually framed. There is here a question

---

PRACTICE FOCUS

So, what needs should be considered when considering Emma, her parents and her grandparents. Case law, as this chapter has shown, has identified that the concept of need includes what may be reasonably foreseen in the future as well as present needs, and has added the concept of psychological needs alongside social and practical needs. Statutory guidance has listed what assessment should cover when considering the needs of children and their families (HM Government, 2013) and both statutory and practice guidance have done likewise for the needs of Emma's grandmother and her carers (DH, 1991; 2004). Any intervention that follows assessment must have a reasonable chance of meeting the needs identified in order to be lawful.

of power, where an authority might wish to deploy managerial and practice expertise to ration scarce resources, by reference to established practice, whilst service users and their advocates might refer to dignity and to preferences for how need should be defined and met (Carr, 2012). It is here particularly, as expressed earlier in this chapter, that social workers must determine the degree to which they will use their assessment and recording skills, and their knowledge of guidance on need, to promote positive liberties (O'Brien, 2012), namely social inclusion and equality as realized through the provision of health and social care.

Organizational resources

Social workers do not necessarily practise in benign and safe working environments. Heavy workloads, in excess of recommended levels (DCSF, 2010), staff shortages, excessive responsibilities when placed alongside a practitioner's work experience and qualifications, lack of management support and neglect of health and safety have been exposed by research (Dickens, 2007; Horwath, 2011; Kline and Preston-Shoot, 2012), inquiries (OFSTED, 2012c), serious case reviews (OFSTED, 2009) and legal judgments (*Bath and North East Somerset v A Mother and Others* [2008]; *A and S (Children) v Lancashire CC* [2012]). Such an organizational context impacts on and corrodes good practice.

The volume and complexity of referrals, investigations, assessments and statutory proceedings appears to be increasing, for example, in child care (Brooks, 2010). Equally, the policy drive to ensure that social workers spend more time with children and their families will create workload pressures, possibly leading to delay in assessments and decision-making, unless additional resources are found or existing resources are used differently (Munro and Lushey, 2012; OFSTED, 2012c).

When organizations encounter difficulties in delivering services to a safe standard, managers must analyse the risks that are present, engage directly with frontline staff and respond to safeguard the lawfulness and security of practice (Kline and Preston-Shoot, 2012). Both social workers and their employers are under an obligation to ensure that what is done is performed safely and appropriately (see Chapter 2). Otherwise, questions about negligence may be asked. Employers must ensure that social workers can meet the requirements of their professional codes, maintain their own safety and well-being, and honour their duty of care towards service users. Social workers must report concerns about the impact of staff shortages, excessive workloads and long working hours. They must be able to work safely according to the *Bolam* standard (see Chapter 2) and excessive or unbalanced workloads may compromise their duty of care towards service users and their ability to meet the requirements of an ordinarily competent member of their profession (Kline and Preston-Shoot, 2012). These obligations are rooted in health and safety legislation (Management of Health and Safety at Work Regulations 1999) and in standards of conduct and proficiency (HCPC, 2012a; 2012b).

Once again, these are not abstract issues. If inexperienced practitioners are undertaking complex child protection work, then important lines of enquiry may well be overlooked (Reder and Duncan, 2004). Equally, the complexity of the work, exacerbated by resource constraint, may lead to organizational practice that remains unquestioned for its lawfulness and ethical propriety until serious abuse is exposed (Wardhaugh and Wilding, 1993; Preston-Shoot, 2011).

Further reading

These three articles explore what factors may conspire to lead social workers and their employing authorities away from lawful and ethical practice:

Preston-Shoot, M (2011) 'On administrative evil-doing within social work policy and services: law, ethics and practice' 14(2) *European Journal of Social Work* 177–94

Series, L and I Clements (2013) 'Putting the cart before the horse: resource allocation systems and community care' 35(2) *Journal of Social Welfare and Family Law* 207–26

Wardhaugh, J and P Wilding (1993) 'Towards an explanation of the corruption of care' 37 *Critical Social Policy* 4–31

7

DECIDING TO SHARE INFORMATION

AT A GLANCE THIS CHAPTER COVERS:

- decision-making around information-sharing in a multi-layered professional and agency context
- reviews of outcomes of professional practice on requesting and sharing information
- Data Protection Act 1998 and guidance on information-sharing and confidentiality
- application of legal rules to cases of child and adult protection
- importance of agencies working collaboratively and sharing information when safeguarding and promoting the welfare of children and adults at risk of significant harm

Uncertainties over sharing information have bedevilled efforts to safeguard and promote the welfare of children and adults at risk. Laming (2009) has observed that, despite government guidance (HM Government, 2008b), the law relating to data protection and privacy is still not well understood by practitioners and managers. He argues that the legal rules surrounding confidentiality should not be used as a barrier to sharing information between professionals when the safety of children is at stake. He urges agencies to have information-sharing protocols and to ensure that practitioners and managers understand when they may lawfully share information about children and families, when in other words it is in the public interest to prioritize children's safety and welfare. The need for a local protocol on sharing information also emerges as a recommendation from some adult protection serious case reviews (Braye et al., 2013b).

On-the-spot questions

1 In the organization in which you currently practise, what protocols exist for discussing with children, families and/or adults at risk the circumstances under which information which they share with you may be disclosed to others?
2 What protocols exist for sharing information between professionals and agencies?
3 How is their effectiveness monitored and by whom?

There appears little doubt that attachment to the principle of confidentiality, and uncertainty or lack of awareness about the legal rules, have impeded collaborative working and information-sharing between professionals and agencies in child protection (Reder and Duncan, 2003; Tiotto, 2012), mental health (Sheppard, 1996) and adult safeguarding (Manthorpe and Martineau, 2011; Braye et al., 2013b). For example, serious case reviews of adult safeguarding in England (Flynn, 2011; Westminster Safeguarding Adults Board, 2011; Braye et al., 2013b) consistently highlight the absence of sustained, formalized and structured information-sharing across agencies, for example, on mental capacity or lack of cooperation with treatment, with the result that agencies and professionals did not have a complete understanding of a situation and, therefore, what should happen next. Often there was no concerted attempt to pull all known information together, including chronologies of significant episodes in someone's life and of involvement with particular services. As a result, potential informative patterns were missed, new issues were not integrated into an ongoing assessment and opportunities for coordinated action lost.

The purpose of this chapter, therefore, is to lay out the legal rules on when information may lawfully be shared.

Information-sharing between agencies and professionals

> **PRACTICE FOCUS**
>
> Emma, aged three, lives with her mother, stepfather and maternal grandparents in a small rented house in poor condition in a deprived neighbourhood. Emma and her mother are being supported by a local children's centre where staff have become concerned about their welfare. Their attendance has become sporadic. Emma has appeared increasingly wary and withdrawn. Staff have seen bruises on her mother's arms and face but she has avoided answering their questions. They refer Emma to children's services but both mother and stepfather are hesitant about engaging with social workers. Shortly thereafter, the police report that they have been called to yet another domestic disturbance at the house, noting in passing that the stepfather is known to them for violent behaviour. The family's GP refers Emma's grandmother for adult social care assessment with a diagnosis of dementia.
>
> - What information can the children's centre staff, police and GP share with the social workers in this case?
> - What information can the social workers request and what may they share with the professionals involved with this family?
> - Can information only be shared if the family consents?
> - What information should be shared with the family?

The Data Protection Act 1998 applies across all four UK jurisdictions. It covers all forms of media in which information may be held, access to personal records, and the use of confidential information about service users and their families. It has been amplified by guidance (DH, 2000; DCA, 2003; HM Government, 2008b), focusing especially on the principles that should guide practice with families on information-sharing and on the circumstances when, and the means by which, knowledge about an individual or family may lawfully be communicated to others. Nonetheless, social workers continue to find the legal rules on sharing information difficult to understand and use (Bichard, 2004; Perkins et al., 2007; Pinkney et al., 2008; Laming, 2009).

Equally, professional codes of practice can impede communication and prove a barrier to inter-professional collaboration (Stanley et al., 2003). Differences in approach across professions may be rooted in values and also status (Richardson and Asthana, 2006). However, where medical and health care professionals are involved, the emphasis they give to confidentiality may be attributed in part to the limited teaching they receive on law within their qualifying training (Preston-Shoot and McKimm, 2010). Perhaps in recognition of the recurring theme of information-sharing in serious case reviews, professional regulatory bodies have felt the need to restate the primary professional duty of safeguarding and promoting the welfare of children and adults at risk. In truth, whilst the law provides the framework, the challenge lies in the willingness of professionals to overcome agency cultures, status issues and questions of trust and respect, and to share what they know (Hudson, 2005).

The Human Rights Act 1998, and specifically the right to private and family life (Article 8 ECHR), is sometimes presented as an obstacle to sharing information. However, Article 8 may be qualified according to law, in this case the Data Protection Act 1998, where such a qualification is necessary for and proportionate to the aim of preventing or detecting crime, preventing or protecting individuals from harm, or facilitating decision-making on what action to take in a case (DH, 2000). Put another way, information that would otherwise be covered by Article 8 may be shared if there is a legal power to do so, there is a public interest to justify it, and what is communicated is proportionate to the need identified.

Similarly, the common law duty of confidentiality is not absolute (Kline and Preston-Shoot, 2012). Information may be passed on with a person's consent or when there is an overriding public interest or when disclosure is required by a statutory function or a court. This general approach has been reinforced by guidance (DCA, 2003; HM Government, 2008b), identifying the questions to be asked and the sequence of decisions to be made about whether, when and with whom to share information.

The sequence of decisions for lawful information-sharing

Is there a legal power? That legal power may reside in legislation relating to child care, youth justice, or mental health, for example, which reinforces one key principle of this book, namely that practitioners and managers must be aware of the content of legislation such as in England the Children Act 1989 and the Crime and Disorder Act 1998.

Is there a clear and legitimate purpose for sharing information? What are the aims behind sharing information and the outcomes sought?

Does the Data Protection Act 1998 allow disclosure? The Data Protection Act 1998 is not a barrier to information-sharing but provides a framework within which to do so (HM Government, 2008b). Guidance allows social workers to disclose information without consent in order to safeguard and promote people's welfare (DH, 2000).

Has consent been given? Consent may be implicitly or explicitly given, the latter being preferred. However, it may not always be safe or appropriate to seek consent, such as in cases where to do so might place a child or adult at risk of significant harm, delay inquiries or prejudice prevention or detection of crime.

Does the public interest balance lie in the sharing of this information or in confidentiality? A strong public interest can override a professional's ordinary duty of confidentiality (*W v Egdell* [1989]; *Re B (Children: Patient Confidentiality)* [2003]), including disclosure of information to employers and professional regulatory bodies (*Woolgar v Chief Constable of Sussex Police and UKCC* [2000]; *Maddock v Devon CC* [2004]). This is a case-by-case decision, based on facts relating to people's safety and well-being, which amount to a pressing need for disclosure (*H and L v A City Council and Another* [2010]; *W v Chief Constable of Northumbria* [2009]). Crime prevention and the protection of children and adults without capacity from significant harm would fall within a definition of public interest (*L v UK (Disclosure of Expert Evidence)* [2000]). Protection of adults with capacity may fall within the public interest depending on the circumstances of the case (see Chapter 5).

Is disclosure proportionate? Considering people's safety and welfare, how much information is it necessary, proportionate, timely and relevant to share to secure the desired objective? Article 8 allows confidential information to be shared if necessary for public safety, the protection of health or the rights of others, and the prevention

of crime and disorder. It should be the minimum necessary to meet the requirements of the case (DH, 2000).
Is the information accurate? For instance, is there a clear distinction between fact and opinion?
Is the information communicated securely? This relates not just to the means of transmitting information but directs attention to whether the manner in which data is shared is likely to be effective and achieve the desired result.
Has the decision-making process about whether or not to share information been recorded? Who took the decision, based on what information and on what advice?

Courts, tribunals and the ombudsman can all order disclosure of records and people's consent is not required, although they should be informed. Children's guardians have statutory rights of access to information relating to children for whom they are responsible (for example, s. 42(1) Children Act 1989; *Manchester CC v T and Another* [1993]). Advocates may examine and take copies of health and local authority records relevant to their work (see, for England and Wales, s. 35(6) Mental Capacity Act 2005; s. 30 Mental Health Act 2007). Sometimes, however, where a statutory right of access to information and records does not exist, requests for disclosure may have to be settled on a case-by-case basis in court, as when a coroner secured access to the individual management reviews and information reviews that had been produced as a prelude to a serious case review involving the death of a child, the overview report for which was already in the public domain (*Worcestershire CC and Another v HM Coroner for the County of Worcestershire* [2013]).

In addition to the Data Protection Act 1998, when working with children, young offenders, people with mental distress and adults in need of care and support, legislation within each national jurisdiction will contain provisions for seeking and providing information, at strategic and operational levels. Thus, at a strategic level, in England LSCBs may request information from agencies in order to perform their statutory functions and the organizations to which the request is made must comply if the request is appropriately made (s. 8 Children, Schools and Families Act 2010). The standards required by the Data Protection Act 1998 for the provision of information must be met in this instance, namely the sequence of questions for lawful disclosure set out above. For England and Wales, the Children Act 2004 includes information-sharing in the strategic arrangements which are established to enable agencies to plan, develop and monitor service provision.

The Children Act 1989, Children (Scotland) Act 1995 and Children (Northern Ireland) Order 1995 permit social workers to seek support, including information, from other agencies who should respond if what is requested falls within their functions. Familiarity with these legal rules, combined with understanding of the provisions of the Data Protection Act 1998 and subsequent guidance, should help to overcome what Richardson and Asthana (2006) have described as over-open sharing (inappropriate disclosures), over-cautious sharing (withholding information inappropriately) and chaotic arrangements. The legal rules therefore provide a framework for good practice that encourages clarity in decision-making surrounding children and adults at risk based on a thorough assessment of all available information (Sinclair and Bullock, 2002). Nonetheless, divergent thresholds about what counts as significant harm will continue to complicate inter-agency working, particularly but not just at operational levels, which underscores the importance of local agency networks having protocols that cover when, how and with whom information may be shared (DH, 2000; DCA, 2003; HM Government, 2013). Equally, it is not enough simply to have technical competence regarding when in law information may or must be shared. What is shared then has to be analysed and that includes not just the information itself but the context in which the communication occurs, and the relationship processes through which data is transmitted (Reder and Duncan, 2004).

Sharing information with service users and their families

Chapter 1 identified the principle in administrative law that relevant information should be shared to enable people to make informed decisions. Guidance issued subsequent to the Data Protection Act 1998 (DH, 2000) reinforces this principle, namely that openness in sharing information is good practice. Thus, in the spirit of transparency, information should be shared in an age-appropriate way and be accessible for people with disabilities and for whom English is not their first language (EHRC, 2011). There should be a full and open discussion about the services available to meet people's needs, including individual budgets and direct payments. Information that is gathered and recorded should be discussed with children and their families and checked for accuracy (HM

Government, 2013). Differences of opinion or interpretation should be recorded and, indeed, may be valuable in challenging dominant views about how something is to be understood (Hope-Hailey et al., 2012), such as the influence of culture and the meaning of silence when an asylum-seeking minor is being interviewed as part of an age assessment (Gower, 2011).

Rules of engagement should be openly discussed with individuals and families, namely here the circumstances when information that could be regarded as confidential will or must be shared with other professionals and agencies, and what this means for children and families in terms of their engagement with social workers should be explored with them (Munro, 2007; HM Government, 2008b; Ferguson, 2010). Children, for example, appreciate the need for confidentiality to be breached when they are at risk of significant harm (Munro, 2007) but want to be consulted where possible, to be assured that positive information as well as concerns will be disclosed, kept safe and used properly, and to know with whom material will be shared (Hudson, 2005).

Where safe and appropriate to do so, obtaining people's consent to the sharing of information shows respect and appropriate acknowledgment of their Article 8 ECHR rights (Munro, 2007; HM Government, 2008b). The policy in Scotland of getting it right for every child (Aldgate, 2013) strongly endorses respect for confidentiality and consent to information-sharing where this safeguards and promotes the child's welfare. Children over 16 will be presumed competent to consent or to refuse to consent, and those over 12 will generally be considered to have sufficient understanding to decide whether or not to consent. For children of any age, the test will be whether they understand the question and the reasons for sharing information, whether they can appreciate the implications of deciding to share or to withhold information, and whether they can give their own view and hold it consistently (HM Government, 2008b).

Particularly careful judgment will need to be exercised when one family member requests information on another. Much will turn on the reason for the request since an individual's right to private and family life is at stake here. In *R (S) v Plymouth CC* [2002] a mother was given information relating to her son who lacked capacity to consent to disclosure so that she could evaluate if action was needed to protect her son's interests. However, in another case a social worker acted lawfully in refusing to disclose the whereabouts of an adult subject to a guardianship order to a relative because of concerns about abuse (*R v Kent CC, ex parte Marston* [1997]). Significant here may be whether the individual has previously stated that their records, holding information about them, are not to be disclosed to relatives and whether personal data about other people would be identified, since the Freedom of Information Act 2000 (and the Freedom of Information (Scotland) Act 2002) would allow non-disclosure in these circumstances (Hasan, 2009).

The obligation of confidentiality is not total, not least because social workers can be compelled to give evidence. Indeed, in care proceedings, the courts will determine what is disclosed. In *Re B (Disclosure to Other Parties)* [2001], a father alleged to be violent was denied access to documents relating to care proceedings in order to protect the mother's Article 8 ECHR rights. In another instance, an opposite decision was reached, namely full disclosure of a report involving what a child had reported in relation to a parent (*A County Council v SB* [2010]). Generally, in legal proceedings, the presumption will be full disclosure by the local authority of its documents and evidence (*Re G (Care: Challenge to Local Authority's Decision* [2003]), and full disclosure by all parties of their material, whether or not supportive of their case (*L v UK (Disclosure of*

PRACTICE FOCUS

The Article 8 (ECHR) right to private and family life may be qualified by the requirements in the Children Act 1989 to safeguard and promote Emma's welfare and by the rules in the Data Protection Act 1998 for the legitimate sharing of information, especially to protect children and adults without capacity. Where this does not involve undue delay and will not put Emma or her grandmother at risk of further harm, obtaining the family's consent to the sharing of personal information is good practice but there are circumstances where social workers can request information and other professionals may share it without the subject's permission. Information-sharing should be proportionate to the risks identified. The question of who has parental responsibility for Emma is relevant when information is being shared with the family. Equally, assumptions should not be made that individual family members will want others to know what they have said. Social workers should be careful to clarify what they may or might have to share from information given in individual meetings.

Expert Evidence) [2000]). Occasionally, a court may order non-disclosure to a party of material relevant to them when the child's welfare is considered against the likelihood and gravity of harm should material be shared (Braye and Preston-Shoot, 2010).

Recording

Recording is a key social work competence (Care Council for Wales, 2002; NISCC, 2002; Scottish Social Services Council, 2009; HCPC, 2012a). However, serious case reviews, research studies and inquiries frequently identify the need for improvements in record-keeping, especially chronologies of agency involvement that would allow agencies to see each incident in the context of the case history, details of risk and capacity assessments, identification of how the views of individuals contributed to decision-making, analysis of significant issues and agreements about roles and responsibilities (OFSTED, 2008; Braye and Preston-Shoot, 2010; Westminster Safeguarding Adults Board, 2011; OFSTED, 2012c; Braye et al., 2013b; Devaney et al., 2013). For example, in one review, the records were silent on whether information had been shared with a carer, when she was engaging with professionals, to help her reach judgments on the health of her partner (Westminster Safeguarding Adults Board, 2011). Statutory guidance requires that records contain a clear analysis of information (for example, HM Government, 2013). Records must allow a clear view of emerging patterns and the extent of a person's needs to appear, and must ensure that the content of decisions, who was involved in taking them, and the rationale behind them are clearly stated.

Recording helps to focus work, monitor practice and maintain continuity when new staff become involved. Objectives, assessments and summaries of progress should be clearly observable, together with how information and, indeed, the record itself have been shared with service users. Files must have an accurate chronology of significant events and provide a clear picture of the problems and needs being addressed, how they were being tackled and why particular theories or methods were being used. Notes of all meetings and discussions should be detailed, clear, accurate, balanced and full to enable transparency (see Chapter 1). They should be contemporaneous to the events described and enable the reasons for, and participants to a decision, to be identified (*Re E and Others (Minors) (Care Proceedings: Social Work Practice* [2000]; *Re C (Care*

Proceedings: Disclosure of Local Authority's Decision-Making Process) [2002]; *Re F (A Child)* [2008]). However, recording practice has often been poor when assessed against these standards (Preston-Shoot, 2003; O'Rourke, 2010).

On-the-spot questions

1 Based on the standards outlined here, how satisfied are you with your own record-keeping?
2 What might you do to improve the standards of what and how you record?

Accessing personal information

The Data Protection Act 1998 covers subject access to files, the current legislative outcome of a process begun with *Gaskin v UK* [1989].

> **KEY CASE ANALYSIS**
>
> *Gaskin v UK* [1989]
>
> Graham Gaskin had been in the care of the local authority. Subsequently he sought access to his files in order to understand his time in care and to appreciate why particular decisions had been taken. He was denied access by UK courts and so took his case to the European Court of Human Rights where he succeeded.
>
> This case established that there must be a specific reason to prevent an individual from seeing information held about them. Such information is an integral part of their Article 8 ECHR rights. For this reason, record-keeping must enable service users to know and understand their development, help them to deal with the emotional and psychological impact of significant events in their lives and appreciate other fundamental and essential aspects of their private and family life, including why professionals took the particular decisions they did (*MG v UK* [2002]).
>
> Access to files legislation was the direct result of the European Court's decision in the *Gaskin* case. The relevant law is now the Data Protection Act 1998.

Specific regulations for social services and guidance have been issued (Data Protection (Subject Access Modification) (Social Work) Order 2000; DH, 2000). Access to personal data may be restricted if it is likely to cause serious harm to the individual or another person, if it is held for the purposes of crime prevention or detection, if it would prejudice social work functions, such as preparing a case for legal proceedings, or if legislation prohibits its disclosure, such as adoption information to children under the age of 18. If other individuals can be identified from the requested information, they must consent to its disclosure or that part of the information should be withheld. Requests for access should be in writing, after which there are clear timescales for responding. Applicants can request amendment of recorded information if they believe it to be inaccurate. If an authority refuses to agree to this request, a note should be attached to the file indicating what is disputed. Ultimately, unresolved disputes may be taken to the Information Commissioner.

There is no minimum age for accessing personal records and so, in relation to children, the relevant test will be whether the young person has sufficient understanding to decide the matter in question (*Gillick v West Norfolk and Wisbech Area Health Authority* [1986]). Young people over 16 will be presumed competent and those over the age of 12 generally expected to have sufficient understanding (HM Government, 2008b). Individuals with parental responsibility may seek access to a child's records if the young person is not competent to make their own application and if access is in the child's best interests, or the child is competent and consents.

The Freedom of Information Act 2000 covers England, Northern Ireland and Wales. In Scotland the relevant provision is the Freedom of Information (Scotland) Act 2002. The right is to information held by public authorities concerning their functions but the legislation may be used by individuals in order to secure information held about their involvement with a particular authority. Requests must be made in writing and specific timescales operate in which organizations should respond either with the information or by claiming an allowed exemption. In England especially there is political pressure to publish serious case reviews of child protection outcomes in full. Significantly, in Northern Ireland the balance to be struck between the public interest in full disclosure of events surrounding cases of child abuse, as reported through case management reviews, and the risks to the family of loss of anonymity and public disclosure of personal data has been tested (*Torney v Information Commissioner and the Regional Health and Social Care Board* [2013]). In this instance, the balance came down on protecting the families from additional distress, with data protection considerations outweighing claims for transparency. Guidance for England and Wales on publication of serious case reviews (HM Government, 2013) accepts that publication must comply with the standards set out in the Data Protection Act 1998. Specifically, published reports must not contain personal information about children and their families, such as chronologies and histories, which would enable them to be identified. Chapter 8 will return to the challenge of learning from the unthinkable and, with Chapter 9, will consider effective mechanisms for holding practitioners and managers accountable and using review reports meaningfully to embed improvements in organizational and inter-agency practice.

Supporting good information-sharing practice

Social workers will depend, in this area as in other fields of practice, on legal advice, supervision and organizational support. The necessity of having inter-agency protocols for information-sharing has already been emphasized. Mechanisms should be in place, perhaps overseen by LSCBs (Child Protection Committees in Scotland) and LSABs (Adult Protection Committees in Scotland), for developing protocols and then monitoring information-sharing practice at strategic and operational levels. Organizational cultures and professional values on confidentiality and information-sharing are likely to remain significant but legislative intention, amplified by guidance, appears clear. The priority behind sharing information is to safeguard and promote the welfare of children and adults at risk.

Getting information-sharing right is part of making sense of what social workers do in direct work with children and families and across networks of inter-agency relationships and services (Ferguson, 2010). It is clear that lack of communication and misunderstood communications between professionals have featured strongly in child and adult protection cases that have had unfortunate outcomes. However, systematic information-sharing between social workers and other professionals is only one component of protecting children and adults at risk, which is why the final two chapters survey what can go wrong within and between organizations and explore practice and organizational governance – the necessary supports for ensuring that the best possible decisions are taken.

Further reading

HM Government (2008b) *Information Sharing: Guidance for Practitioners and Manager.* Clear and accessible guidance of when sharing information is permitted or required.

O'Rourke, L (2010) *Recording in Social Work: Not Just an Administrative Task.* A useful restatement of the importance of and skills involved in compiling social work records.

8

LEARNING FROM THE UNCOMFORTABLE AND UNTHINKABLE

AT A GLANCE THIS CHAPTER COVERS:

- key themes in failing organizations
- attitudes towards complainants and whistleblowers
- organizational negligence
- barriers to inter-agency and inter-professional collaboration

Social work practice does not take place in a vacuum; rather it is held and led within organizations, sometimes nurtured and supported, sometimes mismanaged and neglected. This is explicitly recognized by the regulatory councils that oversee social work and groups which have sought to reform the context for practice, with professional codes having standards for employers alongside those for social workers (Care Council for Wales, 2002; NISCC, 2002; Scottish Social Services Council, 2009; Social Work Reform Board, 2010b). As the preceding chapters have shown, however, social work organizations have sometimes failed the audit of legality (Bingham, 2011), namely judicial review, their decisions quashed or their managers ordered to approach decision-making lawfully. Alternatively, their failings have been dissected by inquiries.

The test of any organization is how it responds to what is discomforting (Sachs, 2009). This test applies equally to social work organizations. However, as this chapter will uncover, some social work organizations have lost sight of professional values and standards of lawful decision-making, demeaning themselves and others in the process. They may not have taken action to prevent the unthinkable or acted swiftly enough when given uncomfortable feedback by service users, carers or practitioners.

This chapter, therefore, moves the focus beyond the contribution of individual social workers to the process of decision-making and turns the spotlight unequivocally on how organizations and networks of agencies, and the systems and cultures within and surrounding them, can distort the standards by which the law and professional values expect decisions to be reached. Four illustrative examples follow of how lawful and professionally accountable practice can be subverted. They are not, sadly, unique. Flynn (2006) has, for example, previously identified inhumane treatment of learning disabled people permitted within the NHS. OFSTED inspection reports of local authority children's services practice sometimes find good and outstanding practice but sometimes the opposite. The remainder of this chapter will pick up the themes that emerge from these case studies.

It couldn't happen here, could it?

The majority of local authorities and health care agencies may be performing at least adequately, which means achieving minimum standards for the effectiveness of safeguarding, and for services for looked after children and for adults requiring support to live in the community (Wallace et al., 2009;

> **KEY CASE ANALYSIS**
>
> **Northamptonshire Children's Services (OFSTED, 2013)**
>
> The inspection found systemic weaknesses and inconsistent practice. There had been extensive turnover and discontinuities in operational and strategic leadership. Senior leaders had not focused sufficiently on ensuring service quality. The LSCB had not exercised leadership and challenge. Agencies were not working together productively. Information-sharing and communication, for instance, to support risk assessments, between organizations were weak due to insufficiently strong inter-agency links.
>
> Risk of harm to children was not consistently recognized or addressed. Too many assessments were of poor quality and shortfalls pointed out by IROs were not leading to effective remedial action. Children were therefore being exposed to harmful experiences, some of which were neither assessed nor tackled. Not all help was made available in a responsive way. There was some evidence of constructive and helpful work but some interventions lacked focus to deliver change. Voices of children were infrequently heard, for example, in assessments and service planning. There were high numbers of unallocated cases. Help to some families was delayed. Performance management focused on compliance rather than qualitative evaluation of service delivery.
>
> Arrangements in Northamptonshire were judged inadequate. Immediate attention was judged necessary to risk assessment and management, decision-making relating to children subject to child protection enquiries, use of all relevant information, and ensuring that children's experiences, wishes and feelings are consistently and explicitly foregrounded in assessments, interventions and planning. Other immediate priorities included the use of advocates for children and the development of determined and effective political, professional and managerial leadership.

Tiotto, 2012; CQC, 2013). However, no health or welfare organization can afford to sit back complacently. Protocols for effective inter-agency work and partnership working with children and young people (Chapter 4) and for information-sharing between professionals are not always developed (Wallace et al., 2009). There remain challenges for community care services in meeting quality and safety standards, including incomplete records, ineffective complaints procedures, lack of monitoring and rushed visits (CQC, 2013). Child protection services are not universally characterized by

Serious case review: Daniel Pelka (Lock, 2013)

Daniel suffered prolonged abuse and neglect. He was assaulted, injured and malnourished. Teachers noticed that he was hungry at school and also bruised but not all their observations were recorded or referred on. A paediatrician was unaware of the injuries witnessed at school and did not consider whether emotional abuse and neglect were the causes for Daniel's low weight. His mother and stepfather, who deliberately misled and deceived professionals, have been convicted of murder.

The serious case review concluded that the child protection risks in a volatile household had not been fully perceived or identified. Work had been insufficiently focused and formalized. There was insufficient enquiry. For example, there was no attempt to address alcohol misuse and no full assessment of the extent of domestic violence and its impact on the children. Some professionals did not perceive domestic violence as a child protection issue. There were missed opportunities by the police, hospital staff and social workers to address the domestic violence issue.

Missed ante-natal and paediatric appointments were not followed up. There were missed opportunities to protect Daniel. Professionals did not think the unthinkable but accepted parental versions of Daniel's injuries and bruises, and of the domestic situation, without robust challenge.

One assessment was thorough. It included unannounced visits. The children were seen and other agencies consulted. However, its findings were compromised by not having all available information. Other assessments lacked analysis, for example, of the domestic violence and the male partners, the family's immigrant status and associated language and cultural factors, and additional risks were not recognized, such as pregnancy. Core assessments were insufficiently probing. The children's experiences and needs appeared to have been minimized. Assessments were not always followed by interventions.

There were delays in information-sharing between agencies and the patterns were not seen. Recording of referrals was poor. There was limited inter-agency liaison regarding the case, for example, between GPs, teachers, health visitors and social workers. Professionals acted on assumptions about what other practitioners were doing. Police responses were insufficiently child-centred. Some meetings were not properly minuted, decisions improperly recorded, and agencies did not challenge children's services about their approach to the case. Decisions were not always followed through. The cumulative effect on Daniel of a chaotic household, scapegoating, planned punishments and emotional abuse was not recognized.

There were severe resource pressures in several agencies. Social workers and health visitors carried high workloads. There was management oversight of the case in health and children's social services but the poor quality of assessments and information-sharing was not tackled.

the completion of timely assessments (Chapter 1), the availability of chronologies of significant events (Chapter 7), the performance of planned and purposeful work (Chapter 2), and clarity about the process and rationale for decision-making (Chapter 1). For example, another child protection inquiry (SWIA, 2005) highlights the importance of challenging entrenched patterns of thinking and observes that adverse work contexts, such as workloads and staffing levels, and failures of supervision and strategic management, impact on professionals' ability to keep children safe and to question organizational decision-making. Delving a little more deeply into the key themes that may be discerned from these four case studies will identify why complacency is unwise.

On-the-spot questions

1 If you think of the organization in which you are currently working, or as a student the agency in which you last undertook practice learning, how open to feedback from service users, family carers, staff members and other professionals did you experience the culture to be?

2 What is/was the attitude of managers to people who complain or make representations?

3 What is/was the attitude towards staff who escalate concerns?

4 How prominent are/were senior managers in providing leadership in multi-agency networks?

5 How accessible are/were senior managers to frontline staff?

Complaints procedures

How agencies respond to representations and complaints is one illustration of the openness of organizational cultures to learning. Unfortunately, some evidence exists of local authorities, networks of professionals handling complex cases, and individual practitioners being

> **KEY CASE ANALYSIS**

Winterbourne View (Flynn, 2012)

Adults with learning disabilities were placed in Winterbourne View. Institutional abuse went unchallenged because of substantial failings by managers, commissioners, regulators and safeguarding agencies. Unlawful and inappropriate restraint was used by staff who were untrained and who did not receive supervision. There was a lack of professional input and patient advocacy, little senior executive oversight and a lack of effective leadership and management.

There was a failure to respond effectively to complaints. Service users did not have unimpeded access to complaints procedures, and their representations were dealt with by staff members whose behaviours and actions were sometimes the focus of what was being complained about. Residents were not listened to or believed. Complaints were not investigated robustly, independently of staff and line management.

For much of the time Winterbourne View did not have a registered manager as required by regulations. Reviews of service users were ineffective, failing to identify concerns about assessment and/or treatment. There was a lack of understanding of people's complex needs. Care plans were poor. Injuries sustained by residents were not followed up.

Staff did not whistleblow. The organization responsible for Winterbourne View and the CQC failed to respond when a staff member did blow the whistle. Commissioners did not have an up-to-date knowledge of the service, including of serious incidents. Regulators were kept at a distance about important events affecting the health and welfare of residents, and about concerns regarding the fitness to practise of some staff members. Inspection was too light-touch, placing heavy reliance on Winterbourne View's self-assessment.

Family members were also kept at a distance, with access to residents tightly controlled.

Forty safeguarding alerts were received by South Gloucestershire Adult Safeguarding but were treated as discrete cases. Safeguarding policies and procedures were inconsistently applied and investigation of referrals was sometimes poor.

Eleven former members of staff have now been convicted of abusing service users at Winterbourne View.

> **KEY CASE ANALYSIS**

Mid Staffordshire NHS Trust (Francis, 2013)

There was a serious failure by the board of the NHS trust to tackle the negative culture in the hospital involving tolerance of poor standards and disengagement by managers from nursing and medical staff. At times the board showed a lack of urgency. Neither the hospital's internal systems nor those of the Strategic Health Authority, safeguarding agencies and regulators, such as the CQC and Monitor, picked up or responded to failures in care.

Targets, particularly financial performance indicators, were placed ahead of acceptable standards of patient care. Staffing levels were inadequate and poor standards were tolerated. Risk assessments of staffing levels were inadequate. Hospital managers appeared to screen out information which would have indicated warning signs and a cause for concern, and were focused on measuring compliance with targets rather than outcomes for patients.

The work environment was unsupportive, with incidents of bullying and a culture of secrecy and fear. There was a lack of openness to criticism. Some staff attempted to raise concerns but these were not acted on internally or by external regulatory bodies. There was a failure of communication between agencies in terms of sharing knowledge of concerns. Inspection was inadequate in uncovering the full extent of the experiences of patients and their families.

Essentially, the hospital was focused on the system's business and not on the patients.

unwelcoming of challenges from service users and family carers. Complaints are unwelcome and poorly investigated. Researchers have identified that people fear reprisals if they complain and may have insufficient information about the process to follow (Manthorpe et al., 2009; EHRC, 2012). Responses are delayed and not always formalized, and the bravery of those who challenge poor practice not recognized (Flynn, 2004; 2006; Manthorpe et al., 2007; Westminster Safeguarding Adults Board, 2011). Complaints are not seen as information about practice standards that should be investigated; rather, attitudes towards complainants are disrespectful, even hostile, service users and family carers experience the procedures as daunting, and recommendations are sidelined (Braye and Preston-Shoot, 2010; Kline and Preston-Shoot, 2012). Thus, complaints procedures may not be operating effectively in challenging poor practice. A more positive attitude and learning orientation are required.

Whistleblowing

Social workers must challenge unacceptable practice responsibly (QAA, 2008). Safe systems depend on people raising concerns. However, they have found it difficult to raise issues because of fear of victimization, uncertainty about their knowledge of law and ethics to challenge the practice of colleagues, unsupportive peers and managers, and the presence of blame cultures (Skinner and Whyte, 2004; Kline and Preston-Shoot, 2012). Indeed, the reality for whistleblowers has often been detriment, victimization, disciplinary action, stress, ill-health and job loss, even when their actions have subsequently been vindicated at employment tribunals. For instance, four social workers who blew the whistle about illegal and/or abusive practice in their organizational settings were all eventually vindicated but all suffered unfair dismissal and ill-health as a result and three have not worked as social workers since (Kline and Preston-Shoot, 2012).

One report concluded that whistleblowers were often ignored by managers, or their concerns were minimized, and in a significant minority of cases there was no positive change as a result of concerns having been raised (Public Concern at Work, 2011). Whistleblowing policies are often not widely known or publicized. One conclusion is that some managers and organizations do not welcome uncomfortable feedback; another is that the Public Interest Disclosure Act 1998 is weak in protecting whistleblowers.

Organizational culture can be insidious, distorting ethical principles and producing a code of silence and tolerance of the unacceptable (Doel et al., 2010; Preston-Shoot, 2010; 2011). Managers too have found difficulty in discussing areas that are not working well, again often because of the presence of blame cultures (Skinner and Whyte, 2004).

Valued knowledge

Inquiries and researchers not infrequently point out that managerialism in social work departments has become a barrier to using professional knowledge, which the standards of accountability, as described in Chapter 2, would expect and value. Sullivan (2009), Munro (2011), Gordon and Cooper (2010), Rixon and Ward (2012) and Skinner and Whyte (2004) all identify that social work practitioners and managers experience difficulty in transferring professional values, knowledge and learning into the workplace. What appears valued is performance of the agency's requirements and procedures, leaving little space for the outcomes of training, research, evidence-based practice and reflection.

Indeed, Skinner and Whyte (2004) found managers to be very uninformed about aspects of their work context, including law. Munro and Lushey (2012) found a lack of reference to research or explicit use of theory in assessments of children and their families. In such environments, learning from and changing practice and its management can prove challenging. OFSTED (2008) has criticized social work for not embedding learning from serious case reviews. However, a more systemic analysis highlights that what is valued in policy terms is what managers provide (Ayre and Preston-Shoot, 2010). It has not been evidence-based practice that has been valued as much as compliance with regulation, targets and procedures, with sometimes resulting compromises in respect of legal principles (Chapter 1) and professional standards for decision-making (Chapter 2).

Governance overview

Some inquiries have found that local authority and multi-agency governance and audit systems have failed to identify problems and risks. For example, in one local authority, neither the Overview and Scrutiny Committee nor the LSCB were appraised of safeguarding incidents and concerns; rather, they were kept at a distance and therefore unable to exercise sufficient oversight of management responses (ESTYN and CSSIW, 2011). Elected members were unsighted on safeguarding issues and unable to hold senior managers to account. The LSCB was unable to consider whether or not to commission serious case reviews and, without regular reports, could not exercise independent judgment of the authority's strategic and operational safeguarding practice.

The LSCB in another local authority has been required to develop more effective oversight of frontline practice and to ensure that its subgroups have effective and realistic work plans (OFSTED, 2012c). It has been charged with ensuring that managers exercise clear leadership and, via audits, with demonstrating the degree to which agencies are complying with guidance. It was judged to have been limited in holding agencies to account for their safeguarding practice, with the objectives in its business plan insufficiently robust.

Good governance includes monitoring procedures and learning from active, complex cases. However, across systems for safeguarding children and adults, not all safeguarding boards (England and Wales) or protection committees (Scotland) have effectively managed this task (France et al., 2010; ESTYN and CSSIW, 2011; Braye et al., 2013b; Cornish and Preston-Shoot, 2013). Rather, they have been found to have poorly developed audit systems and/or to be tardy in pressing for action or challenging the lack of information about serious incidents or compliance with care standards. Local authorities and their NHS partners have been found to be working with outdated procedures, out of line with best practice, for example, in respect of learning disabled people (Flynn, 2006; 2012). Records of supervision and of investigations have been inadequate and engagement with frontline staff and with service users sporadic. Inspections have failed to detect abuse or accurately assess the quality of provision (Kline and Preston-Shoot, 2012). The parallels with the board responsible for Winterbourne View are clear. They surround the quality of leadership in setting fundamental standards and workplace cultures, and then driving through quality provision.

Management engagement

Investigations have been critical of management oversight of professional practice for its lack of rigour and inconsistency in challenging poor standards. Necessary scrutiny has been lacking of risk assessments, for example, surrounding unallocated cases, and of continuity in case management, planning and decision-making (OFSTED, 2012c). Reviews of LSCBs and LSABs (France et al., 2010; Westminster Safeguarding Adults Board, 2011; Braye et al., 2012) and of Adult Protection Committees in Scotland (Cornish and Preston-Shoot, 2013) have noted the challenge of ensuring that managers of sufficient seniority are present to provide strategic leadership in developing and monitoring systems of safe safeguarding practice.

However, effective managers require more than technical competence – knowing *what*. Knowing *how* is also crucial and that requires relationship competence, characterized by empathy and engagement (Morrison, 2007). Just like social workers, managers too benefit from adequate support but it may be absent in some working contexts (Bates et al., 2010). Nonetheless, the dominant culture has been one of surveillance, audit and compliance control, which has created anxiety and defensiveness, impacting negatively on learning (Driscoll, 2009;

Morrison, 2010). Even then, serious case reviews have found insufficient management oversight of complex situations, decisions made without knowledge of the case, and inconsistent auditing of case files (OFSTED, 2008; 2009; 2010). Sometimes the accusation has been more challenging still, namely that managers had no sense of how damaging and impoverished their organization's services were (Flynn, 2006). Perhaps in the context in which they find themselves, managers and indeed practitioners may find it easier to accommodate to an organization's demands, to become socialized into local expectations, than to escalate concerns and to challenge the policy and practice framework within which they are expected to work.

Supervision

One key illustration of the degree of management engagement with frontline practice is supervision. Employers must provide good supervision (GSCC, 2008; Social Work Reform Board, 2010b). With alarming frequency, however, the quality and frequency of available supervision draws criticism from inquiries and researchers (for example, OFSTED, 2008; 2009). For example, in one local authority, formal supervision was not consistently taking place and, when provided, was largely task-focused rather than reflective and offering the necessary challenge on casework decisions (OFSTED, 2012c). Across serious case reviews in adult safeguarding (Westminster Safeguarding Adults Board, 2011; Braye et al., 2013b), staff supervision has been criticized for not offering objectivity and challenge, and for failing to support practitioners in difficult and complex situations, involving having to balance choice with safety, and people's autonomy with a duty of care, with the result that social workers and other staff feel unsupported.

Duffy (2011) found that there were insufficient opportunities for social workers to discuss moral and ethical principles arising in their work. Conversely, Gordon and Cooper (2010) found that team meetings, a team ethos, supervision, access to knowledge and shadowing more experienced members of staff were all helpful in maintaining high standards of practice. The SWTF (2009) found that supervision was process, target and case management-driven at the expense of its supportive, analytical and evaluative possibilities. Perhaps these findings should not surprise since a managerialistic culture will value precisely the kind of supervision that is being criticized in serious case reviews and inquiries into social work (Ayre and Preston-Shoot, 2010).

A helpful statement of good supervision practice (British Association of Social Workers (BASW), 2011) frames it as a right for social workers and an agency responsibility. Supervision should be regular, planned, frequent, systematic and reflective. Done well, it facilitates accountability for practice and helps to ensure quality service provision and uphold professional standards. It builds social workers' confidence and capacity, helping them to make sound judgments, to manage risks whilst respecting rights, and to develop their knowledge, values and skills.

Resources

Employers must provide a suitable work environment for social workers. This includes access to continuing professional development and realistic workloads (GSCC, 2008; Social Work Reform Board, 2010b). Organizations, though, also operate in a context, the most obvious being the resources allocated by central and local government. One manifestation of this context is the reduced capacity of managers to provide the necessary strategic and operational direction of practice because of significant budget cuts (OFSTED, 2012c); another is the high volume of work carried by social workers, coupled with staff shortages, which leads to pressurized staff denying the individuality and uniqueness of service users, disregarding research and implementing policies such as personalization in a routine manner (Dwyer, 2009; Gordon and Cooper, 2010). The IRO involved in one case had over 200 cases, far in excess of recommended levels (DCSF, 2010), coupled with limited training, supervision and access to legal advice (*A and S (Children) v Lancashire CC* [2012]). Child protection tragedies have often involved inexperienced social workers, with heavy workloads making demands beyond their level of competence at that point in their careers, who have also lacked support and adequate supervision (Kline and Preston-Shoot, 2012). Reviews of the experiences of newly qualified social workers similarly report that the reality of the work they encounter deflates their confidence levels and morale, and that the organizational context comprises large workloads, lack of induction and continuing professional development, and negative experiences of supervision (Bates et al., 2010; Jack and Donnellan, 2010).

The SWTF (2009) was clear that too many social workers are overloaded, unsupported and deskilled but its recommendation that employers' standards should be binding has not been implemented. Ultimately, then, individual social workers may be held accountable in law for their practice, through their professional registration, but holding employers accountable for the working environment they provide for their staff is not so clearly established in law.

Laming (2009) identified the negative impact on social work practice and its management of poor supervision, high caseloads, inadequate resources and pressure. Subsequent political intervention in policy-making on social work has done little to ensure the adequacy of investment in staffing and training resources (Driscoll, 2009). Competing demands or priorities at the front door of social services are the result – professional and political encouragement sees social workers spend more time with children and their families, but referrals mount up and there are competing pressures to avoid delay (Munro and Lushey, 2012).

How would you assess the social work organization in which you work on the following criteria?

On-the-spot questions

1 Provision of induction and career appraisal
2 Provision of supervision and continuing professional development
3 Allocation of work and workload management
4 Access to advice, including legal advice
5 Enabling the escalation of concerns
6 Supporting social workers to use professional knowledge and to exercise professional judgment
7 Dealing with workplace bullying
8 Managing unfilled vacancies

Barriers to learning within and across organizations

Wardhaugh and Wilding (1993) identify four themes that potentially distort lawful decision-making and disrupt learning when the unthinkable is uncovered, namely:

1 the characteristics of those with whom practitioners work, which can encourage a neutralization of moral concerns, reflected in the adoption of stereotypes and lack of interest in their needs and well-being;
2 power and process in enclosed, inward-looking organizations, with a command and control bureaucracy stifling criticism and silencing moral considerations;

3 the complexity of the work, with concentration on the most difficult cases exacerbated by resource pressures and preoccupation with outcomes and targets, generating a routinized use of discretion and an institutional rather than individual approach;

4 the absence of accountability and reluctance to challenge professional autonomy, such that ethical practice depends on the values of front-line staff.

Adams and Balfour (1998) describe how organizational authority can erase ethics and how unethical choices (and in this book's focus, unlawful choices) can be redefined through agency procedures into the good or right thing to do. They urge the development of a more critical attitude towards public organizations and the instrumental technical culture in which they are embedded. They caution against perceiving system failures as temporary departures from ethical (and lawful) standards and identify within management a tendency to contain problems rather than to communicate them forward and outwards.

Differences in professional cultures and values, management styles and levels of autonomy enjoyed by staff may affect collaboration and learning within a network of agencies, as may tight budgets, limited resources to meet unpredictable needs, and competing demands (Johnson et al., 2003). Collaboration and, in England especially, moves towards greater integration of health and social care may be affected by legal rules and government policies that are experienced as difficult to implement, lack of trust, and inexperience in formalizing partnership agreements (Audit Commission, 2009). Within individual social work organizations, the behaviour of practitioners and managers may betray the presence of different priorities.

In this context, judicial reviews and ombudsman investigations are mechanisms of redress available to service users and, indeed, organizations. As remedies they restore lawful and/or ethical practice in individual cases. However, they are essentially reactive remedies, reliant on individuals and organizations pursuing their complaints (Braye and Preston-Shoot, 2010) and, arguably therefore, insufficient on their own to embed accountability in decision-making. Indeed, regulation and mechanisms of redress only work when service users and carers have the necessary knowledge to challenge harmful decision-making (Flynn, 2004; Preston-Shoot, 2011). In this context, Flynn's experience of heartless and weak administration of complaints procedures is sobering.

Equally, in less than benign contexts, adherence by individual social workers to their professional codes of practice, and employers to nationally agreed standards (see Chapter 9), may be experienced as challenging in the face of organizational pressures. It is one thing knowing that employment law has established that organizations must not expect staff to behave in an unlawful manner, or to act contrary to their professional ethics and knowledge, as this would undermine the necessary relationship of trust that must exist between employers and employees (Kline and Preston-Shoot, 2012). In addition, however, practitioners and managers will need moral courage to learn from the unthinkable and to uphold professional standards in uncomfortable situations.

Looking forward

Key characteristics emerge from the findings reported in this chapter. They are the presence of isolated, closed and reactive organizational cultures, inflexible and unreflective, and apparently resistant to acknowledging errors, pressures and strain (Kline and Preston-Shoot, 2012). Interestingly, in this context, Francis (2013) identified that the CQC appeared not to be a happy environment in which to work. The impact on the professionalism and accountability of social work practitioners and managers when working in such environments has arguably been given insufficient attention. Optimism may, however, spring from two sources. One is the increasing recognition of the need for whole system change, based on a thorough-going systemic analysis, if repeating lessons from unthinkable tragedies and other events are to finally result in learning. The second is the enforcement of legal principles and professional standards for decision-making, which has been very much the focus of this book. The next and final chapter reiterates these principles and standards, with essentially a focus on 'getting to what good looks like' for the service user, the team around the service user, and organizations around the team, and the regulatory and governance structures around the organizations.

Further reading

Flynn, M (2012) *Winterbourne View Hospital. A Serious Case Review*. A devastating critique of how one agency, the organization of which it was a part, and the surrounding regulatory architecture, failed to safeguard and promote the welfare of patients.

Francis, R (2013) *Report of the Mid Staffordshire NHS Foundation Trust Public Inquiry: Executive Summary*. A similarly devastating forensic analysis of the failings within one NHS hospital, with the organization's management and the agencies which surrounded it in the regulatory architecture of health and social care all severely censured.

Lock, R (2013) *Serious Case Review: Re Daniel Pelka – Overview Report*. An evaluation of practice and multi-agency arrangements that highlights missed opportunities to protect Daniel Pelka from abuse and neglect. It offers some analysis of why agencies failed to safeguard Daniel and makes recommendations. Its findings make familiar reading.

OFSTED inspection reports of local authority arrangements for the protection of children. These are available at www.ofsted.gov.uk.

SWIA (2005) *An Inspection into the Care and Protection of Children in Eilean Siar*. Another inquiry into standards of child protection practice and into the surrounding organizational context. It emphasizes the importance of social workers exploring a range of options, using their knowledge of the law. It highlights the importance of challenging entrenched patterns of thinking and observes that adverse work contexts, such as workloads and staffing levels, and failures of supervision and strategic management, impact on professionals' ability to keep children safe and to question organizational decision-making.

9

EMBEDDING AND ENSURING BEST PRACTICE

AT A GLANCE THIS CHAPTER COVERS:

- legal rules on complaints procedures and whistleblowing
- reinforcing professional, accountable and safe decision-making
- good practice on reviews of decision-making
- good practice on clinical and organizational governance
- good practice on supervision and staff support
- overseeing and monitoring practice and its management – legal rules on safeguarding boards and protection committees

Chapter 8 explored the evidence for the difficulties that some social work organizations have in learning from tragedies, failures in decision-making and departures from the best standards of professional accountability. It is easy to focus on breaches of good governance and workforce support, thereby ignoring the many transactions that take place between social workers and service users, or between agencies, in order to facilitate purposeful and effective work between practitioners and those with whom they work.

The vast majority of local authorities and their statutory partners in England have multi-agency arrangements in place to safeguard children, with clear procedures for reporting concerns and handling complaints by service users (Wallace et al., 2009). Many LSCBs in England and Wales provide strong leadership. Similarly, in Scotland, Adult Protection Committees have established their effectiveness since implementation of the Adult Support and Protection (Scotland) Act 2007 (Cornish and Preston-Shoot, 2013).

Equally, although the numbers appear to be rising slowly, care councils report very few complaints regarding registered social workers and even fewer findings of misconduct (for example, GSCC, 2012). Thus, there is room for some optimism that social workers and their managers attain legal standards for conduct in a public office and the exercise of professional authority, namely that their approach to using discretion, employing statutory authority and making decisions is serious, single-minded, professional and attentive (Bingham, 2011). In line with professional standards articulated in Chapter 2 and legal principles outlined in Chapter 1, practitioners and managers exclude personal feelings from their decision-making and suspend judgment until all the available evidence has been obtained and scrutinized. They also promote equality and both respect and protect human rights (Chapter 3) since reasonableness includes taking account of the dignity of human beings (Sachs, 2009). Expressed alternatively, social work decisions take place within the domain of human experience. Therefore, alongside reasoning and technical competence in the law, social work must be and often is characterized by grace, passion and compassion (Sachs, 2009) and infused with ethical principles and moral resources.

In responding to the events in Mid Staffordshire, summarized in Chapter 8, Francis (2013) identified some key principles for achieving excellence in health care. Their resonance for reclaiming social work is obvious. Service users/patients should be put first. Fundamental standards should be set and no breach should be countenanced. Common values should be emphasized, with openness, transparency and candour throughout organizational and practice systems. Accountability should be embedded through the workforce, with peer review and audit to ensure adherence to best practice.

Francis (2013) also strongly recommends the presence of effective complaints and whistleblowing procedures. Bingham (2011) and Sachs (2009) also recognize that the law requires that decisions should not only be based on stated criteria but also accessible and amenable to challenge, that adjudicative processes should be fair, and that practitioners and managers should stand against abuses of power and authority. This chapter therefore returns initially to the question of complaints procedures and whistleblowing.

Complaints procedures

Good organizational practice welcomes feedback and challenge from service users (Francis, 2013). Indeed, this is recognized in government guidance. IROs must ensure that young people know how to make a complaint (DCSF, 2010). Complaints are an essential part of improving services, of working in partnership with service users, and of developing a learning and listening culture (DH, 2006b).

Complaints procedures for children's services in England and Wales are mandated by the Children Act 1989. The Children (Scotland) Act 1995 and the Children (Northern Ireland) Order 1995 contain similar provisions. Complaints regarding adult services are mandated by the Health and Social Care (Community Health and Standards) Act 2003 for England and Wales, with the legal rules for Scotland being located in the NHS and Community Care Act 1990 and those for Northern Ireland in the Health and Social Care (Reform) Act (Northern Ireland) 2009 and the Health and Social Care Complaints Procedures Directions (Northern Ireland) 2009. There are three stages – informal, formal and review (for adult services in England, contained within the Local Authority Social Services and NHS Complaints (England) Regulations 2009). The further through the stages a complainant progresses, the greater the involvement of panel members independent of the local authority, although the degree to which this independence is effective in holding local authorities accountable is disputed (Braye and Preston-Shoot, 2010).

Service users must receive information about the procedures, and may submit complaints verbally, in writing or electronically. Advocates may use formal complaints procedures on behalf of a service user if so authorized or if the individual lacks capacity. Advocacy can help children, for example, overcome a reluctance to complain and manage the stress of making a complaint. Advocacy appears to promote better understanding and outcomes (Carrigan and Randell, 2006). Procedures themselves must be accessible, efficient, even-handed and managed with courtesy and respect, along the lines of the legal principles for making decisions outlined in Chapter 1. There are timescales for raising a complaint and for its resolution, again according to legal principles, this time of timeliness. Complainants should be reassured that there will not be any adverse consequences as a result of making a complaint and social workers should record the advice they give to potential complainants (Kline and Preston-Shoot, 2012). Organizations must be able to demonstrate what and how they have learned from complaints.

Complaints procedures are to be preferred ahead of judicial review because they offer a cheaper, quicker and less formal means of attempting to resolve a dispute; accordingly, they should normally be the first avenue for seeking redress (*R (S) v Hampshire CC* [2009]). The outcome will be recommendations with reasons, in accordance with the principles in Chapter 1. A local authority may refuse to implement these recommendations but must have good reason; in other words, it must have properly analysed the evidence and reached a defensible, not unreasonable conclusion and alternative way forward (*R v North Yorkshire CC, ex parte Hargreaves* [1997]; *R (A, T and S) v Newham LBC* [2008]). Unjustified procedural obstacles must not be placed in the way of a complaint. Fairness, a key principle in Chapter 1, applies to processes where service users and family members are making representations and seeking redress (*Public Services Ombudsman for Wales v Cardiff Local Health Board* (2009)). Taking a case to judicial review or the ombudsman may follow the completion of complaints procedures in order to scrutinize the reasonableness of a local authority's approach or response to the findings.

Whistleblowing

Managers should regard social workers who communicate honestly about their lived experience of work as a valuable source of feedback and learning (Munro, 2010; DH, 2012; Francis, 2013). Standards for employers (Care Council for Wales, 2002; NISCC, 2002; Scottish Social Services Council, 2009; Social Work Reform Board, 2010b) include fostering a culture where practitioners and managers feel able to raise concerns, for example, about inadequate resources, operational difficulties, workload issues and their own skills and capacities for the work assigned to them. They should feel able to do so without fear. Good organizational practice therefore protects whistleblowers (Hope-Hailey et al., 2012) and promotes well-publicized escalation procedures.

Social work standards (Care Council for Wales, 2002; NISCC, 2002; Scottish Social Services Council, 2009; HCPC, 2012a) require social workers to contribute to the development of services and organizations and to provide leadership for other staff members' learning and development. Despite the difficulties experienced by whistleblowers that were described in Chapter 8, employees who reasonably believe that disclosure of confidential information is in the public interest (to be defined by courts and tribunals) are protected in law providing that they do not act for personal gain (Public Interest Disclosure Act 1998 – England, Scotland and Wales; Public Interest Disclosure Act (Northern Ireland) Order 1998; Enterprise and Regulatory Reform Act 2013). In future staff who harass or bully a whistleblower will become liable for their actions in addition to employers remaining vicariously liable for the actions of employees unless they have taken reasonable steps to prevent victimization. Failure to comply with legal obligations and situations where the health and safety of service users and staff are endangered by the acts or omissions of employers are examples of permitted disclosures. Moreover, the European Court of Human Rights has confirmed that Article 10 ECHR protects freedom of expression and, therefore, whistleblowing. This Article was breached in the case of a nurse who was dismissed after she disclosed in pursuit of a public interest, her employer having ignored her complaints (*Heinisch v Germany* [2011]).

Unless unsafe or impractical to do so, concerns should normally be raised within the organization first. The burden of proof lies with the person raising concerns. To raise concerns effectively requires the employee to be clear regarding what they are concerned about and why, to be fully prepared and to have access to advice and support. Concerns should be set out in writing, with clarity about the outcome sought (Kline and Preston-Shoot, 2012). Employers would be advised to have whistleblowing policies but are not required by law to do so. Within the NHS the right of staff to whistleblow is now enshrined in the NHS Constitution (Health Act 2009) but within social work and social care it remains far from straightforward and safe (Public Concern at Work, 2011), not withstanding the European Court judgment.

Reviews

Reviewing assessments of service users' needs and the outcomes of care plans is a core part of social work practice. Reviewing service users' needs is a requirement in the legal rules that apply to children in need, children requiring protection, children leaving care and adults in need of services or protection. Social workers should be familiar with the requirements embedded in these legal rules relating to the frequency and scope of reviews. They are an opportunity to share information, consider legal options and plan together (Westminster Safeguarding Adults Board, 2011).

Furthermore, to improve standards of decision-making, reviewing practice generally should feature strongly in social work, in order to learn from cases where outcomes have been successful, disappointing or tragic. Increasingly, statutory guidance is encouraging review audits (for example, HM Government, 2013) alongside serious case reviews, appreciating the value of learning from successful work as well as from apparent failures (Carson, 2012). In such reviews, it will be important to understand the working environment and context if positive and negative outcomes are to be fully, that is systemically, understood. This level of analysis includes the organization's systems, history and ways of working (Payne, 2007; Munro, 2010) and should provide information on how well the multi-agency system is working in child and adult protection.

The legal principles outlined in Chapter 1 and the professional practice standards captured in Chapter 2 provide a set of benchmarks for such reviews. Thus, reviews should involve the families concerned, where possible (Chapter 4), and should be proportionate to the scale and complexity of the issues to be examined (Chapter 3) (HM Government, 2013). Carson (2012), however, has built on these benchmarks and proposes a number of principles for reviewers to follow.

Questions for reviewers, adapted from Carson (2012)

1 In the light of what is known about the type of case in question, how appropriate was the assessment and care plan, including the resources made available?

2 Judging by the standards for professional accountability (Chapter 2), what was the quality of the decision-making and the managerial support for it?

3 How thorough was the assessment of need and of risk, and the subsequent intervention?

4 Reviewers have the luxury of time and of hindsight. What, however, is it reasonable to have expected those involved at the time to have considered and why? How would reasonable decision-makers have acted and what leads reviewers to that judgment?

5 What was the quality of the decisions that were taken? The benchmark is not the consequence or outcome of the decision so much as why, how and where it was taken. To what degree do the decision and the practice surrounding it reach the *Bolam* standard?

6 What contributed to difficulties in managing the case, including systemic organizational and policy factors?

7 In addition to what people did, why did they act or not act, and what does this reveal about the policy, practice and organizational context in which they were working?

8 What actions should be taken forward as suggested by the review?

One outstanding challenge may be the effective dissemination of learning from reviews and audits to staff. Noticeable here is the active use by Adult Protection Committees in Scotland of serious case reviews and inquiries in the training and briefings they provide to social workers and other professionals involved in adult safeguarding (Cornish and Preston-Shoot, 2013) and the frequency of recommendations from serious case reviews that their findings be used as part of training and a learning and improvement strategy (for example, Flynn, 2011; 2012).

Professional standards

The Corporate Manslaughter and Corporate Homicide Act 2007 applies across the UK. Senior executives could be prosecuted for failures in a duty of care that led to a person's death. Currently that legislation does not cover situations where service users or staff have been abused or neglected but have survived. This may change following the events at Winterbourne View. The Health and Safety Offences Act 2008 enables prosecutions for breaches of health and safety legislation which may have resulted in reckless disregard of requirements which sometimes have resulted in an employee's death. Mental health, mental capacity, health and social care, and domestic violence legislation, as configured in each of the four UK nations, contains various provisions to prosecute individuals responsible for maltreatment and neglect.

Alongside the legal rules for good decision-making, and for criminal prosecutions where service providers and individuals have abused or neglected people for whom they are responsible, there are professional standards for practice and the management of practice, which social work has set out. When deciding what a *Bolam* standard for social work might look like, these professional standards act as benchmarks. The first seven chapters in this book focused largely on how individual social workers should pay due regard in their practice to particular legal rules and the standards in professional codes of practice. As the book has progressed the focus has been extended to the organizational context within which social work practice occurs. It is the standards for the organizational context that are highlighted here.

In his review of Mid Staffordshire (Chapter 8), Francis (2013) concluded that leadership must reinforce professional values and standards. Munro (2012) similarly has observed that good social work needs good guidance, management, senior support and advice, and records. All four UK nations have been reviewing, indeed reclaiming, social work. Even allowing for jurisdictional and cultural differences, the themes emerging from the reviews are remarkably similar and capture the standards by which organizational support for social work should be judged.

Supervision

Supervision must be open, constructively challenging and supportive, focusing on the quality of risk analysis, care planning and decisions rather than targets (Laming, 2009; HM Government, 2010). Regular and appropriate supervision features strongly in the reviews of social work (for example, SWTF, 2009; OFSTED, 2012a; Devaney et al., 2013), its frequency to be determined by the social worker's level of experience and its focus to be on the quality of practice and decision-making, on the emotional impact of the work, and on sustaining practitioners' resilience when challenging parents and others involved in a case. Supervision should be focused on developing learning and promoting best practice, which includes ensuring that legal rules are being followed, work pressures are tackled, research and other evidence accessed, assumptions challenged and decisions reviewed. It is especially important at critical points in a case, such as the development or conclusion of protection plans.

Supervision should also enable social workers to confront their fears about exercising legal powers and about making mistakes, otherwise over-assessment, delay or paralysis could result, with potentially negative impacts on children and families (Munro and Ward, 2008). Equally, supervision is critical to establishing a realistic and child-centred timescale for completion of a proportionate assessment (Munro and Lushey, 2012). In adult safeguarding, supervision must focus on the tension between a person's autonomy and choices, which may involve degrees of risk, and protection. It should be robust in challenging optimism and scrutinizing work done, and ensure that decisions taken at conferences and reviews are followed through (Braye et al., 2013b). These professional standards align closely with the legal principles highlighted in this book – assessment and intervention should be timely (Chapter 1), proportionate to the needs identified (Chapter 3) and thorough (Chapter 1).

Resources

Social workers should not be allocated work that is beyond their level of experience and competence in terms of their career progression (Munro, 2011; Devaney et al., 2013). Newly qualified social workers are ready to begin practice. Competence as expert practitioners takes time and support to develop. Thus, employers must have transparent systems for managing workloads and for developing and sustaining a competent and confident workforce that is capable of well-informed decision-making (Social Work Reform Board, 2010a; Scottish Government, 2011; WAG, 2011a). Employers must have the right level of skills and experience available to meet demands and ensure that social workers have the resources to practise effectively (SWTF, 2009).

Employers must provide appropriate, high-quality training and support (*Lancaster v Birmingham CC* [1999]; *Fraser v Winchester Health Authority* [1999]; OFSTED, 2012b), a safe place of work that protects social workers from unreasonable behaviour by service users (*R v*

Kensington and Chelsea, ex parte Kujtim [1999]) and looks after their mental and physical well-being (*Walker v Northumberland CC* [1995]). They must prevent and/or minimize the risks to staff (SWTF, 2009) and support newly qualified professionals through supervision, induction, mentoring, appraisal and continuing professional development (DH, 2012; Francis, 2013). Detailed guidance is available for social workers to use when they are concerned about their workloads (Kline and Preston-Shoot, 2012).

Valuing knowledge

The focus is now on supporting staff to exercise professional judgment, providing guidance on how to balance risks, needs and autonomy (Scottish Government, 2011). Priority is given to knowledge for good social work practice, including research and legal advice (SWTF, 2009). Useful in this context are action learning sets, panels, advice sessions, and case study groups that offer time and space for practice-oriented reflection, emotional support, and problem-solving (Morrison, 2010; Clark, 2012; Braye et al., 2013b). Learning and development is well-timed and relevant in local authorities that support social workers effectively (OFSTED, 2012a). Learning is extracted from serious case reviews and robust audits (OFSTED, 2012b).

Case law (*Bolitho v City and Hackney Health Authority* [1997]) also places knowledge centre-stage by stressing that professionals must have a logical basis for their opinions, including the weight given to risks and benefits of proposed courses of action. Thus, in determining an acceptable standard of professional practice, research evidence, practice experience and service-user narratives all have a place as types of knowledge around which a sound body of professional opinion will form.

Management engagement

Where senior managers support staff in developing and exercising skilled judgment and are accessible and visible, child protection outcomes are better (OFSTED, 2012a). Managers must know their organizations well and should engage with frontline staff routinely, taking feedback seriously. Munro (2012) refers to the importance of sustained contact by managers with social workers, Morrison (2010) to hearing frontline narratives so that managers have an accurate and systemic analysis of the state of practice. Senior managers should ensure that social workers are able to meet the requirements of their professional codes of practice and through engagement must understand the impact of their decisions on frontline staff and service users (DH, 2006a; DfE, 2011; 2013). This includes taking responsibility for the health and safety of staff, ensuring that what is done is done safely and appropriately, and being active in identifying and responding to foreseeable risks and actual problems. Managers have a duty of care towards staff and must take appropriate measures to prevent harm caused by inadequate resources. Such measures include engaging with staff about concerns regarding resources and determining priorities and methods for safe working (Kline and Preston-Shoot, 2012).

Senior management involvement is also helpful when social workers are working with highly complex cases. It provides external objective scrutiny on the view taken of a case and should offer robust challenge of work either done or proposed. Senior managers can then ensure follow-through on the decisions that have been taken, based on a clear view of the child or adult at risk (OFSTED, 2009; Westminster Safeguarding Adults Board, 2011; Braye et al., 2013b).

Good governance

External scrutiny enables members of a system to step back and look in upon their work from a different perspective. It is a key activity in ensuring that organizations, and their managers and practitioners, challenge poor practice and promote compassionate care (DH, 2012). Chapter 8 identified concerns that inquiries had uncovered about clinical and organizational governance. For example, Munro (2012) concluded that inspection, one component of external scrutiny, had focused unduly on compliance with procedures rather than on good practice and the judgments and reflections that surround it. Furness (2009) and Laming (2009) have both criticized inspection arrangements for insufficient attention to service development and improvement.

The purpose here is to identify benchmarks for good practice, to which the various boards, committees and regulatory bodies in the four UK nations, responsible for assuring the quality of strategic partnerships and operational practice, should adhere. These boards and committees are configured differently in the various jurisdictions, their mandates originating in primary legislation and amplified in secondary legislation and statutory guidance. For example, England and Wales have LSCBs and LSABs; Scotland has Child and Adult Protection Committees. In Northern Ireland clinical governance is termed clinical and social care governance. Nonetheless, it is the overview and scrutiny function that is important.

In line with the legal principles and professional standards set out in this book, effective governance promotes professional accountability (Chapter 2) by seeking to understand service-user experience, auditing cases and investigating concerns, and using annual reports to present an analysis of the state of practice and its management. It encourages the involvement of service users and of staff from across the agencies responsible for the health and well-being of children and adults in order to share ideas on how to best safeguard and promote people's welfare (Chapter 4). It is proportionate to the risks and needs identified (Chapter 3). It is accompanied by strong and knowledgeable political and corporate support (OFSTED, 2012a).

Standards of good governance have been developed through research and in response to inquiries into serious practice abuses, such as Winterbourne View (Office for Public Management and Chartered Institute of Public Finance and Accountancy, 2004; Audit Commission, 2005; Braye et al., 2012; DH, 2012; HM Government, 2013). Increasingly, the focus is on learning rather than simply on ensuring compliance. The challenge will be the degree to which these standards are made meaningful for, and impact beneficially on, the lived experience of service users and the staff working with them.

Standards for clinical and organizational governance

- How clearly expressed are the purpose and goals for a committee or board that is responsible for ensuring that the tasks of an organization are appropriately accomplished?
- How and why are organizational structures configured to ensure adequate performance of an organization's or a multi-agency network's tasks?
- Is there senior management time and responsibility clearly allocated to quality assurance and reviews of service provision?
- How, where and by whom are decisions taken and recorded on cases and on multi-agency partnership commitments?
- Where and by whom is there scrutiny of these decisions and how effective is that oversight?
- How rigorous are senior managers in holding their own organization and other stakeholder partners to account for the processes and outcomes of their work and the support and resources provided for staff in response to demands on services?
- How effective are committees and boards in pressing for and analysing information, in driving through action plans based on

this analysis and reporting annually the state of practice and its management?

- How are quality standards disseminated within and across organizations responsible for child and adult protection?
- How is performance information collated, analysed, assessed and discussed? This includes robust interrogation of what may lie behind statistical information (DfE, 2011).
- To what degree are all stakeholders engaged in an agency's or network's assessment of its effectiveness, including frontline staff and service users?
- How open is an organization or multi-agency network to external review and commentary, especially from staff and service users, and from independent board and committee members who have to bridge some distance between their outsider position and detailed insider knowledge of daily practice?
- How are boards and committees assisted to exercise independent and effective challenge? This includes the adequacy of resources (staff and budgets) to undertake audits and reviews, the seniority of managers who are present at meetings, and the quality assessment and relationship skills of board and committee members.

Multi-agency working

Legislation provides a framework for multi-agency collaboration and is differently configured across the four UK nations. For example, the Adult Support and Protection (Scotland) Act 2007 lays out the requirements on statutory partners, social services, health services and the police to cooperate with respect to adult protection. In England, the Health Act 1999, the NHS Act 2006 and the Health and Social Care Act 2012 aim to facilitate the achievement of partnership arrangements and integrated service provision across health and social care. However, legislation cannot ensure collaborative practice; rather it can only set a framework for it. Thus, ongoing leadership will be required from senior managers across the multi-agency network regarding developing and monitoring agreements about standards for good practice, goals in response to assessments of a community's needs, and participatory practice with service users and staff. Good interpersonal relationships between managers, flexibility, commitment to team working and positive challenge, shared vision and open communication are amongst the skills and attitudes required to achieve positive outcomes for service users and their communities (Johnson et al., 2003).

Taking good practice forward

Good social work is characterized by individual and collective learning, effective use of knowledge and evidence drawn from a wide variety of sources, and genuine engagement with service users. Good social workers learn from experience and reflection during and outside direct work with service users and other professionals. Good social work practice and its management are built on relationships (Ayre and Preston-Shoot, 2010).

Good social workers know what they must do, understand how they should do it and develop the confidence to do it. They will also know what to do if they have concerns and if these are not acted upon (Kline and Preston-Shoot, 2012). In supporting that endeavour, this book has sought to identify where and how the legal rules align with social work's own standards for practice and the management of practice. Between them the legal principles for good decision-making and social work's own standards set out the landscape for practice and provide pathways through which accounts can be given and representations made. Service users may not always agree with when and how statutory authority is exercised but they do appreciate social workers who possess a detailed knowledge of the legal rules, express awareness of the impact and implications of their use, and are prepared to advocate for best practice standards, even when that requires them to take issue with their own employers (Braye and Preston-Shoot, 2006).

Used effectively and in unison, the legal principles and practice standards provide for social workers, managers and service users a sense of security and consistency (the boundaries and requirements are known and familiar), a sense of purpose (goals that are valued and valuable), a sense of significance (people's involvement and experiences matter) and a sense of achievement (outcomes realized) (Commission on Dignity in Care for Older People, 2012). Decision-making is of crucial and central relevance to social work, involving, as it often does, crises, high-risk situations, lives and liberty (Taylor, 2012). Thus, these legal rules and practice standards need to be operationalized through decision-making models, some analytic and prescriptive, others intuitive and descriptive, each with a potential contribution to offer (Taylor, 2012). Thus, an adjacent task for social workers, alongside an appreciation of the law for good decision-making, is familiarization with what different models of decision-making have to offer.

Alongside different models of decision-making, there is the range of literacies (see Introduction and Chapter 2) from which social workers may draw when navigating complex practice tensions. Law, alone, cannot resolve tensions and dilemmas which originate in resource (staff, money, time) scarcity or different ethical views about what might be a good decision in a particular case. Nor are legal rules themselves necessarily unproblematic; they are, after all, created and implemented by people. Thus, intra and inter-personal dynamics will also enter decision-making as well as rules of evidence (what can be considered as relevant in a situation) and the balance to be desired between prescription, via regulations and procedures, and professional discretion and judgment. Nonetheless, law represents one key guide when seeking to reach good decisions.

The purpose of this book has been to assist social work practitioners and managers to navigate complex terrain. Ultimately, the book's effectiveness will be judged by the degree to which they feel empowered to take good decisions, where good equates to an approach to taking decisions which is both lawful and professionally accountable.

Final on-the-spot question	If law is the mathematics of freedom (Bingham, 2011), what might best describe the purpose and potential of social work?

Further reading

OFSTED (2012a) *High Expectations, High Support and High Challenge.* This report identifies the difference that managers can make when supporting frontline staff to protect children and young people. A range of strategies clearly enable staff to feel supported and lead to better outcomes in child protection.

Taylor, B (2012) 'Models for professional judgement in social work' 15(4) *European Journal of Social Work* 546–62. This article reviews some theoretical models of decision-making and their potential application in social work settings and situations.

USEFUL WEBSITES

www.cqc.org.uk
Inspection reports on local authority adult services and on service provision by healthcare organizations available for download.

www.lgo.org.uk
Website for the local government ombudsman with individual decisions and summaries of cases available for download.

www.local.gov.uk
Website for the Local Government Association, a useful source of publications on children's services and adult social care.

www.ofsted.gov.uk
Inspection reports on local authority children's services available for download.

www.pcaw.org.uk
Website for Public Concern at Work, a charity which campaigns for strong whistleblowing legal rules that protect people when they raise concerns about malpractice.

www.scie.org.uk
Website for the Social Care Institute for Excellence, a useful source of research and knowledge reviews, and of e-learning materials, including on social work and the law.

www.skillsforcare.org.uk
Skills for Care has useful material on workforce development.

www.supremecourt.gov.uk
The UK Supreme Court's website with decisions available for download.

GLOSSARY

Administrative law
Legal rules that regulate the balance of power between the state and individuals. The law allows for review of executive power by the judiciary and sets out the principles to be observed in professionals' decision-making.

Adult Protection Committees
Established by the Adult Support and Protection (Scotland) Act 2007, these committees oversee in Scotland the effectiveness of the work of local authorities and partner agencies in the statutory, private and voluntary sectors relating to adult safeguarding. The committees are required to produce biennial reports which are public documents.

Care Quality Commission
Created by the Health and Social Care Act 2008 for England and Wales, the CQC covers all adult social care services, including mental health, residential and non-residential provision, across local authorities, voluntary organizations and independent agencies. It also covers health, both hospitals and care homes. It registers and inspects service providers and can take enforcement action when agencies have failed to comply with regulations and standards. It uses outcomes for adult services, including health and well-being, quality of life and dignity, when inspecting services, and monitors management, staffing, record-keeping and the handling of complaints. Its remit is broad and its effectiveness has been seriously questioned (Francis, 2013).

Case law
Judicial decisions which may concern the lawfulness and reasonableness of decisions taken by social workers, or which may revolve around how particular sections and clauses in primary and secondary legislation are to be understood, such as the 'likelihood of significant harm'. When interpreting the meaning of particular legal rules, judges may refer to debates in Parliament, to the ordinary and everyday meaning of words, and to the intent of the Act and the particular clause within it. In a decided case, courts distinguish between *ratio decidendi* (the reasons for a decision) and *obiter dicta* (other comments).

Discretion
The ability to decide whether and how to act in a particular case. Decisions must be lawful and reasonable, that is capable of justification. Properly exercised discretion will draw on knowledge of law and ethics, research evidence and other types of knowledge, applied skilfully to the circumstances of a particular case.

Duties
Social work law comprises two types of duties. Absolute duties, such as s. 117 Mental Health Act 1983, require local authorities to act in a particular way. More common are discretionary duties, such as s. 47 NHS and Community Care Act 1990. Here, social workers have to exercise their discretion in order to determine whether the duty to act in a particular way is triggered. Discretion is often indicated in primary legislation by the phrase 'where the local authority considers it necessary'.

Equality and Human Rights Commission
Created by the Equality Act 2006, and covering England and Wales, the EHRC has investigation and enforcement powers with respect to public bodies. It covers all the protected groups under equality legislation. Its mandate includes disseminating awareness of human rights and securing equality and good relations between diverse groups. It may intervene in court cases covering equality and human rights issues.

Independent Reviewing Officer
This role was created in England and Wales by the Adoption and Children Act 2002 and extended by the Children and Young Persons Act 2008. IROs monitor local authorities' performance of care plans for looked after children. They may refer a case to the Children and Family Court Advisory and Support Service, having drawn any shortcomings to the attention of senior managers, where unable to ensure that a local authority is delivering the commitments outlined in an approved care plan. The IRO must ensure that the child's wishes are understood and taken into account. They must assist young people to make representations and complaints, and to obtain legal advice and access to advocacy. Their role now encompasses not just reviews but all local authority functions.

Judicial review
This procedure focuses on the relationship between individuals and the state. It provides for High Court scrutiny of the lawfulness, reasonableness and rationality of decisions taken by public bodies. Decisions are binding and enforceable but also appealable. Various orders may be made. An injunction is an order not

to proceed or to proceed in a particular way. A declaration is a statement of the legal position. An order may be made quashing a decision, rendering it null and void, or prohibiting a particular proposed action. The court may mandate a public body to act in a particular way, essentially giving direction.

Local government ombudsman
A quasi-judicial inquisitorial consideration of an individual complaint or of a series of similar cases. Sometimes undertaken jointly with the PSHO, the outcome can be particularly critical of local authorities and other public bodies. The recommendations are not binding and there is no appeal. Financial remedies are not uncommon.

Local Safeguarding Adults Board
Although not named as such in statutory guidance for England and Wales on adult protection, each local authority was required to establish a body to oversee multi-agency arrangements. The Care Bill, being debated in Parliament 2013–2014, promises to establish LSABs on a statutory footing, with functions and powers closely resembling those of LSCBs.

Local Safeguarding Children Board
Established in England and Wales by the Children Act 2004, and designed to overcome the weaknesses of previous Area Child Protection Committees, their remit has been elaborated by statutory regulations and guidance. The role includes the commissioning and publication of serious case reviews, the provision of multi-agency safeguarding training and the auditing of inter-agency procedures and practices for protecting children. These boards must have an independent chair.

Managerialism
This approach to public sector management gives prominence to agency procedures, instrumental goals and performance measures which demonstrate organizational success. Performance is prescribed, regulated and evaluated, drawing heavily on quantitative data.

Negligence
A social worker or the employer may be held to have been negligent where a duty exists, which has been breached, with damage the result. Damage may be psychological and emotional.

Office for Standards in Education, Children's Services and Skills
OFSTED inspects local authorities and third-sector providers. It monitors compliance with statutory requirements. It produces ratings for providers

across such services as adoption, foster placements, meeting the needs of disabled children and looked after children, and care planning.

Precedent
The principle that the decisions of higher courts are binding on lower courts when hearing similar cases. Thus, in England and Wales, Court of Appeal decisions are binding on all lower courts unless overruled by the Supreme Court, the highest court in the UK. Supreme Court decisions bind all other courts until the Supreme Court changes its own decision or Parliament changes the law. Precedent has the advantage of seeking to ensure consistency in administration of the legal rules but the disadvantage that the law can be very slow to evolve.

Primary legislation
Acts of Parliament that contain the powers and duties to be given to local authorities. Primary legislation sets out the basic framework, for instance, with respect to mental capacity, detention of people with serious mental distress, or child protection. The detail of how, when and with whom powers and duties are to be exercised is elaborated in secondary legislation, policy guidance and practice guidance.

Proportionality
Introduced by the Human Rights Act 1998, this is the principle that, using lawful authority, the state and its officers should only intervene as much as is necessary to achieve a legitimate goal. It is not a new principle. Approved Mental Health Professionals have long had the duty under mental health legislation to look for the least restrictive alternative when seeking lawfully to protect individuals or those around them.

Secondary legislation
Sometimes known as regulations or Statutory Instruments, secondary legislation is made by the relevant secretary of state on the authority of Parliament as given in primary legislation. Acts of Parliament often enable the relevant secretary of state to 'make regulations'. They may contain powers and/or duties. Regulations must be followed by social workers.

Serious case reviews
Commissioned by LSCBs and LSABs (and the equivalent committees in Scotland) where a child or adult dies or sustains significant harm as a result of abuse or neglect by others and where there appears to have been failings in multi-agency collaboration. Statutory guidance (HM Government, 2013) outlines the procedures to be followed in England and Wales by LSCBs.

Social Work Task Force
Established by the New Labour government to review social work practice and social work education in England. Its recommendations were taken forward by the Social Work Reform Board.

Statutory guidance
In England and Wales such guidance is issued by central government departments under s. 7 Local Authority Social Services Act 1970. It requires local authorities to act in accordance with the guidance issued. This is sometimes referred to as policy guidance. Only if there are exceptional reasons should an authority depart from the guidance.

Tribunals
First-tier tribunals have a legally qualified chairperson and two lay members. The procedure is less formal than a court and rules of evidence are less strict. They are subject to judicial review. They cover such matters as special educational needs, immigration, mental health reviews, and employment. An upper tribunal hears appeals from first-tier tribunal decisions.

Vicarious liability
This is the concept that employers are responsible for the actions of their employees rather than staff members themselves being held personally accountable for their actions. Employers may escape this responsibility if they can show that an employee has been fully trained and supported to act in a particular way. Increasingly too, as a result of the Human Rights Act 1998, individual practitioners may have to defend themselves if they have acted outside of lawful authority or practised in such a way that no social work authority would support.

BIBLIOGRAPHY

Adams, G and D Balfour (1998) *Unmasking Administrative Evil* (London: Sage)

Aldgate, J (2013) *UNCRC: Getting it Right for Every Child* (Edinburgh: Scottish Government)

Audit Commission (2005) *Governing Partnerships: Bridging the Accountability Gap* (London: Audit Commission)

Audit Commission (2009) *Means to an End: Joint Financing across Health and Social Care* (London: Audit Commission)

Ayre, P and M Preston-Shoot (eds) (2010) *Children's Services at the Crossroads: A Critical Evaluation of Contemporary Policy for Practice* (Lyme Regis: Russell House Publishing)

Banks, S (2010) 'Integrity in professional life: issues of conduct, commitment and capacity' 40(7) *British Journal of Social Work* 2168–84

BASW (2011) *UK Supervision Policy* (Birmingham: BASW)

Bates, N, T Immins, J Parker, S Keen, L Rutter, K Brown and S Zsiog (2010) '"Baptism of fire": the first year in the life of a newly qualified social worker' 29(2) *Social Work Education* 152–70

Bichard, M (2004) *The Bichard Inquiry Report* (London: The Stationery Office)

Bilson, A (2007) 'Promoting compassionate concern in social work: reflections on ethics, biology and love' 37(8) *British Journal of Social Work* 1371–86

Bingham, T (2011) *The Rule of Law* (London: Penguin Books)

Boylan, J and S Braye (2006) 'Paid, professionalised and proceduralised: can legal and policy frameworks for child advocacy give voice to children and young people?' 28(3–4) *Journal of Social Welfare and Family Law* 233–49

Boylan, J and J Dalrymple (2011) 'Advocacy, social justice and children's rights' 23(1) *Practice* 19–30

Braye, S and A Brammer (2012) 'Law on personalization' in M Davies (ed.) *Social Work with Adults* (Basingstoke: Palgrave Macmillan) 24–47

Braye, S and M Preston-Shoot (2006) *Resource Guide: Teaching, Learning and Assessment of Law in Social Work Education* (London: Social Care Institute for Excellence)

Braye, S, D Orr and M Preston-Shoot (2011) *Self-Neglect and Adult Safeguarding: Findings from Research* (London: Social Care Institute for Excellence)

Braye, S, D Orr and M Preston-Shoot (2012) 'The governance of adult safeguarding: findings from research' 14(2) *Journal of Adult Protection* 55–72

Braye, S, D Orr and M Preston-Shoot (2013b) *A Scoping Study of Workforce Development for Self-Neglect Work* (Leeds: Skills for Care)

Braye, S and M Preston-Shoot (2007) *Law and Social Work E-Learning Resources* (London: Social Care Institute for Excellence)

Braye, S and M Preston-Shoot (2010) *Practising Social Work Law* 3rd edn (Basingstoke: Palgrave Macmillan)

Braye, S, M Preston-Shoot and A Thorpe (2007) 'Beyond the classroom: learning social work law in practice' 7(3) *Journal of Social Work* 322–40

Braye, S, M Preston-Shoot and V Wigley (2013a) 'Deciding to use the law in social work practice' 13(1) *Journal of Social Work* 75–95

Brooks, C (2010) *Safeguarding Pressures Project: Results of Data Collection* (Manchester: Association of Directors of Children's Services)

Buckinghamshire Safeguarding Vulnerable Adults Board (2011) *Executive Summary: The Murder of Mr C – A Serious Case Review* (Aylesbury: Buckinghamshire County Council)

Burke, T (2010) *Anyone Listening? Evidence of Children and Young People's Participation in England* (London: Children's Rights Alliance England and National Children's Bureau)

Campbell, M and D Chamberlin (2012) 'A pilot project: evaluating community nurses' knowledge and understanding of the Adult Support and Protection (Scotland) Act 2007' 14(4) *Journal of Adult Protection* 188–96

Care Council for Wales (2002) *Codes of Practice for Social Care Workers and Employers of Social Care Workers* (Cardiff: Care Council for Wales)

Care Council for Wales (2011a) *Annual Report and Accounts 2010–11* (Cardiff: Care Council for Wales)

Care Council for Wales (2011b) *National Occupational Standards for Social Work* (Cardiff: Care Council for Wales)

Carpenter, J, S Hackett, D Patsios and E Szilassy (2010) *Outcomes of Inter-Agency Training to Safeguard Children: Final Report to the Department for Children, Schools and Families and the Department of Health* (London: DCSF)

Carr, H (2012) 'Rational men and difficult women – *R (on the application of McDonald)* v *Royal Borough of Kensington and Chelsea* [2011] UKSC 33' 34(2) *Journal of Social Welfare and Family Law* 219–30

Carrigan, D and J Randell (2006) 'Complaints from children and young people: the Local Government Ombudsman' 230 *Childright* 20–23

Carson, D (2012) 'Reviewing reviews of professionals' risk-taking decisions' 34(4) *Journal of Social Welfare and Family Law* 395–409

Carson, D and A Bain (2008) *Professional Risk and Working with People: Decision-Making in Health, Social Care and Criminal Justice* (London: Jessica Kingsley Publishing)

Cestari, L, M Munroe, S Evans, A Smith and P Huxley (2006) 'Fair Access to Care Services (FACS): implementation in the mental health context of the UK' 14(6) *Health and Social Care in the Community* 474–81

Charles, M and J Horwath (2009) 'Investing in interagency training to safeguard children: an act of faith or an act of reason?' 23 *Children and Society* 364–76

Charles, N and J Manthorpe (2007) 'FACS or fiction? The impact of the policy Fair Access to Care Services on social care assessments of older visually impaired people' 19(2) *Practice* 143–57

Clark, C (1998) 'Self-determination and paternalism in community care: practice and prospects' 28(3) *British Journal of Social Work* 387–402

Clark, C (2007) 'Professional responsibility, misconduct and practical reason' 1(1) *Ethics and Social Welfare* 56–75

Clark, C (2012) 'From rules to encounters: ethical decision-making as a hermeneutic process' 12(2) *Journal of Social Work* 115–35

Commission on Dignity in Care for Older People (2012) *Delivering Dignity: Securing Dignity in Care for Older People in Hospitals and Care Homes – A Report for Consultation* (London: Local Government Association, NHS Confederation and Age UK)

Corkhill, R and C Walker (2010) *Improving the Safeguarding of Vulnerable Adults in the North East* (Teesside: North East Improvement and Efficiency Partnership and ADASS North East Branch)

Cornish, S and M Preston-Shoot (2013) 'Governance in adult safeguarding in Scotland since the implementation of the Adult Support and Protection (Scotland) Act 2007' 15(5) *Journal of Adult Protection* 223–36

CQC (2011) *The State of Health Care and Adult Social Care in England* (London: The Stationery Office)

CQC (2013) *Not Just a Number* (London: CQC)

CSCI (2007) *Growing Up Matters: Better Transition Planning for Young People with Complex Needs* (London CSCI)

CSCI (2008a) *Putting People First: Equality and Diversity Matters 1 – Providing Appropriate Services for Lesbian, Gay and Bisexual and Transgender People* (London: CSCI)

CSCI (2008b) *Putting People First: Equality and Diversity Matters 2 – Providing Appropriate Services for Black and Minority Ethnic People* (London: CSCI)

CSCI (2009) *Putting People First: Equality and Diversity Matters 3 – Achieving Disability Equality in Social Care Services* (London: CSCI)

Daniel, B and N Baldwin (2010) 'Safeguarding children: the Scottish perspective' in P Ayre and M Preston-Shoot (eds) *Children's Services at the Crossroads: A Critical Evaluation of Contemporary Policy for Practice* (Lyme Regis: Russell House Publishing) 18–27

DCA (2003) *Public Sector Data Sharing: Guidance on the Law* (London: DCA)

DCA (2007) *Mental Capacity Act 2005: Code of Practice* (London: DCA/The Stationery Office)

DCSF (2008) *Safeguarding the Young and Vulnerable: The Government's Response to the Third Joint Chief Inspectors' Report on Arrangements to Safeguard Children* (London: DCSF)

DCSF (2010) *IRO Handbook: Statutory Guidance for Independent Reviewing Officers and Local Authorities on their Functions in relation to Case Management and Review for Looked After Children* (London: The Stationery Office)

Devaney, J, L Bunting, D Hayes and A Lazenbatt (2013) *Translating Learning into Action: An Overview of Learning Arising from Case Management Reviews in Northern Ireland 2003–2008* (Belfast: Queen's University Belfast, National Society for the Prevention of Cruelty to Children Northern Ireland and Department of Health, Social Services and Public Safety)

Devo, J (2009) 'Life in the midst of the misconduct machine' (May) *Professional Social Work* 10–12

DfE (2011) *A Child-Centred System: The Government's Response to the Munro Review of Child Protection* (London: The Stationery Office)

DfE (2013) *Statutory Guidance on the Roles and Responsibilities of the Director of Children's Services and the Lead Member for Children's Services* (London: The Stationery Office)

DH (1990) *Community Care in the Next Decade and Beyond: Policy Guidance* (London: HMSO)

DH (1991) *Care Management and Assessment: Practitioners' Guide* (London: HMSO)

DH (2000) *Data Protection Act 1998: Guidance to Social Services* (London: DH)

DH (2002) *Fair Access to Care Services: Guidance on Eligibility Criteria for Adult Social Care* (London: DH)

DH (2004) *Community Care Assessment Directions* (London: DH)

DH (2006a) *Statutory Guidance on the Strategic Chief Officer Post of the Director of Adult Social Services* (London: Department of Health)

DH (2006b) *Learning from Complaints: Social Services Complaints Procedure for Adults* (London: DH)

DH (2008) *Code of Practice: Mental Health Act 1983* (London: The Stationery Office)

DH (2009) *The Second Year of the Independent Mental Capacity Advocacy Service 2008/2009* (London: DH)

DH (2010) *Local Authority Circular on the Personal Care at Home Act 2010 and Charging for Re-ablement* LAC (2010) 7 (London: DH)

DH (2011) *Enabling Excellence: Autonomy and Accountability for Healthcare Workers, Social Workers and Social Care Workers* (London: The Stationery Office)

DH (2012) *Transforming Care: A National Response to Winterbourne View Hospital – Department of Health Review: Final Report* (London: DH)

DH (2013) *The Fifth Year of the Independent Mental Capacity Advocacy (IMCA) Service: 2011–2012* (London: DH)

DHSSPS (2010) *Deprivation of Liberty Safeguards (DOLS): Interim Guidance* (Belfast: DHSSPS)

Dickens, J (2007) 'Child neglect and the law: catapults, thresholds and delay' 16(2) *Child Abuse Review* 77–92

Dickens, J (2012) *Social Work, Law and Ethics* (London Routledge)

Doel, M, P Allmark, P Conway, M Cowburn, M Flynn, P Nelson and A Tod (2010) 'Professional boundaries: crossing a line or entering the shadows?' 40(6) *British Journal of Social Work* 1866–89

Driscoll, J (2009) 'Prevalence, people and processes: a consideration of the implications of Lord Laming's progress report on the protection of children in England' 18 *Child Abuse Review* 333–45

Drury-Hudson, J (1999) 'Decision-making in child protection: the use of theoretical, empirical and procedural knowledge by novices and experts and implications for field-work placement' 29(1) *British Journal of Social Work* 147–69

Duffy, J (2011) 'Explicit argumentation as a supervisory tool for decision making in child protection cases involving human rights issues' 23(1) *Practice* 31–44

Duffy, J and M Collins (2010) 'Macro impacts on caseworker decision-making in child welfare: a cross-national comparison' 13(1) *European Journal of Social Work* 35–54

Duffy, J, B Taylor and S McCall (2006) 'Human rights and decision-making in child protection through explicit argumentation' 12(2) *Child Care in Practice* 81–95

Dwyer, S (2009) 'The good news and the bad news for frail older people' 21(4) *Practice* 273–89

EHRC (2011) *Personalisation in the Reform of Social Care: Key Messages* (Manchester: EHRC)

EHRC (2012) *Human Rights Review 2012: How Fair is Britain? An Assessment of How Well Public Authorities Protect Human Rights* (Manchester: EHRC)

EHRC Scotland (2011) *Meeting the Public Sector Equality Duty in Scotland: Interim Guidance for Scottish Public Authorities on Meeting the General Duty* (Glasgow: EHRC Scotland)

Ellis, K (2004) 'Promoting rights or avoiding litigation? The introduction of the Human Rights Act 1998 into adult social care in England' 7(3) *European Journal of Social Work* 321–40

ESTYN and CSSIW (2011) *Joint Investigation into the Handling and Management of Allegations of Professional Abuse and the Arrangements for Safeguarding and Protecting Children in Education Services in Pembrokeshire County Council* (Cardiff: The Stationery Office)

Fairgrieve, D and S Green (eds) (2004) *Child Abuse Tort Claims against Public Bodies: A Comparative Law View* (Aldershot: Ashgate)

Ferguson, H (2010) 'The understanding systemic caseworker: the (changing) nature and meanings of working with children and families' in P Ayre and M Preston-Shoot (eds) *Children's Services at the Crossroads: A Critical Evaluation of Contemporary Policy for Practice* (Lyme Regis: Russell House Publishing) 28–35

Flynn, M (2004) 'Challenging poor practice, abusive practice and inadequate complaints procedures: a personal narrative' 6(3) *Journal of Adult Protection* 34–44

Flynn, M (2006) 'Joint investigation into the provision of services for people with learning disabilities at Cornwall Partnership NHS Trust' 8(3) *Journal of Adult Protection* 28–32

Flynn, M (2011) *The Murder of Adult A: A Serious Case Review* (Stockport: Stockport Safeguarding Adult Board)

Flynn, M (2012) *Winterbourne View Hospital. A Serious Case Review* (Bristol: South Gloucestershire Safeguarding Adults Board)

Forum for a New World Governance (2011) *World Governance Index: Why should World Governance be Evaluated and for What Purpose?* (Paris: Charles Léopold Mayer Foundation for the Progress of Humankind)

France, A, E R Munro and A Waring (2010) *The Evaluation of Arrangements for Effective Operation of the New Local Safeguarding Children Boards in England: Final Report* (London: DfE)

Francis, R (2010) *Independent Inquiry into Care Provided by Mid Staffordshire NHS Foundation Trust January 2005–March 2009* (London: The Stationery Office)

Francis, R (2013) *Report of the Mid Staffordshire NHS Foundation Trust Public Inquiry: Executive Summary* (London: The Stationery Office)

Furness, S (2009) 'A hindrance or a help? The contribution of inspection to the quality of care in homes for older people' 39(3) *British Journal of Social Work* 488–505

Fyson, R and D Kitson (2007) 'Independence or protection: does it have to be a choice? Reflections on the abuse of people with learning disabilities in Cornwall' 27(3) *Critical Social Policy* 426–36

Fyson, R and D Kitson (2010) 'Human rights and social wrongs: issues in safeguarding adults with learning disabilities' 22(5) *Practice* 309–20

General Teaching Council, GSCC and Nursing and Midwifery Council (2007) *Values for Integrated Working with Children and Young People* (London: General Teaching Council)

Goldsmith, L (2005) 'A daughter's battle' (January) *Professional Social Work* 8–9

Gordon, J and B Cooper (2010) 'Talking knowledge–practising knowledge: a critical best practice approach to how social workers understand and use knowledge in practice' 22(4) *Practice* 245–57

Gower, S (2011) 'How old are you? Ethical dilemmas in working with age-disputed young asylum seekers' 22(5) *Practice* 325–39

GSCC (2008) *Social Work at its Best: A Statement of Social Work Roles and Tasks for the 21st Century* (London: GSSC)

GSCC (2011) *Annual Report 2010–2011* (London: GSCC)

GSCC (2012) *Regulating Social Workers (2001–11)* (London: GSCC)

Guthrie, T (2011) *Social Work Law in Scotland* 3rd edn (Haywards Heath: Bloomsbury Professional)

Hale, B (2009) 'Dignity' 31(2) *Journal of Social Welfare and Family Law* 101–08

Hamilton, C (2007) 'Smacking children: has the government implemented the judgment of the European Court of Human Rights in *A v UK*?' 238 *Childright* 10–13

Harwin, J and N Madge (2010) 'The concept of significant harm in law and practice' 5(2) *Journal of Children's Services* 73–83

Hasan, I (2009) 'What's freedom of information got to do with social work?' (October) *Professional Social Work* 26–27

HCPC (2012a) *Standards of Conduct, Performance and Ethics* (London: HCPC)

HCPC (2012b) *Social Workers in England: Standards of Proficiency* (London: HCPC)

Heath, J (2011) 'A career on the line' (January) *Professional Social Work* 20–21

HM Government (2008a) *Safeguarding Children: The Third Joint Chief Inspectors' Report on Arrangements to Safeguard Children* (London: The Stationery Office)

HM Government (2008b) *Information Sharing: Guidance for Practitioners and Managers* (London: The Stationery Office)

HM Government (2010) *Building a Safe and Confident Future: Implementing the Recommendations of the Social Work Task Force* (London: The Stationery Office)

HM Government (2013) *Working Together to Safeguard Children. A Guide to Inter-Agency Working to Safeguard and Promote the Welfare of Children* (London: The Stationery Office)

Hope-Hailey, V, R Searle and G Dietz (2012) *Where Has All the Trust Gone?* (London: Chartered Institute of Personnel and Development)

Horwath, J (2011) 'See the practitioner, see the child: the framework for the assessment of children in need and their families ten years on' 41(6) *British Journal of Social Work* 1070–87

Hudson, B (2005) 'Information sharing and children's services reform in England: can legislation change practice?' 19(6) *Journal of Interprofessional Care* 537–46

Hussein, S, S Martineau, M Stevens, J Manthorpe, J Rapaport and J Harris (2009) 'Accusations of misconduct among staff working with vulnerable adults in England and Wales: their claims of mitigation to the barring authority' 31(1) *Journal of Social Welfare and Family Law* 17–32

Jack, G and H Donnellan (2010) 'Recognising the person within the developing professional: tracking the early careers of newly qualified child care social workers in three local authorities in England' 29(3) *Social Work Education* 305–18

Johnson, P, G Wistow, R Schulz and B Hardy (2003) 'Interagency and interprofessional collaboration in community care: the interdependence of structures and values' 17(1) *Journal of Interprofessional Care* 69–83

Jones, R (2012) *Mental Capacity Act Manual* 5th edn (London: Sweet and Maxwell)

Kennedy, R with J Richards (2007) *Integrating Human Service Law and Practice* 2nd edn (South Melbourne: Oxford University Press)

Keywood, K (2010) 'Vulnerable adults, mental capacity and social care refusal' 18(1) *Medical Law Review* 103–10

Kline, R and M Preston-Shoot (2012) *Professional Accountability in Social Care and Health: Challenging Unacceptable Practice and its Management* (London: Sage/Learning Matters)

Laming, H (2009) *The Protection of Children in England: A Progress Report* (London: The Stationery Office)

Law Commission, Scottish Law Commission and Northern Ireland Law Commission (2012) *Regulation of Health Care Professionals: Regulation of Social Care Professionals in England – Summary of Joint Consultation Paper* (London: The Stationery Office)

LGO (2002) *Report Summaries: Social Services* (London: LGO)

LGO (2007) *Report Summaries: Social Services* (London: LGO)

LGO (2008) *Injustice in Residential Care: A Joint Report by the Local Government Ombudsman and the Health Services Ombudsman for England – Investigations into Complaints against Buckinghamshire County Council and Oxfordshire and Buckinghamshire Mental Health Partnership* (London: HMSO)

LGO (2009) *13th Annual Digest of Cases* (London: LGO)

LGO and PHSO (2009) *Six Lives: The Provision of Public Services to People with Learning Disability* (London: The Stationery Office)

Lock, R (2013) *Serious Case Review: Re Daniel Pelka – Overview Report* (Coventry: Coventry Safeguarding Children Board)

Manthorpe, J and S Martineau (2011) 'Serious case reviews in adult safeguarding in England: an analysis of a sample of reports' 41(2) *British Journal of Social Work* 224–41

Manthorpe, J, M Cornes, J Moriarty, J Rapaport, S Iliffe, J Wilcock, R Clough, L Bright and OPRSI (2007) 'An inspector calls: adult protection in the context of the NSFOP review' 9(1) *Journal of Adult Protection* 4–14

Manthorpe, J, J Rapaport and N Stanley (2009) 'Expertise and experience: people with experiences of using services and carers' views of the Mental Capacity Act 2005' 39(5) *British Journal of Social Work* 884–900

McDermott, S (2011) 'Ethical decision-making in situations of self neglect and squalor among older people' 5(1) *Ethics and Social Welfare* 52–71

McDonald, A (2007) 'The impact of the UK Human Rights Act 1998 on decision making in adult social care in England and Wales' 1(1) *Ethics and Social Welfare* 76–94

McDonald, A, K Postle and C Dawson (2008) 'Barriers to retaining and using professional knowledge in local authority social work practice with adults in the UK' 38(7) *British Journal of Social Work* 1370–87

MoJ (2008) *Mental Capacity Act 2005: Deprivation of Liberty Safeguards: Code of Practice to Supplement the Main Mental Capacity Act 2005 Code of Practice* (London: MoJ/The Stationery Office)

Morris, K (2010) 'Children in need: the challenge of prevention for social work' in P Ayre and M Preston-Shoot (eds) *Children's Services at the Crossroads: A Critical Evaluation of Contemporary Policy for Practice* (Lyme Regis: Russell House Publishing) 64–73

Morrison, T (2007) 'Emotional intelligence, emotion and social work: context, characteristics, complications and contribution' 37(2) *British Journal of Social Work* 245–63

Morrison, T (2010) 'The strategic leadership of complex practice: opportunities and challenges' 19 *Child Abuse Review* 312–29

Munby, Lord Justice (2010) 'What price dignity?' speech to the Legal Action Group Community Care Conference, July

Munro, E (2007) 'Confidentiality in a preventive child welfare system' 1(1) *Ethics and Social Welfare* 41–55

Munro, E (2010) 'Learning to reduce risk in child protection' 40(4) *British Journal of Social Work* 1135–51

Munro, E (2011) *The Munro Review of Child Protection: Final Report – A Child-Centred System* (London: The Stationery Office)

Munro, E (2012) *The Munro Review of Child Protection: Progress Report – Moving Towards a Child Centred System* (London: The Stationery Office)

Munro, E R and Lushey, C (2012) *The Impact of More Flexible Assessment Practices in Response to the Munro Review of Child Protection: Emerging Findings from the Trials* (Loughborough: Loughborough University Childhood Wellbeing Research Centre)

Munro, E R and H Ward (2008) 'Balancing parents' and very young children's rights in care proceedings: decision-making in the context of the Human Rights Act 1998' 13 *Child and Family Social Work* 227–34

Newton, J and L Browne (2008) 'How fair is fair access to care?' 20(4) *Practice* 235–49

NISCC (2002) *Codes of Practice for Social Care Workers and Employers of Social Care Workers* (Belfast: NISCC)

NISCC (2011) *National Occupational Standards for Social Work* (Belfast: NISCC)

O'Brien, N (2012) 'Social rights and civil society: "giving force" without "enforcement"' 34(4) *Journal of Social Welfare and Family Law* 459–70

OFSTED (2008) *Learning Lessons: Taking Action: OFSTED's Evaluations of Serious Case Reviews 1 April 2007 to 31 March 2008* (Manchester: OFSTED)

OFSTED (2009) *Learning Lessons from Serious Case Reviews: Year 2* (Manchester: OFSTED)

OFSTED (2010) *Learning Lessons from Serious Case Reviews: Interim Report 2009–10* (Manchester: OFSTED)

OFSTED (2012a) *High Expectations, High Support and High Challenge* (Manchester: OFSTED)

OFSTED (2012b) *Inspection of Safeguarding and Looked After Children Services: London Borough of Lambeth* (Manchester: OFSTED)

OFSTED (2012c) *Inspection of Local Authority Arrangements for the Protection of Children: Doncaster Metropolitan Borough Council* (Manchester: OFSTED)

OFSTED (2013) *Inspection of Local Authority Arrangements for the Protection of Children: Northamptonshire* (Manchester: OFSTED)

Office for Public Management and Chartered Institute of Public Finance and Accountancy (2004) *The Good Governance Standard for Public Services* (London: Independent Commission on Good Governance in Public

Services (Office for Public Management/Chartered Institute of Public Finance and Accountancy/Joseph Rowntree Foundation)

Orme, J and G Rennie (2006) 'The role of registration in ensuring ethical practice' 49(3) *International Social Work* 333–44

O'Rourke, L (2010) *Recording in Social Work: Not Just an Administrative Task* (Bristol: Policy Press)

Patrick, H and N Smith (2009) *Adult Protection and the Law in Scotland* (Haywards Heath: Bloomsbury Professional)

Payne, M (2007) 'Performing as a "wise person" in social work practice' 19(2) *Practice* 85–95

Perkins, N, B Penhale, D Reid, L Pinkney, S Hussein and J Manthorpe (2007) 'Partnership means protection? Perceptions of the effectiveness of multi-agency working and the regulatory framework within adult protection in England and Wales' 9(3) *Journal of Adult Protection* 23

Pike, L, T Gilbert, C Leverton, R Indge and D Ford (2011) 'Training, knowledge and confidence in safeguarding adults: results from a postal survey of the health and social care sector in a single county' 13(5) *Journal of Adult Protection* 259–74

Pinkney, L, B Penhale, J Manthorpe, N Perkins, D Reid and S Hussein (2008) 'Voices from the frontline: social work practitioners' perceptions of multi-agency working in adult protection in England and Wales' 10(4) *Journal of Adult Protection* 12–24

Pithouse, A and A Crowley (2007) 'Adults rule? Children, advocacy and complaints to social services' 21 *Children and Society* 201–13

Preston-Shoot, M (2000) 'Making connections in the curriculum: law and professional practice' in R Pierce and J Weinstein (eds) *Innovative Education and Training for Care Professionals: A Providers' Guide* (London: Jessica Kingsley)

Preston-Shoot, M (2003) 'A matter of record?' 15(3) *Practice* 31–50

Preston-Shoot, M (2010) 'On the evidence for viruses in social work systems: law, ethics and practice' 13(4) *European Journal of Social Work* 465–82

Preston-Shoot, M (2011) 'On administrative evil-doing within social work policy and services: law, ethics and practice' 14(2) *European Journal of Social Work* 177–94

Preston-Shoot, M and S Cornish (2014) 'Paternalism or proportionality? Experiences and outcomes of the Adult Support and Protection (Scotland) Act 2007' 16(1) *Journal of Adult Protection* 5–16

Preston-Shoot, M and J McKimm (2010) 'Prepared for practice? Law teaching and assessment in UK medical schools' 36(11) *Journal of Medical Ethics* 694–99

Preston-Shoot, M and J McKimm (2012a) 'Tutor and student experiences of teaching and learning law in UK social work education' 31(7) *Social Work Education* 896–913

Preston-Shoot, M and J McKimm (2012b) 'Perceptions of readiness for legally literate practice: a longitudinal study of social work student views' 31(8) *Social Work Education* 1071–89

Preston-Shoot, M, G Roberts and S Vernon (2001) 'Values in social work law: strained relations or sustaining relationships' 20(2) *Journal of Social Welfare and Family Law* 137–50

Public Concern at Work (2011) *Speaking Up for Vulnerable Adults: What the Whistleblowers Say* (London: Public Concern at Work)

QAA (2008) *Subject Benchmark Statements: Social Work* (Gloucester: QAA)

Reder, P and S Duncan (1999) *Lost Innocents: A Follow-up Study of Fatal Child Abuse* (London: Routledge)

Reder, P and S Duncan (2003) 'Understanding communication in child protection networks' 12 *Child Abuse Review* 82–100

Reder, P and S Duncan (2004) 'Making the most of the Victoria Climbié inquiry report' 13 *Child Abuse Review* 95–114

Richardson, B, G Kitchen and G Livingston (2002) 'The effect of education on knowledge and management of elder abuse: a randomized controlled trial' 31 *Age and Ageing* 335–41

Richardson, S and S Asthana (2006) 'Inter-agency information sharing in health and social care services: the role of professional culture' 36(4) *British Journal of Social Work* 657–69

Rights of the Child UK (no date) *Why Incorporate? Making Rights a Reality for Every Child* (London: Rights of the Child UK)

Rixon, A and R Ward (2012) 'What difference does it make? Social work practice and post-qualifying awards' 24(3) *Social Work Education* 147–59

Roche, D and J Rankin (2004) *Who Cares? Building the Social Care Workforce* (London: Institute for Public Policy Research)

Sachs, A (2009) *The Strange Alchemy of Life and Law* (Oxford: Oxford University Press)

Sawyer, C (2006) 'The child is not a person: family law and other legal cultures' 28(1) *Journal of Social Welfare and Family Law* 1–14

Scottish Executive (2003) *Standards in Social Work Education: Framework for Social Work Education in Scotland* (Edinburgh: Scottish Executive)

Scottish Government (2011) *Practice Governance Framework: Responsibility and Accountability in Social Work Practice* (Edinburgh: Scottish Government)

Scottish Social Services Council (2009) *Codes of Practice for Social Services Workers and Employers* (Dundee: Scottish Social Services Council)

Scottish Social Services Council (2010) *Annual Reports and Accounts 2009–2010* (Dundee: Scottish Social Services Council)

Scottish Social Services Council (2011) *National Occupational Standards for Social Work* (Dundee: Scottish Social Services Council)

Seddon, D, C Robinson, C Reeves, Y Tommis, B Woods and I Russell (2007) 'In their own right: translating the policy of carer assessment into practice' 37(8) *British Journal of Social Work* 1335–52

Series, L and I Clements (2013) 'Putting the cart before the horse: resource allocation systems and community care' 35(2) *Journal of Social Welfare and Family Law* 207–26

Sheppard, D (1996) *Learning the Lessons* 2nd edn (London: Zito Trust)

Sheppard, M and K Ryan (2003) 'Practitioners as rule using analysts: a further development of process knowledge in social work' 33(2) *British Journal of Social Work* 157–76

Sinclair, R and R Bullock (2002) *Learning from Past Experience: A Review of Serious Case Reviews* (London: DH)

Skinner, K and B Whyte (2004) 'Going beyond training: theory and practice in managing learning' 23(4) *Social Work Education* 365–81

Social Work Reform Board (2010a) *Building a Safe and Confident Future: One Year On* (London: Department for Education)

Social Work Reform Board (2010b) *Standards for Employers of Social Workers in England and Supervision Framework* (London: Social Work Reform Board)

Stanley, N and J Manthorpe (eds) (2004) *The Age of Inquiry* (London: Routledge)

Stanley, N, P Miller, H Richardson Foster and G Thomson (2011) 'A stop-start response: social services' interventions with children and families notified following domestic violence incidents' 41(2) *British Journal of Social Work* 296–313

Stanley, N, B Penhale, D Riordan, R Barbour and S Holden (2003) 'Working on the interface: identifying professional responses to families with mental health and child-care needs' 11(3) *Health and Social Care in the Community* 208–18

Stevens, M and J Manthorpe (2007) 'Barring "inappropriate people"? The operation of a barring list of social care workers: an analysis of the first referrals to the Protection of Vulnerable Adults List' 15(4) *Health and Social Care in the Community* 285–94

Sullivan, M (2009) 'Social workers in community care: ideologies and interactions with older people' 39(7) *British Journal of Social Work* 1306–25

Swain, P (2009) 'Procedural fairness and social work practice' in P Swain and S Rice (eds) *In the Shadow of the Law* 3rd edn (Sydney: Federation Press)

Swain, P and S Rice (eds) (2009) *In the Shadow of the Law: The Legal Context of Social Work Practice* (Sydney: The Federation Press)

SWIA (2005) *An Inspection into the Care and Protection of Children in Eilean Siar* (Edinburgh: Scottish Executive)

SWTF (2009) *Building a Safe and Confident Future: The Final Report of the Social Work Taskforce* (London: DCSF)

Tanner, D (2003) 'Older people and access to care' 33(4) *British Journal of Social Work* 499–515

Taylor, B (2012) 'Models for professional judgement in social work' 15(4) *European Journal of Social Work* 546–62

Taylor, B (2013) *Professional Decision Making and Risk in Social Work Practice* 2nd edn (London: Sage/Learning Matters)

TCSW (2012) *Professional Capabilities Framework* (London: The College of Social Work)

Thomas, N (2011) 'Care planning and review for looked after children: fifteen years of slow progress?' 41(2) *British Journal of Social Work* 387–98

Timms, J and J Thoburn (2006) 'Your shout! Looked after children's perspectives on the Children Act 1989' 28(2) *Journal of Social Welfare and Family Law* 153–70

Tiotto, J (2012) *A New Inspection Framework: The Multi-Agency Arrangements for the Protection of Children,* presentation to London Safeguarding Children Board, December

van Heugten, K (2011) 'Registration and social work education: a golden opportunity or a Trojan horse?' 11(2) *Journal of Social Work* 174–90

WAG (2011a) *Sustainable Social Services for Wales: A Framework for Action* (Cardiff: WAG)

WAG (2011b) *Guidance on the Equality Duty for the Welsh Public Sector* (Cardiff: WAG)

Wallace, E, E Sapsed and A Magill (2009) *Safeguarding and Promoting the Welfare of Children: Perceptions of Senior Stakeholders on how Public Organisations have Responded to Section 11 of the Children Act 2004* (London: DCSF)

Wardhaugh, J and P Wilding (1993) 'Towards an explanation of the corruption of care' 37 *Critical Social Policy* 4–31

Westminster Safeguarding Adults Board (2011) *A Serious Case Review in Respect of Mr BB: Executive Summary* (London: Westminster Safeguarding Adults Board)

White, C (2014) *Northern Ireland Social Work Law* 2nd edn (Haywards Health: Bloomsbury Professional)

Zifcak, S (2009) 'Towards a reconciliation of legal and social work practice' in P Swain and S Rice (eds) *In the Shadow of the Law: The Legal Context of Social Work Practice* (Sydney: The Federation Press)

SUBJECT INDEX

access to files 122
accountability 2, 4, 11, 15, 17, 20,
    22, 37, 41, 42, 43, 46, 48, 56,
    67, 87, 88, 94, 124, 127, 133,
    137, 138, 139, 140, 142, 143,
    144, 148, 153, 156
action learning sets 151
administrative law 2, 14, 15, 19,
    21, 69, 118, 158
adoption 9, 34, 38, 45, 123
adult protection/safeguarding 5, 6,
    7, 13, 16, 29, 32, 49, 59, 61,
    78, 82, 88, 96, 112, 113, 124,
    131, 136, 147, 154, 160
Adult Protection Committees 79,
    80, 124, 135, 143, 148, 152,
    158
advance declaration 94
advocacy 27, 50, 51, 59, 72, 73,
    78, 85, 86, 88, 94, 95, 96, 97,
    98, 110, 128, 131, 145
age assessment 10, 31, 34, 38, 73,
    119
appropriate adult 57
Approved Mental Health
    Professionals 43
assessment 5, 7, 8, 11, 12, 22, 24,
    25, 26, 27, 28, 29, 30, 31, 32,
    35, 39, 41, 43, 48, 50, 56, 59,
    60, 66, 73, 74, 75, 76, 77, 78,
    79, 81, 82, 83, 87, 90, 91, 92,
    94, 97, 98, 101, 103, 104,
    105, 106, 107, 109, 110, 114,

    118, 121, 128, 129, 130, 131,
    134, 148, 150
audit 46, 127, 134, 135, 136, 144,
    147, 148, 151, 153, 154, 160
autonomy 3, 12, 16, 32, 50, 85,
    86, 87, 88, 90, 98, 136, 139,
    150, 151

bias 29, 30, 42

Care Bill 160
care plans 6, 7, 10, 23, 24, 25, 26,
    27, 29, 34, 38, 40, 50, 59, 61,
    62, 72, 74, 78, 79, 83, 94,
    107, 108, 131, 147, 148, 149,
    159, 161
Care Quality Commission 131,
    132, 140, 158
Care Standards Tribunal 46
carers 9, 23, 26, 34, 36, 40, 49,
    71, 76, 77, 78, 79, 90, 92,
    93, 95, 97, 99, 104, 106,
    107, 109, 121, 127, 130, 132,
    139
case study groups 151
charges 25, 33, 101
child protection/safeguarding 5, 6,
    7, 9, 14, 16, 17, 18, 23, 24,
    28, 29, 34, 38, 40, 43, 44, 45,
    56, 59, 64, 72, 74, 75, 80, 82,
    103, 104, 106, 111, 113, 123,
    128, 129, 130, 137, 141, 151,
    154, 156, 161

Child Protection Committees 80, 124, 135, 152
Children and Families Bill 58
Children and Family Court Advisory and Support Service 159
Children and Young Persons (Scotland) Bill 66
Children's Commissioners 58, 67
children's guardians 117
chronology 8, 81, 113, 121, 124, 130
Commissioners for Older People 58
complaints 3, 13, 17, 94, 95, 105, 128, 130, 131, 132, 139, 142, 143, 144, 145, 158
confidentiality 4, 16, 82, 112, 113, 115, 116, 119, 120, 124
consultation 33, 35, 65, 76, 77, 98, 108
criminal responsibility 67

data protection 5
delay 21, 27, 28, 29, 48, 49, 62, 78, 103, 107, 108, 110, 128, 129, 138, 150
deprivation of liberty 16, 24, 85, 93, 94, 95
directors of adult services 103
directors of children's services 103
discretion 5, 11, 21, 22, 26, 32, 33, 101, 103, 108, 139, 143, 156, 159
domestic violence 51, 74, 129, 149
due regard 63, 65, 73, 149
duty of care 12, 40, 43, 45, 47, 58, 64, 86, 87, 88, 110, 111, 136, 148, 152

early help/prevention/support 74, 81, 106
eligibility criteria 15, 16, 32, 33, 65, 76, 106, 108

emotional literacy 50, 51
employment law 140
employment tribunals 133
empowerment 2, 70, 89
equality 4, 9, 15, 22, 41, 49, 51, 54, 57, 58, 62, 63, 64, 65, 66, 77, 102, 110, 143, 159
Equality and Human Rights Commission 102, 159
ethical literacy 49

fairness 21, 22, 26, 38, 60, 106, 108, 144, 145
fitness for practice 15, 37, 47, 56, 131

Gillick principle 96, 98
governance 3, 17, 35, 82, 96, 124, 134, 135, 140, 142, 143, 152, 153

Health and Care Professions Council 15, 20
history 51, 147
human rights 2, 4, 5, 9, 15, 22, 23, 25, 32, 41, 49, 51, 54, 57, 58, 59, 60, 62, 67, 73, 88, 93, 102, 103, 106, 108, 143, 159

impact assessments 15, 53, 63, 64, 65
impartiality 22
incompatibility 55, 57
Independent Reviewing Officers 40, 44, 62, 72, 73, 95, 128, 137, 144, 159
induction 46, 48, 137, 138, 151
Information Commissioner 123
information-sharing 3, 7, 12, 16, 22, 33, 73, 76, 78, 81, 94, 96, 98, 112, 113, 114, 115, 116, 117, 118, 120, 124, 128, 129, 130, 147

inspection 131, 132, 135, 152
institutional abuse 131
involvement 33, 61, 67, 69, 70, 73, 78, 79, 83, 88, 90, 94, 153

judicial review xxvi, 14, 16, 64, 76, 127, 139, 145, 159, 162

knowledge literacy 51

lawfulness 21, 22, 23, 158, 159
leadership 64, 128, 130, 131, 134, 135, 143, 146, 149, 154
legal literacy 49, 98
literacy 156
Local Safeguarding Adults Boards 79, 80, 124, 135, 152, 160, 161
Local Safeguarding Children Boards 80, 117, 124, 134, 135, 143, 152, 160, 161

management 3, 5, 7, 8, 17, 46, 47, 48, 49, 95, 110, 130, 131, 134, 135, 136, 138, 139, 141, 142, 149, 151, 152, 153, 154, 155, 158, 160
managerialism 11, 17, 60, 70, 73, 133, 136, 160
mental capacity (assessments) 3, 5, 6, 16, 50, 51, 83, 85, 86, 87, 88, 89, 90, 91, 92, 93, 94, 96, 97, 98, 113, 116, 121, 145
Mid Staffordshire NHS Trust 132, 141, 143, 149
monitor 132
multi-agency working 79, 80, 81, 82, 83, 115, 118, 124, 126, 128, 129, 147, 153, 154

negligence 12, 17, 44, 45, 47, 104, 110, 126, 160
NHS Constitution 147
Northern Ireland 14, 15, 18, 23, 41, 46, 58, 62, 77, 86, 93, 123, 144, 152

Office for Standards in Education, Children's Services and Skills 160
ombudsmen 13, 14, 21, 22, 24, 70, 73, 102, 103, 117, 139, 145, 160
openness 22, 30, 42, 63, 118, 119, 130, 131, 132, 144, 149, 154
organizational context/culture 8, 46, 48, 50, 73, 82, 110, 115, 124, 127, 130, 132, 133, 137, 138, 140, 148, 149
orientations 30, 31, 42, 106

parental responsibility 23, 24, 40, 96, 97, 98, 120, 123
participation 22, 33, 34, 35, 56, 57, 67, 72, 73, 75, 78, 87, 92, 97, 98
partnership 3, 15, 34, 49, 50, 51, 69, 70, 71, 72, 74, 77, 78, 79, 128, 144, 154
poverty 30, 64, 75
precedent 14, 161
Professional Capabilities Framework 4
professionalism 2, 11, 15, 26, 37, 38, 39, 41, 48, 60, 75, 140
proportionality 15, 53, 59, 60, 61, 62, 66, 87, 88, 90, 92, 94, 115, 116, 120, 147, 150, 153, 161

rationality 21, 22, 23, 26, 27, 43, 61, 106, 108, 159

reasonableness 22, 23, 26, 27, 33, 34, 35, 38, 41, 43, 61, 103, 106, 107, 108, 143, 148, 158, 159

recording 5, 8, 27, 34, 38, 40, 41, 45, 47, 48, 56, 63, 65, 73, 78, 94, 110, 114, 117, 119, 121, 122, 123, 128, 129, 135, 145, 149, 153, 158

redress 25, 36, 139

reflection 8, 30, 41, 134, 151, 155

registration 47, 103, 138

relational literacy 50, 98

relationships 70, 71, 72, 73, 74, 78, 79, 83, 87, 98, 118, 135, 154, 155

resources 3, 9, 16, 27, 32, 42, 47, 48, 50, 54, 57, 70, 77, 82, 100, 101, 102, 103, 104, 105, 106, 107, 108, 109, 110, 130, 137, 138, 139, 146, 148, 150, 152, 153, 154, 156

reviews 3, 8, 10, 11, 12, 25, 26, 28, 34, 40, 44, 60, 61, 72, 73, 76, 78, 79, 81, 82, 92, 93, 94, 95, 96, 106, 107, 108, 109, 131, 137, 142, 144, 147, 148, 150, 153, 154

risk 4, 5, 6, 8, 13, 27, 30, 32, 33, 36, 38, 41, 43, 44, 45, 46, 47, 48, 49, 51, 56, 60, 61, 66, 67, 70, 78, 79, 80, 81, 82, 85, 88, 89, 90, 91, 94, 97, 99, 103, 106, 107, 110, 119, 120, 121, 123, 128, 129, 132, 134, 135, 137, 148, 149, 150, 151, 152, 153, 155

rule of law 57

Scotland 13, 15, 16, 18, 23, 39, 41, 46, 58, 61, 62, 63, 66, 74, 78, 79, 80, 86, 88, 93, 96, 98, 106, 119, 123, 124, 135, 143, 144, 148, 152, 158, 161

secondary legislation 21, 22, 24, 29, 47, 49, 55, 72, 77, 152, 158, 161

self-neglect 13, 38, 88, 89

serious case reviews 7, 22, 27, 29, 30, 32, 48, 72, 78, 80, 88, 90, 104, 110, 113, 115, 117, 121, 123, 124, 129, 134, 136, 141, 147, 148, 151, 160, 161

statutory guidance 11, 14, 15, 16, 21, 22, 24, 25, 29, 35, 49, 55, 72, 76, 77, 86, 103, 105, 108, 109, 121, 147, 152, 162

stereotyping 92, 97

supervision 5, 7, 8, 17, 30, 40, 42, 47, 48, 62, 75, 124, 130, 131, 135, 136, 137, 138, 142, 149, 150, 151

targets 101, 132, 134, 136, 139, 149

time 22, 23, 27, 28, 29, 35, 61, 73, 106, 130, 145, 150

training 46, 47, 48, 62, 64, 82, 134, 137, 138, 148, 150, 160

transition 28

transparency 28, 35, 38, 118, 121, 124, 144

unaccompanied asylum seekers 24, 31, 58, 119

United Nations Committee on the Rights of the Child 67

values 9, 19, 21, 22, 41, 42, 43, 46, 49, 51, 54, 59, 62, 72, 82, 83, 88, 92, 97, 115, 124, 127, 134, 137, 139, 144, 149

vicarious liability 146, 162

Wales 13, 15, 24, 25, 41, 46, 58, 62, 63, 64, 66, 67, 75, 77, 79, 80, 86, 88, 90, 92, 93, 94, 95, 97, 98, 103, 117, 123, 124, 135, 143, 144, 152, 158, 159, 160, 161

whistleblowing 35, 126, 131, 133, 142, 144, 145, 146, 147

Winterbourne View 96, 131, 135, 140, 149, 153

workloads 8, 17, 41, 46, 47, 50, 62, 104, 110, 111, 130, 137, 138, 146, 150, 151

AUTHOR INDEX

Adams and Balfour 139

Aldgate 66, 71, 72, 74, 80, 119

Audit Commission 139, 153

Ayre and Preston-Shoot 11, 17, 70, 73, 134, 136, 155

Banks 49

Bates et al. 135, 137

Bichard 115

Bilson 70

Bingham 21, 26, 29, 36, 40, 42, 54, 57, 127, 143, 144

Boylan and Braye 95, 98

Boylan and Dalrymple 98

Braye and Brammer 12

Braye and Preston-Shoot 17, 34, 36, 49, 57, 62, 66, 70, 94, 101, 106, 121, 132, 139, 144, 155

Braye, Orr and Preston-Shoot 7, 13, 49, 70, 79, 81, 82, 88, 89, 91, 113, 121, 135, 136, 150, 151, 152, 153

Braye, Preston-Shoot and Thorpe 6, 101

Braye, Preston-Shoot and Wigley 6, 30, 31, 42, 43, 49, 50, 59, 60, 80, 86, 101, 105

British Association of Social Workers 137

Brooks 110

Buckinghamshire Safeguarding Adults Board 32, 79, 80

Burke 34, 72

Campbell and Chamberlin 82

Care Council for Wales 4, 41, 46, 47, 80, 121, 127, 146

Care Quality Commission 78, 128

Carpenter et al. 82

Carr 54, 102, 110

Carrigan and Randell 145

Carson 42, 50, 147, 148

Carson and Bain 36

Cestari et al. 106

Charles and Horwath 82, 106

Clark 30, 42, 43, 49, 50, 70, 88, 151

Commission for Social Care Inspection 28, 60, 64

Commission on Dignity in Care for Older People 78, 155

Corkhill and Walker 96

Cornish and Preston-Shoot 79, 82, 135, 143, 148

Daniel and Baldwin 106

Department for Children, Schools and Families 9, 72, 95, 110, 137, 144

Department for Constitutional Affairs 91, 92, 97, 114, 115, 118

Department for Education 11, 67, 80, 103, 152, 154

Department of Health 24, 25, 47, 48, 77, 78, 80, 96, 103, 108, 109, 114, 115, 116, 117, 118, 122, 144, 146, 151, 152, 153

Department of Health, Social
    Services and Public Safety 93
Devaney et al. 41, 46, 72, 74, 80,
    121, 149, 150
Devo 48
Dickens 5, 6, 50, 59, 68, 76, 110
Doel et al. 43, 60, 133
Driscoll 50, 80, 135, 138
Drury-Hudson 6, 49, 51
Duffy 35, 59, 74, 136
Duffy and Collins 4, 8
Duffy et al. 59, 62
Dwyer 50, 78, 137

Ellis 60, 68
Equality and Human Rights
    Commission 57, 64, 96, 118,
    132
Equality and Human Rights
    Commission Scotland 63
ESTYN and Care and Social Services
    Inspectorate Wales 48, 134,
    135

Fairgrieve and Green 52
Ferguson 119, 124
Flynn 70, 90, 113, 127, 131, 132,
    135, 136, 139, 140, 148
Forum for a New World Governance
    57
France et al. 135
Francis 101, 132, 140, 141, 143,
    144, 146, 149, 151, 158
Furness 152
Fyson and Kitson 32, 50, 60, 88

General Social Care Council 4, 47,
    58, 80, 136, 137, 143
General Teaching Council, GSCC
    and Nursing and Midwifery
    Council 83
Goldsmith 70

Gordon and Cooper 42, 133, 136,
    137
Gower 31, 106, 119
Guthrie 18

Hale 68
Hamilton 56
Harwin and Madge 74, 75
Hasan 120
Health and Care Professions Council
    4, 41, 58, 64, 71, 80, 102,
    111, 121, 146
Heath 48
HM Government 4, 20, 24, 34, 72,
    80, 82, 108, 109, 113, 114,
    115, 116, 118, 119, 121, 123,
    124, 125, 147, 149, 153, 161
Hope-Hailey et al. 21, 119, 146
Horwath 50, 72, 73, 74, 110
Hudson 115, 119
Hussein et al. 48

Jack and Donnellan 46, 51, 137
Johnson et al. 82, 139, 155
Jones 99

Kennedy with Richards 52
Keywood 90
Kline and Preston-Shoot 42, 43,
    52, 58, 63, 64, 108, 110, 111,
    115, 132, 133, 135, 137, 140,
    145, 146, 151, 152, 155

Laming 5, 8, 11, 46, 50, 70, 104,
    113, 115, 138, 149, 152
Law Commission et al. 48
Local Government Ombudsman
    60, 73, 103, 106, 108
Local Government Ombudsman
    and Parliamentary and Health
    Service Ombudsman 60
Lock 129, 141

Manthorpe and Martineau 49, 113

Manthorpe et al. 132

Manthorpe, Rapaport and Stanley 86, 96, 98, 132

McDermott 88

McDonald 54, 60, 62

McDonald et al. 6, 49, 51, 75

Ministry of Justice 94

Morris 106

Morrison 8, 50, 70, 135, 136, 151

Munby 86, 87, 92

Munro 8, 11, 17, 30, 42, 46, 49, 50, 74, 119, 133, 146, 147, 149, 150, 151, 152

Munro and Lushey 51, 73, 75, 76, 82, 110, 134, 138, 150

Munro and Ward 28, 59, 82, 150

Newton and Browne 33

Northern Ireland Social Care Council 4, 41, 46, 80, 121, 127, 146

O'Brien 102, 110

O'Rourke 122, 125

Office for Public Management and Chartered Institute of Public Finance and Accountancy 153

OFSTED 5, 7, 24, 28, 30, 46, 48, 49, 72, 74, 76, 80, 103, 104, 110, 121, 127, 128, 134, 135, 136, 137, 141, 149, 150, 151, 152, 153, 156

Orme and Rennie 43

Patrick and Smith 78, 88

Payne 42, 147

Perkins et al. 5, 59, 115

Pike et al. 82

Pinkney et al. 5, 82, 115

Pithouse and Crowley 95

Preston-Shoot 2, 9, 60, 70, 101, 106, 111, 122, 133, 139

Preston-Shoot and Cornish 88, 96

Preston-Shoot and McKimm 6, 80, 115

Preston-Shoot, Roberts and Vernon 12, 21, 59

Public Concern at Work 133, 147

Quality Assurance Agency 4, 41, 58, 64, 133

Reder and Duncan 28, 111, 113, 118

Richardson and Asthana 115, 118

Richardson et al. 82

Rights of the Child UK 67

Rixon and Ward 51, 133

Roche and Rankin 47

Sachs 42, 50, 51, 54, 57, 67, 68, 70, 102, 127, 143, 144

Sawyer 98

Scottish Executive 41

Scottish Government 11, 41, 46, 150, 151

Scottish Social Services Council 4, 41, 46, 47, 80, 121, 127, 146

Seddon et al. 9, 78, 82, 106

Series and Clements 111

Sheppard 113

Sheppard and Ryan 4

Sinclair and Bullock 30, 48, 72, 74, 80, 118

Skinner and Whyte 133, 134

Social Work Inspection Agency 84, 130, 141

Social Work Reform Board 17, 46, 127, 136, 137, 146, 150

Social Work Task Force 4, 5, 8, 41, 46, 48, 136, 137, 149, 150, 151
Stanley and Manthorpe 80
Stanley, Miller et al. 30, 50
Stanley, Penhale et al. 82, 115
Stevens and Manthorpe 48
Sullivan 34, 42, 50, 51, 78, 82, 133
Swain 36
Swain and Rice 18, 36

Tanner 106
Taylor 18, 84, 155, 156
The College of Social Work 4
Thomas 34, 72

Timms and Thoburn 62, 72
Tiotto 28, 113, 128

van Heugten 43

Wallace et al. 127, 128, 143
Wardhaugh and Wilding 111, 138
Welsh Assembly Government 4, 11, 41, 46, 63
Westminster Safeguarding Adults Board 29, 79, 81, 87, 91, 113, 121, 132, 135, 136, 147, 152
White 18

Zifcak 5